contents

acknowledgements

I am indebted to Jonathan Gorsky for all his help and advice. A more generous consultant would be very hard to imagine. He is not responsible for any personal viewpoint expressed or for any remaining inaccuracies which I would be glad to have pointed out to me for correction.

Most biblical quotations are from the New Revised Standard Version of the Bible, Oxford University Press, 1989.

Most quotations from the Mishnah are from the translation by Herbert Danby, Oxford University Press, 1933.

There are numerous references to the Talmud which is a body of rabbinic literature. A page of the Talmud is called a folio, of which the recto side is designated 'a' and the verso 'b'. References are to the names of particular volumes of the Talmud and to the page numbers printed according to the folios (e.g. Shabbat 31a). The Soncino English translation is available in scholarly libraries.

All photographs are reproduced by kind permission of C. M. Pilkington.

To Jonathan Gorsky

There are sophisticated systems of transliterating Hebrew words into English. In keeping with the purpose of this volume, a simple system has been adopted which, it is hoped, is generally consistent but which also allows for common usage. Many words beginning (or ending) with 'h' are often spelt with 'ch' (e.g. Hanukah or Chanukah) suggesting a sound rather like the 'ch' of the Scottish word 'loch'. 'H' has been adopted here as less misleading to pronunciation.

The theologically neutral BCE (Before the Common Era) and CE (Common Era) are used here instead of BC and AD.

01

approaching Judaism

In this chapter you will learn:

- about the origins of the term 'Judaism'
- the importance of history in the development of the Jewish religion
- about the way in which Judaism centres on God, the Torah, and the Jewish people.

Judaism and Jewishness

It is said that it is the outsider who is anxious to name and to define a religious system. Those within a religion tend not to see it as a system, an 'ism'. Nothing could be more true of the Jewish religion. Strikingly, the sacred language of Jews, Hebrew, contains no word for 'Judaism'. Indeed the Hebrew language does not really have a word for 'religion'. These facts are significant and should make us cautious about defining and describing Judaism as a religion.

It was in the 1880s that the term 'Judaism' became widely used and this because social and political emancipation then made it necessary for Jews to work out for non-Jews, and to a lesser extent themselves, what it was distinguished them from adherents of other religions. It was particularly against the backdrop of Christianity that describing Judaism as a religion, with specific beliefs and practices, began. To a large extent, this is still the case. It is often within university and college departments of Theology or Religious Studies that the study of Judaism takes its place alongside the study of other religions, and predominantly Christianity.

The very title of this series of books, *Teach Yourself World Faiths*, assumes that there are recognizable faith systems which can, if desired, be studied comparatively. The series does not, however, want to superimpose on the major world religions an artificial system by approaching each of them under uniform headings such as Beliefs, Scriptures, Ceremonies, Festivals, and so on. Such an approach runs the severe risk of missing what is distinctive about a religion as understood by its adherents and thus of seriously distorting it. This is done all too commonly when trying to put Christianity and Judaism side by side. Even more dangerous is the tendency to regard Judaism simply as the forerunner of Christianity (as if Judaism were not a living religion) or as Christianity unfulfilled. Christians tend to define their religion in terms of beliefs, a creed. Flowing from their beliefs are practices, moral and ritual. Apart from when the term 'Christian' is used in the vaguest sense of good or humane (with unfortunate implications for non-Christians), a Christian means someone who holds specific theological beliefs. Can the same be said of a Jew?

According to Jewish Law, as codified in the Talmud and defined by rabbis from late antiquity to the present day, a Jew is a person who is born of a Jewish mother or has been converted to Judaism. This definition is important for determining legal status as in Jewish marriage (see Chapter 9) or the right to an Israeli passport (see Chapter 17). Yet it is a circular definition, for the question can still be asked: what constitutes the Jewishness of the mother? The definition of a Jew has, therefore, been formulated in terms of someone who, besides having a Jewish mother or having converted to Judaism, adheres to no other religion and gives indication of affirming identity with other Jews.

Difficulties in treating Judaism as a religion

It is when we try to work out precisely what this means that we see some difficulties with regarding Judaism as a religion. There are things about Judaism which challenge conventional ideas of what we mean by a religion. If we define Judaism in terms of conviction, centred on belief in one God, we have to acknowledge at least two apparent contradictions. First, it is an undeniable fact that there are Jews who deny the tenets of the Jewish religion, however basically formulated. A Jew who repudiates Judaism is not regarded as having severed all links with the Jewish community. Someone with a Jewish mother might reject both belief and observance but still be accounted a member of the Jewish people (albeit, in some cases, virtually excluded from religious rights and consideration in matters pertaining to synagogue or burial). Such a person is not spoken of as 'a lapsed Jew'. If such a person returns to the faith (according to most but not all authorities) no 'conversion' procedure is applied. By contrast, a Roman Catholic or a Baptist who gives up his or her religion is indeed likely to be described as 'lapsed'. There may be remaining influences, but he or she is unlikely to feel closely linked to the community of those who may be described as 'practising' Roman Catholics or Baptists. The defining factor of a Christian community is belief and once the belief has been removed no one is likely to state: 'I am a Roman Catholic' or whatever, in response to a question about what matters to his or her identity. The defining factor of a Jewish community is belonging to a people and someone might well assert: 'I am Jewish' even when no belief is present.

Second, there are many Jews who describe themselves as secular but who take part in activities which are, on the face of it, religious. In Israel, for example, there are members of non-religious kibbutzim who observe the Sabbath and other Jewish festivals. In North America and other Diaspora (outside Israel) communities, there are branches of what is called the International Federation of Secular Humanistic Jews. The British *Jewish Chronicle* newspaper of 21 January 1994 reported that a meeting of this federation at King's College, London opened 'with the traditional lighting of candles . . . but with a kibbutz-style blessing instead of a religious prayer'. A professor from the Hebrew University in Jerusalem remarked, in the report, that some people want to take part in secular celebrations of Jewish festivals, while others 'want to get away from religion entirely'. The previous year, the same newspaper ran many pages headed: 'Can you be Jewish without Judaism?' The debate reflected a wide range of opinion from the secularists to the Chief Rabbi who asked: 'Who would want to be Jewish without Judaism?' He may be puzzled and so may many non-Jews trying to understand what Judaism is, but the fact remains that there are Jews who call themselves secular or humanistic, but who light the Sabbath candles, and there are also Jews who reject the term secular and even call themselves 'religious', but who may have difficulty in defining precisely what is religious in their lives. This should reinforce our determination to avoid forcing Judaism into categories which are alien to it.

Judaism as a religion

Yet the inadequacies of viewing Judaism as a religion can be greatly exaggerated. There are, after all, many aspects of Judaism which can be described as religious in the normal sense of the word.

Peoplehood

Judaism does not replace religion by peoplehood but combines the two distinctively. Judaism is the religion of the Jewish people, upon whom its faith and obligations are binding. The relationship between God and the people of Israel is fundamental. Someone who converts to Judaism does enter the Jewish people, but the affirmation of the Jewish faith is crucial and decisive. In its absence, the conversion process is nullified, even if the formalities are correctly administered (see Chapter 9). Ruth's famous declaration, on adopting the faith of her Israelite mother-in-law, is the paradigm: 'Your people shall be my people, and your God my God' (Ruth 1:16). Conversely, someone who converts from Judaism to another religion, rather than simply ceases to practise Judaism, ceases to be part of the community as understood by those who have not converted. Culturally and historically, the convert (to, say, Christianity) may retain a strong affinity with the Jewish people into whose life he or she was born. Though much debated in the Middle Ages, a differentiation can be made between belonging to the *am* ('people') of Israel and belonging to the *kehillah* ('community') of Israel. The kehillah has a collective set of meanings and these incorporate belief. If someone converts and, therefore, changes at a critical point of belonging, he or she leaves the community. It is sometimes objected that what might be described as 'choosing to love God in a different way' (as when a Jew becomes a Christian) should not exclude people from their former community. But, as we shall see when looking at the Law of Return in Israel (Chapter 17), converting from Judaism is judged to change one of the meanings of what it is to be Jewish. What was said earlier about remaining part of the Jewish people is true but what this belonging amounts to has very little practical significance and this is because the community's self-definition includes belief.

Belief

Furthermore, it is not correct to reduce Judaism to ethics, to describe it as simply 'a way of life', as if beliefs are incidental. Early self-definition, showing how the people of Israel saw themselves as different in a pagan world, expresses distinctiveness through theological belief and the practice that goes with it. One striking expression of this is Deuteronomy 26 where a declaration of belonging to a people brought out of Egypt by God accompanies the offering of the first fruits in recognition of this fact. Another is the ancient prayer known as the Alenu (see Chapter 10). In the Alenu, Jews state their difference from other peoples in terms of the God they worship: 'For we bend the knee and offer worship and thanks before the supreme King of kings.' Both passages focus on the relationship between God and Israel. Further, the same rabbinical tradition that clarified peoplehood (where there was debate as to whether someone with one Jewish and one non-Jewish parent was Jewish) in terms of matrilineal descent was equally concerned with the boundaries of the faith. The *locus classicus* for fundamental beliefs is the Mishnah (Sanhedrin 10:1). It is stated that Israelites who deny certain doctrines stand to forfeit their 'share in the world to come'.

A monotheistic religion

In addition, Judaism can reasonably be regarded as one of what is called the 'monotheistic family' of religions, along with Christianity and Islam. In terms of both geographical origins and theological beliefs, these three religions have much in common. The Christian theologian, Hans Küng, makes much of this as he writes about the crucial need for dialogue between Jews, Christians, and Muslims today. (*Judaism: the Religious Situation of our Time*, SCM, 1992). However, Küng's own writing demonstrates one of the major difficulties here. Though he purports to be presenting Judaism on its own terms 'as an independent entity with amazing continuity, vitality, and dynamism', his approach, his phraseology, his conclusions, and the amount of space he devotes to Christian comparisons all betray a desire to appraise Judaism from a Christian theological standpoint. He does, in fact, impose one religion upon another. That this is an unfortunate tendency does not, however, alter the fact that Judaism can rightly be regarded as a religion. It simply makes more vital the need to approach this religion in terms of how it is lived by Jewish people rather than as others might perceive it.

Faith and history

We have observed that the Hebrew language lacks a word for 'religion'. The nearest is *dat*, which more commonly belongs to the realm of law or custom. It is used in rabbinic writings, for example, of the requirement for a married woman to have her head covered in the street (Ketubot 7:6). This practice is, however, associated with religion and, in rabbinic commentary on Esther 8:17, 'dat' clearly means a faith (Megillah 12a). We have also noted that the word 'Judaism' came into common use only in the nineteenth century when it needed to distinguish itself from the religions of Christianity and Islam. Like so much of Jewish religious terminology in English (such as 'Bible', 'synagogue', 'Pentateuch', 'prophet', 'phylactery'), it has its origin among Greek-speaking Jews. Significantly, it is a word coined, late BCE (Before the Common Era) and early CE (Common Era), to distinguish what is Jewish from other systems. The Greek *Judaismos* appears in 2 Maccabees 2:21; 8:1; 14:38 and Galatians 1:13–14. Its Hebrew equivalent is *Yahadut*, an abstract noun from the word *Yehudi*, 'Jew'. It is found only occasionally in medieval literature and has no parallels in the

Bible or in rabbinic literature. Yet something suggesting Jewishness that includes faith appears in the Bible, again in Esther 8:17. There we find the term *mityahadim*, used for 'becoming Jews', which is a short step from *Yahadut*. There is also *Yiddishkeit*, a term which includes both a sense of peoplehood and belief and which better captures the warmth of this combination than can the 'ism'of Judaism.

Faith in action

A word which is incontrovertibly part of ancient Hebrew vocabulary and Jewish religious terminology is *emunah* ('faith'). This means not so much 'belief' (as in 'I believe that . . .') as 'trust' (as in 'I believe in . . .'). Faith, in the Hebrew Bible, refers not to a set of doctrines which can be described without being believed but to a stance adopted and acted upon. It involves inward trust, commitment, and obedience, as seen in the life of Abraham (Genesis 15:6). It is 'being faithful'. So the famous phrase from the prophet Habakkuk: '. . . the righteous live by their faith' (2:4) refers both to belief in God and to the morality which follows from it. In our passion for a system, we might label this 'ethical monotheism'. It is perhaps this ancient word 'faith' which gives us our best clue to approaching Judaism. Faith is something active. It is something done by people and involves trust in something or someone else. It is to do with experience. What happens in the historical life of the Jewish people is what determines the nature and content of Judaism. As the very name indicates, Judaism should be defined in terms of the Jewish people and a people is defined historically as a group of people sharing a common history.

History experienced

In 1937, American Rabbis of the growing Reform movement in Judaism met for conference at Columbus, Ohio. Their declaration of principles opens with one of the few modern attempts at a concise definition of Judaism: 'Judaism is the historical religious experience of the Jewish people.' This and the titles of studies of Judaism (such as Trepp's *A History of the Jewish Experience* in 1973; Seltzer's *Jewish People, Jewish Thought: The Jewish Experience in History* in 1980 and his *Judaism: A People and its History* in 1987; and Rayner and Goldberg's *The Jewish People: Their History and their Religion* in 1989) recognize the value of the historical approach to Judaism.

10 principal centres of Jewish Population			
(world population =13 million)			
USA	5,800,000	UK	285,000
Israel	5,300,000	Brazil	250,000
Former USSR	879,800 (approx)	Argentina	240,000
France	650,000	Hungary	100,000
Canada	362,000	Australia	97,000

We have already seen why a theological approach, defining Judaism in terms of ideas or beliefs, is suspect. A sociological approach, starting from observable phenomena of worship and ritual, might also produce an inappropriate picture of Judaism. It is more likely to give us 'Judaism', since Jews worldwide live under very different conditions and amongst many non-Jewish majorities. It might try to reduce Judaism to whatever a group of people say and do at a given time or place, which is surely inadequate when representing a religion which appeals to revelation contained in holy writings and passed on by holy teachers. By contrast, the historical approach is particularly suited to the study of Judaism. It is not simply the history of the Jewish people that is studied, but the reflection on this history. Judaism can no more be reduced to history than it can to ethics. It is the religious significance of the history, the way in which Jews perceive in it a divine purpose, that constitutes its importance. A literal history of a religion tends to tell you everything but what you want to know about it, that is, what does the religion mean to those who practise it? It is what might be called 'sacred history' which is vital to Judaism. Jewish ceremonies, notably the Passover celebration, re-enact historical experience and affirm its ever present meaning. Indeed, it is an attachment to this experience which, as we have seen, makes someone a Jew.

Further, Jewish beliefs not only express historical experience but have been formed by it. We cannot understand contemporary Judaism in isolation from the past. All the different movements, however innovatory, are deeply aware of their roots in the Judaism of past generations. The historical approach takes account of this variety of Jewish expression and, at the same time, of the geographical and cultural diversity of the Jewish people.

The essence of Judaism

Attempts to summarize Judaism

Can the historical approach also help us gain a sense of the unity of the Jewish experience? Is it possible for us, as we try to 'teach ourselves Judaism', to have at least a simple starting point, a summary of what Judaism is? This is an ancient quest. The Talmud tells the story of a prospective convert who comes to Rabbi Hillel, asking to be taught the whole of the Torah (the whole body of Jewish teaching) while standing on one leg. Hillel responds to his request with the words:

> *That which is hateful unto thee do not do unto thy neighbour. This is the whole of the Torah. The rest is commentary. Go and study.*

> (Shabbat 31a)

The reply (which has become known as the 'golden rule') is, of course, striking in its emphasis on doing rather than on intellectual believing. But the question is also interesting. Presumably if the Greek-speaking Jews had told the story they would have made the convert ask to be taught 'Judaism' while standing on one leg. For this is, in effect, what is being requested. The student of every age, not surprisingly, wants to discover the guiding principle of Judaism, its main thrust, its particular viewpoint.

There have been other talmudic attempts to distil the essence of Judaism. In one passage (Makkot 23b–24a), it is said that God gave to Moses 613 precepts, but that later teachers reduced these to certain basic principles: David to eleven (Psalm 15); Isaiah to six (Isaiah 33: 15–16); Micah to three (Micah 6:8); Isaiah, again, to two (Isaiah 56:1), and finally, Amos and Habakkuk to one: 'Seek me and live' (Amos 5:4) and 'The righteous live by their faith' (Habakkuk 2:4). In the twelfth century, the great talmudic scholar and philosopher Maimonides (his full name is Rabbi Moses Ben Maimon and he is sometimes known by the acronym 'Rambam') lays down 13 principles of faith which, in his view and that of many later Jewish teachers, are essential to Judaism. Originally in Arabic (the language used by intellectuals of his day in Spain and other Muslim countries), they represent not so much a bare formal statement or creed as a response to the challenges presented to Judaism by Islam and Christianity. They can be summarized as:

- God exists
- God is one
- God is not in bodily form
- God is eternal
- Jews must worship him alone
- God has communicated through the prophets
- Moses is the greatest of the prophets
- the Torah is of divine origin
- the Torah is eternally valid
- God knows the deeds of human beings
- God punishes the evil and rewards the good
- God will send a Messiah
- God will resurrect the dead.

Though much criticised and variously interpreted in different Jewish traditions, this attempt at a summary of the foundations of Jewish belief has found its way into Jewish liturgy. In hymnic form, it is sung in synagogue worship. (The hymn is called the *Yigdal*, from its opening word in Hebrew, meaning 'exalt'. In English, it begins: 'The living God we praise, exalt, adore'.)

History and varieties of Judaism

In the past two centuries, new factors have been operative in the search for the essence of Judaism. One was the rise in the nineteenth century of a movement aimed at the objective investigation into the sources and history of Judaism. This demonstrated the range of Jewish thought and the fact that it developed in response to outside stimuli. No longer would it be possible to view it as a self-contained unchanging entity. Another was political emancipation. Emerging into western society, Jews needed to adapt Judaism to make it viable in the new situation and capable of meeting new challenges. The power of Jewish institutions got lost in the integration of Jews into the structure of the modern state. Questions about the character of the Jewish community, the authority of the Jewish leadership now without political power, and the role of Jewish law led to great uncertainty and readjustment. This social uprooting was often combined with physical uprooting which, although not a new experience for Jews, could not be anything but deeply disorientating. The Holocaust and the establishment of the State of Israel in 1948 have had a profound effect not just on Jewish population but also on Jewish self-perception and self-confidence. In the modern period, starting with the French Revolution of 1789, the Jewish world has been transformed.

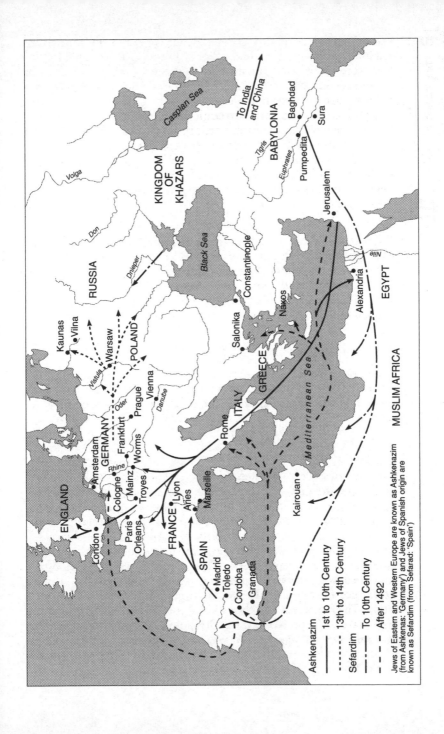

All this has made it hard to detect what is permanent in Judaism. Indeed, some would maintain that it is no longer possible to give a simple account of Judaism in our time. There are different movements in Judaism, each claiming authenticity for itself, but none recognised as definitively authentic by the others. There is no longer a widely accepted yardstick for measuring any particular belief practice. The relatively homogeneous tradition of 200 years ago has gone, making it impossible to say: 'This is Judaism'. There are Jewish thinkers, however, who think that it is possible, even after much of the impact just outlined. The leader of German Jewry, Leo Baeck, entitled his book *The Essence of Judaism*. In it he writes:

> *The essence is characterised by what has been gained and preserved. And such constancy, such essence, Judaism possesses despite its many varieties and the shifting phases of its long career. In virtue of that essence they all have something in common, a unity of thought and feeling, and an inward bond.*

(3rd edition, 1948)

Earlier this century, the talmudic scholar, Ahad Ha-Am, suggested that the essence of Judaism consists in the elevation of the ideal above all material or physical forms or conceptions. He observed that if Hillel's convert had come to him demanding to be taught the whole of the Torah while standing on one leg, he would have replied:

> *Thou shalt not make unto thee a graven image, nor any manner of likeness* (Exodus 20:4). *This is the whole of the Torah. The rest is commentary.*

Is it or is it not possible then to establish the essentials of Judaism? It is clearly precarious to think of Judaism in monolithic terms. Differing civilisations: Egyptian, Canaanite, Babylonian, Persian, Greek, Roman, Christian, and Muslim have made their influence felt on Jews and through them on Judaism itself. As it has developed and adapted to changing circumstances throughout its long history, Judaism naturally contains varying emphases, as well as outright contradictions. If one speaks of the essence of Judaism, or 'normative Judaism', as it is sometimes called, what are the objective grounds for determining what is essential or normative and what is peripheral or ephemeral? A strongly subjective element will surely creep in here.

God, the Torah, and the people of Israel

Perhaps, however, as long as caution is exercised and no exaggerated claims are made for it, it is legitimate to seek such a thing as normative Judaism or an essence. The most important work of Jewish mysticism, the *Zohar* ('illumination') speaks of three elements bound to one another. These are: God, the Torah, and Israel. For all that interpretation of these three ideas has varied from age to age and though there are real differences of emphasis springing from different cultures and outlooks, there does emerge among the faithful a kind of consensus that God, the Torah, and the people are vital to Judaism. As the Jewish theologian, Louis Jacobs, succinctly has it:

> *A Judaism without God is no Judaism. A Judaism without Torah is no Judaism. A Judaism without Jews is no Judaism.*

A distinction between secular and religious Judaism may be helpful. 'Secular Judaism' describes the philosophy of Jews who accept specific Jewish values and even some practices but without attributing religious significance to them. They would describe themselves as Jewish, whilst rejecting any religious philosophy. Some scholars propose other terms to make this distinction clear. Jacob Neusner, for example, has spoken of the 'Judaist' as distinct from the Jew. The latter is one who belongs to the ethnic group of the Jews. His Jewishness comprises what is Jewish *about* his culture, whichever part of the world he lives in. A 'Judaist', on the other hand, is a Jew who, in addition, affirms the Judaic tradition in important ways. Neusner is here differentiating between Jewishness and Judaism, which he calls 'the Judaic tradition'. In his book, *The Way of Torah: An Introduction to Judaism*, he writes:

> *Jewishness refers to the conglomeration of those traits which, in various settings, are regarded as peculiarly and characteristically Jewish; but those traits may have little, if anything, to do with the Judaic tradition. Judaism consists of the religious tradition enshrined in the holy books, expressed by the holy words, deeds, way of living, principles of faith, subsumed under the word Torah.*

(Dickenson Publishing Company, 1974)

Writing in 1992, Neusner admits the difficulty of this distinction. From a survey of 5.5 million north Americans who called themselves 'Jewish' in 1990, four million declared that they were Jewish because they practised their religion. Yet it emerged that much of this was a sort of 'civil religion', a supporting of the land of Israel, something which unites Jews of all persuasions in a way which sometimes makes the ancient Judaism of the Torah hard to locate. Neusner now inclines to speaking of 'Judaisms' as what he calls 'a family of religions'.

The history of Judaism can be divided into five periods:

1 Ancient Israel before Judaism, from the beginnings to 586 BCE.
2 The Beginning of Judaism, after the destruction of the Temple in 586 BCE.
3 The Formative Age of Rabbinic Judaism, after the destruction of the Second Temple in 70 CE.
4 The Domination of Rabbinic Judaism, from 600–1800 CE.
5 The Age of Diverse Judaisms, from the American and French Revolutions of 1776 and 1789 to the present.

Judaism as a world faith

This book is entitled not *Teach Yourself Being Jewish*, but *Teach Yourself Judaism*, and it treats Judaism as a world faith. For a world faith is precisely what it is. Judaism centres on faith, the faith of the people of Israel in God. This God, Jews believe, is not an absent or indifferent God, but one who has conveyed his will to humanity. This will is to be discovered in the Torah, God's direction for living. The Jewish faith is in the love and power of God to bring about his purpose for all humankind. In this purpose, Jews believe, the people of Israel have a special part to play. The Torah has been given to them for the benefit of the world. They, the Jewish people, are the vehicle for communicating God's will. Judaism is thus a world faith, not only in its geographical spread, but in its horizons. It is a faith for the world not in the conviction that all must become Jewish, for this is emphatically not the aim of Judaism, but in the conviction that the world is God's and humanity must conform to his will.

The starting point for any study of this faith is the Bible. Here we find the record of the key ideas, practices, and institutions which became prominent in the faith. We cannot, strictly speaking, refer to the biblical faith, the faith of ancient Israel, as Judaism.

For one thing, the term *Yehudi* ('Jew') did not come to be used of the whole people of Israel until late in biblical history. It originally meant 'someone belonging to the tribe of Judah'. More importantly, there are distinctive features which mark off later Judaism from some of the forms, ideas, and worship found in the Bible. Nonetheless, most Jews would recognise sufficient continuity to enable them to regard Judaism as the same faith. It is in the Bible that our attention is drawn immediately to the essence of Judaism as a faith, an activity, what people do. We see there the sort of religion that we are approaching. As Baeck states in *The Essence of Judaism*:

> *This is the principle of Judaism in its deepest meaning: through action we shall preach our religion. Our lives shall speak of the greatness of our faith.*

02

the roots of belief and practice – the Bible

In this chapter you will learn:

- about the structure of the Jewish Bible
- about key Jewish beliefs as found in the Bible
- about the way the Bible is read, studied, and interpreted.

A people's history and its significance

By referring to Jews as 'people of the book', Islamic texts rightly draw attention to the centrality of holy books in Judaism. These books are the Bible, the Talmud (rabbinic writings), and the siddur (prayer book), but it is the first of these on which all expressions of the Jewish faith depend. Not only is the Bible chronologically the first to be formed, but it is also the root of all that comes after.

The religion portrayed in the Bible cannot be simply equated with Judaism. The religion of the Bible represents diverse circles with diverse viewpoints developed over centuries. Neither is there one circle or viewpoint which can be said to represent modern Judaism. Nonetheless, certain key ideas can be identified as assuming crucial importance in the Bible and as being influential in shaping Judaism. As we have seen in Chapter 1, these revolve round the triangle of people, God, and Torah. Inextricably linked to the people is the land. These key ideas are expressed in the Bible not in the form of creed but in the form of history. Some say that Judaism begins with Abraham, the first person with whom God makes a covenant and to whom God promises the land (Genesis 15:18; 17:2, 19). Certainly, he is regarded as the father or patriarch of the Jewish people. (His son, Isaac, and grandson, Jacob, are also regarded as patriarchs and their wives as matriarchs.) Others consider it more appropriate to locate the beginning of Judaism in the formation of Scripture, in the period after the destruction of the first Temple in 586 BCE. Though most of the events described in the Bible take place before this date, some writing and most collecting of the writing occurs after it. It is the written record which seeks to give enduring significance to the ancient history of a particular group of people.

Simply telling the story of this people, according to the biblical books, does not in itself give us Judaism. There are many books about Jewish history which remain just history and do not go on to show how the religious record of events laid the foundations for the Judaism which evolved from it. What the Bible offers is history *and* an interpretation of its significance. Its opening words: 'In the beginning God' set the tone for a presentation of history which is going somewhere. Jews believe that their own history is a continuation of this, that they are the inheritors of the covenant and, therefore, obligated by the Bible's commands, albeit in reinterpreted ways. It is a tenet of rabbinic Judaism, the

Judaism which eventually became the norm, that all the features of contemporary Judaism have their ultimate source in the Bible. Rabbinic literature and the principles of interpretation which it contains revolve around establishing the biblical authority behind each feature.

The structure of the Jewish Bible

A sense of authority deriving from divine inspiration is the key to understanding the formation and influence of the Jewish Bible. The Latin word *biblia*, 'little books', (ultimately linked to the Greek *Byblos*, an ancient Syrian city renowned for its papyrus industry) indicates that the Bible is not one book but many. A range of books (sometimes considered to number 24 with some in the list below being counted as one book) was finally accepted as particularly authoritative for Judaism, but not all at the same stage and not all carrying the same weight. The order in which the various books or collections of books gained acceptance corresponds to the priority afforded them in Jewish life. The books fall into three main sections. The section which comes first, both in its formation and in its importance, is *Torah*, often translated as 'Law' but better rendered as 'Teaching' or 'Direction'. This comprises the first five books (known, therefore, also by the Greek name, the *Pentateuch*). The second section comprises the *Neviim*, 'Prophets', which is sometimes subdivided into Former and Latter Prophets and which altogether comprises 19 books, though one book can be subdivided into 12 smaller units (the Minor Prophets). The third section comprises all the remaining books. Of very varied character, this section is known as the *Ketuvim*, 'Writings'. The Torah plays a vital role in Jewish worship, a portion being read at every Sabbath morning service from specially prepared parchment scrolls. The Prophets play a complementary role at this service, with selected excerpts being read from printed texts, whilst the Writings do not figure in the public readings, except notably on certain special days for which a particular book has particular significance, for example, Esther at the Festival of Purim (see Chapter 13).

The books of the Bible according to the traditional Jewish arrangement

Torah, Teaching		Genesis Exodus Leviticus Numbers Deuteronomy
Neviim, Prophets: Former Prophets		Joshua Judges 1 & 2 Samuel 1 & 2 Kings
Latter Prophets	Major Prophets	Isaiah Jeremiah Ezekiel
	Minor Prophets	Hosea Joel Amos Obadiah Jonah Micah Nahum Habakkuk Zephaniah Haggai Zachariah Malachi
Ketuvim, Writings		Psalms Proverbs Job
	Hamesh Megillot, Five Scrolls	Song of Songs Ruth Lamentations Ecclesiastes Esther
		Daniel Ezra & Nehemiah 1 & 2 Chronicles

Differences between the Jewish Bible and the Christian Old Testament

This ancient division into three sections is obscured in the Christian arrangement of the books, where the material is divided into 39 books with the Former Prophets separated from the Latter Prophets and the Writings scattered at various points in the list. The Jewish arrangement is what gives the usual Hebrew name for the Bible, the *Tenakh* (also transliterated as Tanach), which is an abbreviation composed of the initial letters of the words: Torah, Neviim, and Ketuvim. The term 'Old Testament' is not used by Jews. 'Testament' means 'Covenant', a key term in Jewish belief, denoting the special relationship between God and the people of Israel. Christians speak of the Old Testament to differentiate between the covenant with the people of Israel and a further covenant which they believe to have been established by Jesus and which lies at the root of the 27 books known collectively as the New Testament. From the Jewish point of view, the original covenant stands and is, therefore, not referred to as 'old'. When Christians refer to the Bible, they mean both the collection of 39 (which correspond to the Jewish 24 books, only subdivided and differently arranged) and the collection of 27 books from the first and second centuries CE. The latter were written in Greek whilst the former were written in Hebrew (apart from a section of the Book of Daniel which was written in Aramaic, a very similar Semitic language). A clear way of referring to the Jewish Bible is, therefore, 'the Hebrew Bible'. To Jews, the Hebrew Bible is simply 'the Bible'. Jews may study the New Testament to learn about Christianity, but they do not regard it as sacred scripture and so it has no place in Jewish belief and practice. There are other books which are part of the canon ('yardstick' or 'standard') in the Roman Catholic and Eastern Orthodox Churches and which are known as the Apocrypha, which is Greek for 'hidden books'. Jewish tradition refers to them as 'external books'. Among them are I and II Maccabees, of historical interest for the Maccabean revolt commemorated at the festival of Hanukah, and one, occasionally cited in rabbinic literature, which is known variously as 'The Wisdom of Jesus Son of Sirah', 'Ben Sira', or Ecclesiasticus. This is not to be confused with the biblical book of Ecclesiastes, also known as 'Kohelet', which is one of the Ketuvim.

The content of the Torah

The term 'Torah' can be used of the entire Hebrew Bible and indeed of the Bible together with the rabbinic teachings which evolved during the first five or six centuries CE. Its most specific use, however, is for the first five books of the Bible. This use is both a little misleading and highly appropriate. It is misleading in that it perhaps suggests that all of the five books are written in the same style and have the same concerns. The reality is that many different strands of material are here collected together. To call the whole lot 'Torah', 'Direction' or 'Teaching' is, however, appropriate in that its unifying concern is God's direction for the people of Israel. Many passages in it are introduced by such phrases as: 'The Lord said to Moses' and this ancient belief in Mosaic authorship is still part of Orthodox Jewish faith.

God the creator of the world

It is all the more striking that this handbook for Jewish living opens with an account of the creation of the world as a whole. Genesis 1–2 contains, in fact, two different accounts but both concerned to stress the sovereign purpose of God and the responsibility given to humankind for the care of the created world. The stories in the first 11 chapters of Genesis raise deep questions about the relationship between God and human beings. God's despair characterizes the 10 generations between Adam and Noah and then God's waiting for humanity to acknowledge him as creator characterizes the next 10 generations from Noah to Abraham. The focus then narrows to Abraham, his wife, Sarah, and their descendants. Through their responsiveness to God's commands, the people of Israel is formed. The name 'Israel' is the one given to Jacob (Genesis 35:10) and so the descendants are literally the 'children of Israel'. The term 'Hebrews' is used of this original group of Semites, as in Genesis 14:13 (others, such as Arabs, are also Semites) and the term 'Jews' historically belongs to Israelites from the sixth century BCE. They (the 'Yehudi') were the people from the southern kingdom of *Yehuda* ('Judah'), a term used of the province of 'Judea' in Maccabean times and still used by Jews to denote this area south of Jerusalem. The name of 'Israel' comes also to be applied to the land which when promised to Abraham is called 'Canaan' and is occupied by the Canaanites (see, notably, Genesis 12 and 17).

The book of Genesis thus gives the setting for the religion which ultimately developed into Judaism. The one creator God has all humanity within his interest. Noah, as its representative (Genesis 9:18–19) is, according to the Talmud, given seven basic principles by which to live. This 'Noahide Code' forbids idolatry, blasphemy, incest, murder, robbery, and cruelty to animals. It requires honesty and fairness, including the establishment of lawcourts to dispense justice. Only then is attention focused on Abraham and the promises made to his descendants. Hence, Genesis transforms the history of this particular group into something not only of enduring consequence for all succeeding children of Israel but also of universal interest and significance.

Obligations of a chosen people

This perspective is most clearly expressed in a vital passage in the second book of the Torah:

> *You have seen what I did to the Egyptians, and how I bore you on eagles' wings and brought you to myself. Now therefore, if you obey my voice and keep my covenant, you shall be my treasured possession out of all the peoples. Indeed, the whole earth is mine, but you shall be for me a priestly kingdom and a holy nation.*

> (Exodus 19:4–6)

The notion of a 'chosen people' is open to serious misunderstanding, by Jews if they forget the conditional nature of this covenant struck with Moses on their behalf and by non-Jews if they see it as limiting God's concern to the children of Israel exclusively. The point of this passage, and of others in the Torah and the Neviim (Prophets), is that the children of Israel are chosen to play a special role in God's plan for 'the whole earth'. It is not that they are better than other people, any more than priests, who in ancient Israel represented the people before God and God before the people, were better than non-priests. They are simply called to a different task. Their task is to be a holy nation, a nation set apart. So before the Torah reading in the synagogue, the prayer spoken is:

> *Blessed art thou, O Lord our God. King of the universe, who hast chosen us from all peoples, and hast given us thy Torah.*

No reason has ever been found for why *this* people should have been given the responsibility. According to rabbinic comment on Exodus 24:7, the Torah was offered to the nations of the world, but only Israel accepted it. It is made plain, however, that God's love and not Israel's deserving was the foundation for this choice. In Deuteronomy 7:7–8, we read:

> *It was not because you were more numerous than any other people that the LORD set his heart on you and chose you – for you were the fewest of all peoples. It was because the LORD loved you and kept the oath that he swore to your ancestors, that the LORD has brought you out with a mighty hand and redeemed you from the house of slavery, from the hand of Pharaoh king of Egypt.*

The fundamental question might still be raised: why should God choose one people at all? Why could not the whole human race be the means of fulfilling his purpose for the world? Perhaps the best answer is that suggested by the British theologian, Rabbi Louis Jacobs, who remarks that 'all the great achievements of humanity have been made by particular people living in a particular way'. Shakespeare's plays could not be produced in the abstract but needed an Englishman writing in English. Yet their value extends far beyond England. So God has to confine his choice to the Jewish people with their particular experience. Yet, 'what came out of it all and, Judaism believes, what will come out of it, is for all humanity' (*The Book of Jewish Belief*, Berhman House, 1984).

Especially in periods of persecution, the Jewish approach has been nationalistic or particularist in the sense of stressing God's favouring the Jews against the other nations. It is, nonetheless, accurate to describe Judaism as universalist in outlook. We see, especially in passages in the Prophets, a notion of the Israelite people being a blessing to the world (e.g. Isaiah 19:24–25). Certainly Jewish liturgy and philosophical thought emphasize Israel's special role in the redemption of humankind (e.g. Saadiah Gaon in the ninth and tenth centuries CE, Halevi in the eleventh and twelfth centuries and the Kabbalah (mystical teaching)).

To indicate the special obligations laid on Israel is the central purpose of the book of Exodus. The early chapters present the story of the slavery of Jacob's descendants in Egypt and their liberation to 'a land flowing with milk and honey' (3:8) under the leadership of Moses. This 'exodus' (the Greek for 'going out') from Egypt is the major event in Jewish history, celebrated annually at Passover and recalled constantly in Jewish liturgy. The culmination of the exodus is the affirmation of the covenant at Mount Sinai (also called Horeb) described in Exodus 19. The following chapter states 10 of the commandments involved in keeping the covenant. These 'commandments' or 'obligations' (in Hebrew *mitzvot*, singular *mitzvah*) are both positive (e.g. 'Honour your father and your mother') and negative (e.g. 'You shall not murder'). The first of these 10 words (as the Greek term *Decalogue* calls them) is actually a statement which sets all the other commandments in context:

> I am the LORD your God, who brought you out of the land of Egypt, out of the house of slavery.

> (Exodus 20:2)

The second (verses 3–6) puts starkly the main consequence of the Israelites' redemption by God, namely, that they must have no other God or make any physical representation of God. This belief in an incomparable God, as the sole creator and sustainer of everything that exists, lies at the heart of the Jewish faith. It is proclaimed with crystal clarity in: 'Hear, O Israel: the LORD is our God, the LORD is one' (Deuteronomy 6:4).

The mitzvot of Exodus 20 (also found in Deuteronomy 5) concern both worship and morality. 'Remember the Sabbath day' is a ritual mitzvah, whilst 'You shall not bear false witness against your neighbour' is an ethical mitzvah. There is a tradition that the mitzvot found in the Torah number 613. They divide into positive (248) and negative (365). A further distinction can be made between mitzvot for which the reason is obvious, such as not murdering, and those for which the reason is not obvious, such as not eating certain kinds of poultry. The first sort are called *mishpatim* ('judgements') and the second *hukim* ('statutes'). Some Jews think that it is good to try to work out reasons for the hukim, notably Maimonides, who, in his *Guide for the Perplexed*, says that they, like the mishpatim, have a rational basis. Others think that they should not attempt to find reasons for the apparently unreasonable. The Bible does not itself offer reasons for the mitzvot. They are simply to be kept in obedience to God's Torah.

Legislation occupies a major place in the remainder of the Pentateuch. The book of Leviticus specifies the rules and regulations by which the people must live to attain 'holiness'.

Many of these concern the sacred calendar and laws of ritual purity. The role of the priests in offering sacrifices on the people's behalf is described. The holiness of the promised land of Genesis and Exodus is emphasized, with sacrifices seen as the produce of this land. Other mitzvot are general moral precepts such as not taking vengeance or bearing a grudge (Leviticus 19:17–18). The book of Numbers tells stories of the people's wandering in the wilderness between Sinai and the land of Canaan, but again the emphasis is upon Moses as a teacher of the Torah and on the responsibility of the priesthood. The Book of Deuteronomy restates the rules of the covenant and also some of the narratives of the preceding books. These are presented in the form of a long sermon by Moses, with whose death the book ends.

The Torah in study and prayer

Divided into portions (*sidrot*), the Torah is read in the synagogue each Sabbath and festival. Each *sidra* takes its name from its opening word(s) in Hebrew. So Genesis 1:1–6:8 is called *Bereshit*, 'In the beginning'. Bereshit constitutes also the name by which the whole book of Genesis is known in the Hebrew Bible. In printed form, the Torah is at the centre of both prayer and study in the synagogue and the home. The term for this printed version of the five books of Moses, as distinct from the handwritten scroll (the *sefer Torah*, plural *sifrei Torah*), is the *humash* (from *hamesh*, 'five').

The content of the Neviim

In popular speech 'prophecy' is a prediction about the future. When we turn to prophecy in the Hebrew Bible, however, we see that the future is not its major concern. The first four books of the Neviim ('Prophets') are predominantly concerned with the past and the implications for the present. The writers of the books of Joshua, Judges, Samuel, and Kings relate events in the people's history from their entry into Canaan until the destruction of Jerusalem some 500 years later. But as they do so, they interpret the events in terms of their theological perspective. The books are prophetic rather than historical in that they evaluate history according to the divine guidance it shows and the moral lessons to be learned from it. The dominant thought is that obedience to God brings prosperity whilst disobedience brings disaster. The Neviim begin where the Pentateuchal history leaves off, describing the Israelite conquest of Canaan under the leadership of Joshua, Moses' successor. They describe how, especially in times of crisis, a leader, known as a 'judge', rises up to guide the people. These national heroes include Samson and Deborah.

The Former Prophets

Of particular importance is the formation of the monarchy in the time of the prophet Samuel. Not all the stories reflect a favourable attitude to this, but those which do suggest that the Twelve Tribes felt the need of a king as a unifying force. 1 Samuel 10:1 recounts Samuel's anointing of the first king, Saul. As an 'anointed one' (in Hebrew, *mashiah*), each king, beginning with Saul, was to be God's representative in ruling his people according to God's laws. The principal figure is David, not least because he captured the city of Jerusalem and made it his capital (2 Samuel 5:1–10). Though not always shown in a good light (as in the story of his adultery and subsequent rebuke by the prophet Nathan in 2 Samuel 11–12), David becomes the model of a just ruler (e.g. Isaiah 11:1–5). His son, Solomon, builds the Temple in Jerusalem, a permanent building to replace the earlier temporary sanctuary (Exodus 25–27).

In the reign of Solomon's son, Rehoboam, the kingdom divides; the tribes of Benjamin and Judah forming the southern kingdom of Judah and the remaining 10 tribes forming the northern kingdom of Israel. The remainder of 1 and 2 Kings traces the histories of the two kingdoms down to the Assyrian destruction of Israel's capital, Samaria, in 721 BCE and the Babylonian destruction of Judah's capital, Jerusalem, in 586 BCE. Prophets, essentially spokesmen for God, appear at critical times to recall the people and their kings to the worship of one God and to the moral standards of the Israelite religion (e.g. Elijah in 1 Kings 18 and 21).

The Latter Prophets

The names of prophetic figures living between the eighth and the fifth centuries BCE, whose messages have been committed to writing either by themselves or by their disciples, constitute the names of the books of the Latter Prophets. The books of Isaiah, Jeremiah, and Ezekiel are substantial and are, therefore, referred to as the 'Major Prophets'. The 'Minor Prophets' are much shorter books, counted in the Hebrew Bible as one book, 'The Book of the Twelve'. The prophetic message varies according to the particular crisis being addressed, but there are some recurrent features. Chief amongst them are savage criticisms of Israel and Judah for betraying the covenant by relying on power politics and idolatry and by breaking its moral demands, as in Hosea where he rebukes Israel (here called by the name of the largest of the northern tribes, Ephraim):

> *When Ephraim saw his sickness, and Judah his wound, then Ephraim went to Assyria, and sent to the great king. But he is not able to cure you or heal your wound. (5:13)*
> *They made kings, but not through me;*
> *they set up princes, but without my knowledge.*
> *With their silver and gold they made idols for their own destruction. (8:4)*
> *Hear the word of the LORD, O people of Israel;*
> *for the LORD has an indictment against the inhabitants of the land.*
> *There is no faithfulness or loyalty, and no knowledge of God in the land.*
> *Swearing, lying, and murder, and stealing and adultery break out; bloodshed follows bloodshed. (4:1–2)*

The values of the Torah are appealed for, such as active compassion for the vulnerable. The fatherless, the widow, and the foreigner are the objects of God's particular care in the Pentateuch (e.g. Exodus 22:21–24; Deuteronomy 10:17–19). So Isaiah pleads to his people to avert divine retribution:

> *Wash yourselves; make yourselves clean;*
> *remove the evil of your doings from before my eyes;*
> *cease to do evil, learn to do good;*
> *seek justice, rescue the oppressed,*
> *defend the orphan, plead for the widow. (1:16–17)*

The hope for a messiah

We see, especially in the book of Isaiah, the development of the idea that when Israel fulfils her role of being truly loyal to God all the universe will enjoy a new age of peace (notably 2:2–4, 9:6–7; 11:1–9). From continued disappointment with nearly all their kings after David there developed the hope for a ruler who would demonstrate the qualities of an 'anointed one' (messiah). Under Roman rule this Messianic hope, whose roots are in the Hebrew Bible, grew and in the thinking of the rabbis there emerged the idea of a human figure who would be sent by God to usher in a golden age. In the first century CE, the Pharisees believed that the dead would then be resurrected.

There have been Messianic claimants at various times in Jewish history, for example, Simon bar Kosiba (known as Bar Kokhba, 'son of a star'), who in 132 CE freed Jerusalem from Roman rule for three years until his revolt was crushed, and a Turkish Jew named Shabbetai Zevi in 1665 CE who subsequently converted to Islam. Jews believe, however, that the Messianic Age has clearly not dawned. They, therefore, reject the claim at the heart of Christianity that Jesus was the Messiah (the Greek equivalent of this title for the 'anointed' is the 'Christ'). There are groups, known as 'Messianic Jews' or 'Jews for Jesus', who today believe that they can maintain their Judaism whilst accepting Jesus as the Messiah. It is hard to see why they simply do not call themselves Christians, as did those Jews who came to believe in Jesus as the Messiah in New Testament times. From the point of view of mainstream Judaism, be it Orthodox or non-Orthodox, these groups are confusing the fundamental beliefs of both Judaism and Christianity. Christianity rests on the figure of Jesus as having fulfilled the Messianic hope and as having replaced the Torah as the focus for obedience. Judaism sees obedience to the Torah as the remaining precondition for the Messianic Age. Many Jews pray daily for the coming of the Messiah and for the accompanying restoration of the Temple and sacrifice. Others, especially non-Orthodox Jews, put the emphasis on a new age rather than on an individual figure and pray for human transformation rather than a return to the sacrificial system.

The content of the Ketuvim

The destruction of the First Temple in 586 BCE was one of two definitive events in the development of the Hebrew Bible, as there arose the need to explain the course Jewish history had taken. The second definitive event was the restoration of Jerusalem and the building of the Second Temple, between 538 and 450 BCE. When the Persian ruler, Cyrus, defeated the Babylonians in 538, he allowed people who had been exiled to return to their native lands. Some Jews chose to stay in Babylon, forming the beginnings of an important Diaspora community. Those who returned to Judah included Ezra who was a scribe, an expert in the Torah, and Nehemiah who became governor. The books of Ezra and Nehemiah describe this crucial period, partly in the form of autobiographical memoirs. Vitally significant for the future development of Judaism is Ezra's public reading of the Torah and the people's commitment to its commands, including one against intermarriage with non-Jews (Nehemiah 10:29). Maintaining the purity of the religion, and thus avoiding renewed unfaithfulness to God and consequent exile, became of paramount importance.

The content and literary genre of the third division of the Hebrew Bible is so diverse that essentially the Ketuvim ('Writings') comprise all the books that are left when the Torah and the Neviim are removed. Written at about the same time as the books of Ezra and Nehemiah (counted as a single book), are 1 and 2 Chronicles which retell history from Adam to the Babylonian exile but with an emphasis on the priesthood rather than on the monarchy of the Samuel-Kings account. The Book of Daniel tells the story of faithfulness in time of persecution. It is set in the Babylonian period though modern scholarship believes it to relate to the Maccabean period.

The first of the Ketuvim is the Book of Psalms, a collection of 150 poems, all or most of which were perhaps composed for worship in the Temple. They still play a prominent part in Jewish worship, representing as they do, often with great literary beauty, the vast range of experiences which confront people of faith. God is thanked and protested to, praised for individual and communal blessings and questioned about individual and communal suffering. Tradition ascribes them to King David. Other books in this miscellany of Ketuvim include Proverbs which is largely a collection of wise maxims and Job which is an exploration of a man's continued faith in God in spite of his experience of innocent suffering. This constitutes a challenge to the predominant biblical association of faithfulness with prosperity.

A challenge to the exclusivist position of post-exilic Judaism is offered by the book of Ruth which tells of its Moabite heroine's devotion to her Jewish mother-in-law and God. This is one of five very short books known collectively as *Hamesh Megillot* ('The Five Scrolls'). Each one is read in the synagogue at a point in the Jewish year considered appropriate to its season or theme: Ruth at the Festival of Weeks, Ecclesiastes at the Festival of Tabernacles, Lamentations on the Fast of Av lamenting the destruction of Jerusalem, the Song of Songs (which is a series of erotic poems, sometimes interpreted as an allegory of the love between God and Israel) at the Festival of Passover and Esther at the Festival of Purim.

Interpreting the Bible

Midrash

Even as the Bible was being written and translated, interpretation was going on. Interpretation is vital if the words of a sacred text are to exercise any significant influence on a people's religious tradition. Words can be ambiguous and even contradictory. Without comment, they might well be ignored. The Greek word used for such interpreting or explaining the meaning of a text is 'exegesis' and the Hebrew word used for biblical exegesis by ancient Jewish authorites is *midrash*. There are different kinds of *midrashim* (plural) coming from different rabbinic authorities. Some are quite fanciful whilst others keep closely to the text. Some try to draw out the meaning in the form of a sermon on the readings for the sabbaths and festivals of the year (homiletical midrashim) whilst other midrashim offer a verse by verse commentary (exegetical midrashim). To understand scripture and the way in which it contains the teachings of Judaism entails understanding midrash and it is to this end that much study, whether in the children's *heder* ('religion school') or in the adults' *shiur* ('religion class'), is devoted.

There are two major collections of midrashim. The first, dating from about 300 CE, is the *Mekhilta* ('rules of interpretation') on the book of Exodus, the *Sifra* ('book') on Leviticus, and the *Sifrei* ('books') on Numbers and Deuteronomy. The second and largest collection, dating from the fifth century CE, is called *Midrash Rabbah* ('The Great Midrash'). It is a compilation of commentaries which were originally separate, one on each of the five books of the Pentateuch and one on the *Megillot* ('[five] scrolls'). Just as the Pentateuch is divided into 54 *sidrot* ('orders'), with each sidra known by its opening words in the Hebrew, so the Pentateuchal commentaries are divided into corresponding sections. Thus, for example, in the commentary on Genesis, *Genesis Rabbah*, we find the section *Toledot* ('generations' or 'descendants'). This contains comments on Genesis 25:19–28:9, a portion which begins: 'These are the descendants of Isaac . . .'.

They come from a variety of authorities offering a variety of perspectives. Some are downright contradictory. For instance, in Genesis Rabbah 63:4 (on Genesis 25:20) Rabbi Yitzhak emphasises the pagan Aramean origins of the matriarch Rebekah, making the point that people can rise above their background. By contrast, in 63:6 (on 25:22), Rabbi Yohanan says that when the pregnant Rebekah passed by the synagogue, Jacob would rub on the walls of the womb as he was in such a hurry to get out to pray, whilst Esau would run to worship idols, making the point that the conflicting characters and lifestyles of the two brothers were prenatally determined. With no attempt made to harmonize this point, in 63:10 (on 25:24) Rabbi Levi says that both Esau and Jacob were keen to go to synagogue.

Principles of interpretation

We see here the creativity of the Rabbis as they try to bring out the many-sidedness of reality. We see here also the way in which later institutions, for example, the synagogue, are read back into the Genesis account. Similarly in the midrashic comment on Genesis 25:25 we see reflected the later hostility between Christendom and Jewry traced back through Rome, Herod, the Idumeans, and the Edomites whose progenitor was Esau. (The line is traced back further to Ishmael as distinct from Isaac.) This alerts us to the way in which later interpretation can give out hostile messages and can lead to a dangerous nationalism. We see this process of demonising Esau already begun in the Bible. Thus the Prophetic reading to follow this Torah portion, Malachi 1:1–2:7, includes the words: 'Yet I have loved Jacob but I hated Esau.' The Jewish scriptures have the potential to be interpreted in an anti-Gentile fashion, just as the Christian Gospels can be interpreted anti-Semitically. Aware of these dangers, however, we can appreciate how the importance of the book of Genesis to the Rabbis of the midrash lay not just in its message to Israel in the past but in its meaning to Israel in the present, viz. in the centuries of subservience to Rome. The hope expressed is that Israel will succeed against the pagan and hostile power, like her eponymous ancestor Jacob-Israel who supplanted Esau. So, the midrash maintains, the rules are laid out at the very start of human history.

Transmitting and translating the Bible

Because of the Bible's importance in determining Jewish belief and practice, the greatest care has been exercised throughout the centuries by those transmitting the Hebrew text. The present text is known as the Masoretic text, from *masorah* ('tradition' or 'what is passed on'). Its editors, known as Masoretes, established by the tenth century CE this universally accepted Hebrew edition. We can see textual variants in older texts, but the accuracy of the Masoretic copying is demonstrated by the fact that the Dead Sea Scroll of Isaiah, dating from at least eight centuries earlier, is virtually the same. Until very recently, this scroll constituted the oldest biblical manuscript. From excavations in the 1970s and 1980s, two silver amulets have been discovered whose Hebrew inscriptions antedate this manuscript by about 400 years, going back to the First Temple period. The most striking example is the inscription of an early version of the priestly benediction of Numbers 6:24–26, a prayer which remains a vital part of synagogue liturgy today.

one of the beautiful stained glass windows in Singers Hill Synagogue, Birmingham depicts the building of the walls of Jerusalem and the reading of the Torah

the Hebrew text from Nehemiah 8:2–3 reads: *the priest Ezra brought the law before the assembly . . . and read from it*

We have mentioned the commentaries in the form of midrashim and we shall later note medieval commentaries on the Bible. There is a sense in which commentary goes back to the time of Ezra. Nehemiah 8:8 says that the Torah was read publicly 'with interpretation', giving 'the sense, so that the people understood the reading'. The Talmud concludes from this that an Aramaic translation was already established (Megillah 3a). The term for such translation which, it is believed, included interpretation of the text, is *Targum*. There are some of the Aramaic *targumim* (plural) still in existence which give us an insight into the way the Bible was interpreted in public worship in the early synagogue. The earliest translation of the Bible into a non-Semitic language is the *Septuagint*, a Greek version made over a long period beginning in the third century BCE. Though widely used by Jews in the Graeco-Roman period, it is no longer part of Jewish life, except in the sort of biblical scholarship we shall mention in Chapter 4.

03
the chain of tradition – the Talmud

In this chapter you will learn:

- about the way in which Jewish belief and practice are expressed in the written and the oral Torah
- about the detailed discussion by the Rabbis of the Second Temple period
- about the summaries of the oral Torah in important Law Codes, notably *Shulhan Arukh*.

The written and the oral Torah

Judaism emphasizes not credal formulations nor a central institutional authority but the Torah. The very wideness with which this term is used indicates the flexibility and dynamism of this faith. What is vital is the direction which God is believed to have given for Jewish living and it is this direction, with all its possibilities for the varied and changing circumstances in which the Jewish people find themselves, which must be handed on. We have noted the word *masorah* ('tradition') for the text of the Hebrew Bible as carefully copied. We have encountered the word *midrash* for the written commentary on the biblical text. Coming from a Hebrew root meaning 'to search' or 'to root out', midrash is the investigation of scripture to discover its full meaning. It is no accident that the terms for the classics of Jewish literature are all connected with Hebrew or Aramaic words for teaching, that is, with what one person learns from another, going back ultimately to God. Besides midrash, we have *mishnah*, from a root meaning 'to repeat' and by implication 'to learn', *talmud*, from the verb 'to learn', and *gemara* from the Hebrew for 'to complete' by studying repeatedly. The teachers of the Torah before the written Mishnah are called *Tannaim* ('teachers') – though in their own day they were more usually referred to as 'sages' – and those after the written Mishnah *Amoraim* ('interpreters').

What lies behind all this is the conviction that what was revealed at Sinai was the Torah not only in the sense of the five books of Moses, but also in the sense of a detailed elaboration of the laws and beliefs contained in these five books. The former came to be referred to as the 'written Torah' and the latter as the 'oral Torah'. (The Hebrew term means literally 'Torah in memory'.) The oral Torah was formulated and transmitted in memory, handed on from prophets to sages, from masters to pupils, from the time of Moses himself until it was eventually written down in the Mishnah, about 200 CE, and in successor documents, above all the Talmud.

The key figures in the chain

This belief in an unbroken chain of tradition, in which Ezra (the first of the 'Men of the Great Assembly') around 444 BCE and all teachers coming after were the links, is expressed most famously in the opening words of a tractate which was added to the Mishnah in about 250 CE. Printed in many prayer books because of the importance and accessibility of its ethical teaching, this tractate is known as *Pirke Avot* ('Sayings of the Fathers', sometimes rendered 'Ethics of the Fathers', because of its character). It begins:

> Moses received the Torah on Sinai, and handed it down to Joshua; Joshua to the elders; the elders to the prophets; and the prophets handed it down to the Men of the Great Assembly. They said three things: Be deliberate in judgement; raise up many disciples; and make a fence round the Torah. Simon the Just was one of the last survivors of the Great Assembly. He used to say, Upon three things the world is based: upon the Torah, upon Divine service, and upon the practice of charity. Antigonos of Socho received the tradition from Simon the Just . . .

Many verses later we read:

> Rabban Yochanan, the son of Zakkai, received the tradition from Hillel and Shammai. He used to say, If thou hast learnt much Torah, ascribe not any merit to thyself, for thereunto was thou created. Rabban Yochanan, the son of Zakkai, had five disciples; and these are they, Rabbi Eliezer, the son of Hyrcanus, Rabbi Joshua, the son of Chananya, Rabbi José the Priest, Rabbi Simeon, the son of Nathaniel, and Rabbi Elazar, the son of Arach. (2:9–10)

This list includes key figures in the development of rabbinic Judaism or the 'Judaism of the dual Torah', as the scholar, Jacob Neusner, calls it. The central figure of Yohanan ben Zakkai is its supposed founder. A survivor of the Roman conquest of Jerusalem, he set up a centre at Yavneh (in Greek, Jamnia) in northern Palestine where, about 100 CE, it was decided which books were accepted as sacred scripture. Little is known about him personally, but his importance lies in his emphasis on the study of the Torah.

The varieties of Second Temple Judaism

The two rabbis mentioned before him, Hillel and Shammai, both founded schools for the study of the Torah. Judaism in the first century CE was far from homogeneous. This highly creative phase produced a number of diverse sects or movements. The one whose influence was to prove most lasting in the development of Judaism was the Pharisaic movement and Hillel and Shammai were two of its earliest and most famous teachers. The title which came to be given to these teachers was *rabbi* ('my master' in the sense of 'my teacher'), hence the term 'rabbinic Judaism'. Hillel and Shammai often differed and the opinions of their rival schools are recorded extensively. In the tractate of the Mishnah (rabbinic writings) relating to Blessings (in Hebrew, *Berakhot*), for example, we see discussion about the order of the blessings to be recited at a meal. In the tractate relating to divorce documents (in Hebrew, *Gittin*), we find different interpretations of Deuteronomy 24:1, rendered in the Revised Standard Version of the Bible:

> *When a man takes a wife and marries her, if then she finds no favour in his eyes because he has found some indecency in her, and he writes her a bill of divorce . . .*

What constitute grounds for divorce rests on the meaning of 'some indecency in her'. Adding one or two words to make the meaning clear, we may translate the Mishnah passage on this:

> *The School of Shammai say, A man is not to divorce his wife unless he has found in her some indecency as it is said, 'Because he has found some indecency in her'. But the School of Hillel say, Even if she spoiled the cooking, as it is said 'Because he has found some indecency in her'. Rabbi Akiva says, Even if he has found another more beautiful than she is, as it is said.*

The followers of Shammai took divorce to be permissible only on the ground of a sexual relationship outside marriage, those of Hillel on far less serious grounds and those of Akiva for any reason at all. No final judgement is offered in the Mishnah, but divorce is clearly discouraged by later rabbis, as represented in the Talmud (discussion of the Mishnah), for example: 'If a man divorces his first wife, even the altar sheds tears' (Gittin 90b).

Following Hillel and Yohanan, Akiva is the third in the trilogy of rabbis whose development of the legal traditions of Judaism produced the Mishnah. He is credited with the collection of some of its sayings. He died a martyr's death following the Bar Kokhba Revolt against Rome in about 135 CE.

The lasting importance of the Pharisees

In contrast with the Pharisees in the first century were the Sadducees. The point of conflict between these two groups was precisely the nature and authority of tradition. The Sadducean movement taught that only the written Torah was to be considered authoritative. The Sadducees rejected all practices and beliefs which they found to be absent from the books of Moses, such as the resurrection of the dead. (Beginning seven centuries later in Babylonia, the Karaite movement similarly demanded a return to the authority of the Bible, decrying rabbinic interpretation.) A hereditary sect, the Sadducees were ceremonial functionaries, their head being the High Priest. Indeed, they took their name from Zadok, priest in the reigns of David and Solomon. It is the Pharisaic viewpoint which prevails and which comes to maintain, in one late commentary, that God revealed to Moses the whole Bible, the Talmud, the Midrash, and even the answers which would be given at any future time to the questions of a serious student. The claim is not that the whole of the oral Torah has been transmitted without change from Moses but rather that the principles of interpretation and the dominant ideas can be traced back to him. Whilst the written Torah is fixed and inviolable, the oral Torah is open-ended and continually evolving. What is vital, therefore, is an unbroken succession of rabbis to *Moshe Rabbenu* ('Moses our Teacher'). This is the position of Orthodox Judaism to this day (see Chapter 4) where the written Torah cannot be altered but where it is constantly being brought to bear on the realities of changing life.

We know that there were other Jewish groups in the Second Temple period, including one at Qumran, near the Dead Sea. The vast majority of scholars identify this group as one branch of the Essenes. Information about the Essenes derives from the writers Josephus and Philo, but the picture of the practices and beliefs of the Qumran sect is largely built up from some of the scrolls found mostly between 1947 and 1960 in caves in that region. These groups differed not only in their theological beliefs but also in their relationship to the Roman power. The Romans ended Jewish self-government, which had been established by the Maccabees in 164 BCE, when they occupied Jerusalem in 63 CE. Of the two major groups whose origins seem to lie in this period, the Pharisees were frequently critical of sources of power, whilst the Sadducees were afforded secular authority by the Romans as they had been earlier by the Ptolemaic Greeks. Their power and wealth were quite disproportionate to their numbers.

Living as a holy people without the Temple

The families who returned from Babylonia after the exile were priestly families. That the Temple was the pivot of the renewed health of the nation is reflected not only in the books of Leviticus and Numbers but in other biblical books which raised high walls of separation between the Jew and the non-Jew. It became vital to establish what was distinctive about the Jewish people and this distinctiveness centred on being sanctified, made holy, set apart. This was to be expressed in the social and the natural order of Jewish life but above all it was to be realized in the Temple service. It was this service, with the altar as its focus, which defined holiness, which offered separateness and which, therefore, gave meaning to Jewish life.

The destruction of the Second Temple

With the Roman destruction of the Second Temple in 70 CE came the urgent need to redefine this holiness. The Temple and the active priesthood were gone and attention was now devoted to working out how the whole life of the entire nation could be sanctified. Though the continuity between pre-destruction and post-destruction figures may have been exaggerated to emphasize authority, most of the evidence suggests that it was the Pharisees, with their fundamental emphasis on the holiness of everyday life, who provided the necessary approach. In this, they were assisted by the professional group of the scribes, those with detailed knowledge of the Bible, interpreting the tradition with its correct procedures. The term 'scribes' relates to their task of copying the Torah and of preparing the documents required for the conduct of society according to its rules. Some scribes were Pharisees, though not all, as they were essentially a profession rather than a sect. The Pharisees practised a wide range of occupations, including manual ones, and only some were scribes.

The resulting Mishnah

In the Judaism which emerged in the crucial centuries following the loss of the Temple, detailed guidance was offered for how every aspect of Jewish life was to be sanctified. The holy men providing this were 'sages' and their first and principal work was the Mishnah, completed around 200 CE. The Mishnah's essential message is that the Jewish people, in spite of the absence of the

Temple, retains its sanctity. The farmer must obey the rules of order and structure laid down in Leviticus (such as the laws of the sabbatical year) and the priests, even without being able to carry out their sacrificial task, must observe the rules which Leviticus lays out for them (such as the caste rules governing marriage). Remaining from Temple days are the holy times, the weekly Sabbath, the monthly new moon, and the annual festivals. Especially the meals at these 'appointed times' become sacred as the table replaces the altar. It is this which gives the meaning to the rituals (such as hand washing) and to the liturgy (such as grace after meals) which remain important expressions of the Jewish identity as a holy people.

The Mishnah covers six principal areas of life showing how they can be sanctified in the here and now of Jewish existence. Four of these concern the Temple service. 'Seeds' centres on the designation of portions of the crop for the use of the priesthood, and others specially classified, such as the poor. 'Appointed Times' is largely concerned with conduct on special occasions like the Day of Atonement, Passover, and other festivals. 'Holy things' focuses on the Temple and the sacrificial system. 'Purities' concerns the laws of ritual contamination and the means of purification, taking up laws specified in Leviticus (especially Leviticus 12–15). The middle two areas focus on the everyday affairs of 'Damages', which concerns civil and criminal law, and 'Women', which concerns matters of family, home and personal status.

The six orders of the Mishnah

Zeraim	–	Seeds
Moed	–	Appointed Times
Nashim	–	Women
Nezikin	–	Damages
Kodashim	–	Holy Things
Tohorot	–	Purities

Each order (*seder*, plural *sedarim*) is subdivided into shorter units known as tractates. Altogether these tractates number 63.

Loving your neighbour

We have already seen some examples from the order (*Nashim*) 'Women' but examples from the order (*Nezikin*) 'Damages' might further exemplify this expansion of the written Torah. We noted in Chapter 1 the summary attributed to Hillel: 'That which is hateful unto thee do not do unto thy neighbour' (Shabbat 31a). This relates to a crucial passage:

> *You shall not hate in your heart anyone of your kin; . . . You shall not take vengeance or bear a grudge against any of your people, but you shall love your neighbour as yourself.*

> (Leviticus 19:17–18)

Christian sermons too often attribute the last phrase to Jesus, as if he originated the concept of love of neighbour rather than quoted it (Matthew 22:39). Alternatively, they acknowledge the quotation but stress a Jewish interpretation of the Leviticus passage which limits love to fellow-Jews and argue that Jesus uniquely widened this to include non-Jews, even enemies, making a point about the inadequacy of Judaism's humanitarianism.

Christian preachers, and more frequently the media when reporting some trial, have been known to do similar things to another passage in Leviticus, i.e. 24:17–24, which says that 'one who kills a human being shall be put to death' and anyone 'who maims another shall suffer the same injury in return: fracture for fracture, eye for eye, tooth for tooth'. (Compare Exodus 21:23–25 and note the concession already surfacing if the killing is 'not premeditated'.) There is much complex discussion of the principle (the *lex talionis*), first in the Mishnah (in the first tractate of 'Damages', Bava Kama 8:1ff.) and then in the Talmud (Bava Kama 83b–84a). It has never been a matter of literal 'eye for eye . . .' but rather one of establishing compensation for an injury to a neighbour. The concern with liability for injury, for pain, for healing, for loss of time, for indignity suffered sound remarkably enlightened. (See Talmud extract below.) It is a pity that the text is so often cited as encouraging revenge. Love of neighbour in the sense of acknowledging that he is 'a man like you' or in the sense of 'putting yourself in his place' is of the essence here. Nursing hatred or anger 'to keep it warm' (as Robert Burns tellingly puts it in his poem, *Tam O'Shanter*) is precisely the sort of dangerous precursor to violent conflict discouraged by the injunction to behave towards others as we would like them to behave towards us. The sort of love commanded in Leviticus 19:17–18 is dependent not on liking but on this capacity to remember everyone's common humanity.

A fascinating exploration of what love of neighbour amounts to in practical terms is found in the third tractate of 'Damages' (Bava Batra 2:1–5). Here the other person to be considered is literally a neighbour:

> None may dig a cistern near his fellow's cistern; nor may he dig a trench, vault, water-channel, or washerman's pool unless it is three hand-breadths away from his fellow's wall; and he must plaster it with lime . . . None may open a baker's shop or a dyer's shop under his fellow's storehouse, nor [may he keep] a cattle-stall [near by] . . . A man may protest against [another that opens] a shop within the courtyard and say to him, 'I cannot sleep because of the noise of the hammer' or 'because of the noise of the mill-stones' or 'because of the noise of the children.' . . . If one man's wall adjoins his fellow's wall he may not build another wall adjoining it unless it is at a distance of four cubits . . . A man's ladder must not be kept within four cubits of [his neighbour's] dovecot, lest the marten should jump in. His wall may not be built within four cubits from [his neighbour's] roof-gutter, so that the other can set up his ladder [to clean it out]. A dovecot may not be kept within fifty cubits of a town, and none may build a dovecote in his own domain unless his ground extends fifty cubits in every direction . . .

Apart from the words of the translation (by Danby), this all sounds strangely modern in days of dispute over people keeping smelly or fierce animals in spaces which are too small or too near to the house next door; running a noisy business from their house; and building extensions which take the neighbour's light, spoil the view, or make access difficult. The concrete cases which form the heart of the Mishnah offer not hair-splitting distinctions, but ones which are vital to social co-existence.

The ninth tractate of 'Damages' provides further examples of down-to-earth advice. Though untypical of the Mishnah in its character and style, *Pirke Avot* ('Sayings of the Fathers'), is the most accessible and most quoted section, some of its phrases having passed into folklore:

> If I am not for myself, who will be for me? And if I am only for myself, what am I? And if not now, when?

> (Avot 1:14)

... do not judge your neighbour until you come to his place ... do not say when I have leisure, I will study – perhaps you will not have leisure ... In a place where there are no men, strive to be a man.

(Avot 2:5–6).

Discussing the Mishnah – the Talmud

Though not collected together in published form until 200 CE, the Mishnah represents the discussions of sages on the written Torah from a long period. Hillel and Shammai, both late first century BCE and early first century CE, are much cited. Though the historical Hillel may be rather elusive, many prevailing views are attributed to him, as are all the sayings from Pirke Avot just quoted. The collection we now have in the Mishnah was edited by Rabbi Judah the Prince (*Ha-Nasi*), who lived from 135 to 217 CE. Other discussions (especially of the Tannaim) which did not find their way into the Mishnah, are called *Tosefta* ('addition'). The Tosefta is divided into the same six orders as the Mishnah.

The completion of the Mishnah

Rabbinic discussion for the purposes of clarifying the Torah for new and specific circumstances did not end here. 'Oral' is indeed an apt description of the Torah which followed the written Torah because it was essentially a record of oral discussion in court-rooms and academies. Between 200 and 400 CE, the Rabbis of the Palestinian academies, chiefly at Tiberias, Caesarea, and Sepphoris, discussed the teaching of the Torah, largely in the form of case studies. These discussions also eventually came to be written down. They were printed alongside the section of the Mishnah being discussed and were known as the *Gemara* (Hebrew for 'completion' and Aramaic for 'learning'). These explorations of the Mishnah, often running to several pages, were thought of as completing the Mishnah. The written record of the Mishnah and the Gemara combined was called the *Talmud* (from the Hebrew 'to learn'). Compiled in Palestine by about 400 CE, this work is commonly referred to as *Yerushalmi*, the Jerusalem Talmud (though the academies were situated in northern rather than southern Palestine). It covers 39 of the 63 tractates of the Mishnah.

Even more detailed discussions of the Mishnah went on in the Babylonian academies of Sura and Pumbedita. These were eventually edited (according to tradition, by Rabbi Ashi and his disciple Rabbi Avina by 500 CE, though many think that the process went on well into the next century) to form the Babylonian Talmud, known as the *Bavli*. Though it contains Gemara on several fewer tractates of the Mishnah than the Jerusalem Talmud, the Babylonian Talmud is very much longer, each discussion being longer than its Palestinian equivalent. An English translation of it, published by the Soncino Press, runs to over 15,000 pages. The outcome of three centuries of rabbinic scholarship, its vastness and depth have led to its being compared to a deep sea. When the Talmud is quoted or cited without qualification, it is the Babylonian Talmud which is meant. Attracting the best commentators and the most intelligent and comprehensive interpreters, it has come to be the principal source of authoritative law and theology.

The layout of the Talmud

The text printed on page 46 is folio 83b, the opening page in the Talmud of tractate Bava Kama. The Hebrew text of the Mishnah begins with the word in heavy type at the top right of the central column. This paragraph is itself called a mishnah, as is each paragraph of the Mishnah. After the two letters printed in bold type (which transliterate into GM for Gemara), in the middle of the sixteenth line, the Aramaic Gemara text on this mishnah begins. It occupies the rest of the centre of the page. The text of the Mishnah (as in the Soncino Talmud, ed. I Epstein, 1938) reads:

> One who injures a fellow man becomes liable to him for five items: for depreciation, for pain, for healing, for loss of time and for degradation. How is it with 'depreciation'? If he put out his eye, cut off his arm or broke his leg, the injured person is considered as if he were a slave being sold in the market place, and a valuation is made as to how much he was worth [previously] . . . if he has struck him, he is under obligation to pay medical expenses. Should ulcers [meanwhile] arise on his body, if as a result of the wound, the offender would be liable, but if not as a result of the wound, he would be exempt.

The much longer Gemara text begins:

> *Why [pay compensation]? Does the Divine Law not*
> *say 'Eye for eye'? Why not take this literally to mean*
> *[putting out] the eye [of the offender]? Let not this*
> *enter your mind, since it has been taught: You might*
> *think that where he put out his eye, the offender's eye*
> *should be put out, or where he cut off his arm, the*
> *offender's arm should be cut off, or again where he*
> *broke his leg, the offender's leg should be broken. [Not*
> *so; for] it is laid down, 'He that smiteth any man . . .'*
> *'And he that smiteth a beast . . .' just as in the case of*
> *smiting a beast compensation is to be paid, so also in*
> *the case of smiting a man compensation is to be paid.*

The Gemara goes on to differentiate between loss of a limb or organ and loss of human life. No compensation but only the death penalty is possible for murder.

To the left (or to the right on folio 'a' rather than 'b') of the Mishnah and Gemara text comes commentary by Rashi (Rabbi Shelomo ben Yitzhak) who lived in France, 1040–1105. Rashi is a towering figure in the history of Judaism, composing immensely influential commentaries on the whole of the Bible and the Babylonian Talmud. His talmudic commentary is lucid and very concise, showing both the process of argument and the conclusion. To the right on this page come additions or supplements to Rashi's commentary, the *Tosafot* (not to be confused with the Tosefta, the supplement to the Mishnah). These begin where Rashi's comments leave off – the first Tosafists were, in fact, his sons-in-law and grandsons. This work spread from France to Germany and ended in the early fourteenth century.

As is evident from the extract printed above, the Talmud is con-cerned with the commonplace (e.g. the consequences of physical injury) as the place where the divine may be discovered. Its unifying truth is holiness and so its concerns are not solely ethical. As Jacob Neusner (*Invitation to the Talmud*, revised edition, Harper and Row, 1984) writes:

> *To the Talmudic way of thinking a person is liberated,*
> *not imprisoned, by reason, which opens the way to*
> *true creativity, that is, the work of finding, or*
> *imposing, form and order upon chaos. The where-*
> *withal of creativity is triviality . . . and what is to be*

החובל

החובל בחבירו **חייב** עליו חמשה דברים בנזק בצער בריפוי בשבת ובבושת. בנזק כיצד כיפר את עינו קטע את ידו שיבר את רגלו רואין אותו כאילו הוא עבד נמכר בשוק ושמין כמה היה יפה וכמה הוא יפה. צער כואה (או) בשפוד או במסמר ואפילו על ציפורנו מקום שאינו עושה חבורה אומרין כמה אדם כיוצא בזה רוצה ליטול להיות מצטער כך. ריפוי הכהו חייב לרפאותו עלה בו צמחים אם מחמת המכה חייב שלא מחמת המכה פטור חייתה ונסתרה חייתה ונסתרה חייב לרפאותו חייתה כל צרכה אינו חייב לרפאותו. שבת רואין אותו כאילו הוא שומר קשואין שכבר נתן לו דמי ידו ודמי רגלו. בושת הכל לפי המבייש והמתבייש:

גמ' אמאי עין תחת עין אמר רחמנא אימא עין ממש לא סלקא דעתך דתניא יכול סימא את עינו מסמא את עינו קטע את ידו מקטע את ידו שיבר את רגלו משבר את רגלו ת"ל מכה אדם ומכה בהמה מה מכה בהמה לתשלומין אף מכה אדם לתשלומין ואם נפשך לומר הרי הוא אומר לא תקחו כופר לנפש רוצח אשר הוא רשע למות לנפש רוצח אי אתה לוקח כופר אבל אתה לוקח כופר לראשי אברים שאין חוזרין. רבי מכה בהמה ישלמנה ומכה אדם יומת. מקיש הכאה בהמה להכאת אדם מה מכה בהמה בתשלומין אף מכה אדם בתשלומין. כי יתן מום בעמיתו כאשר עשה כן יעשה לו מה הכאה לתשלומין אף מום לתשלומין.

מכה

...

מ"ט חיים ללמוד ממכה בהמה

מכה

...

לנפש רוצח אי אתה לוקח כופר אבל אתה לוקח כופר למעותי ראשי אברים שאין חוזרין...

תורה אור

החובל בדברים חייב...

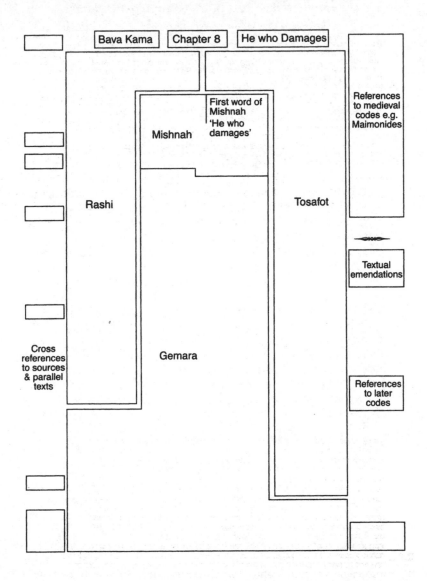

Bava Kama | Chapter 8 | He who Damages

References to medieval codes e.g. Maimonides

Rashi

Mishnah

First word of Mishnah 'He who damages'

Tosafot

Textual emendations

Cross references to sources & parallel texts

Gemara

References to later codes

done with triviality is to uncover, within or beyond the simple things of chaos, the order, the complex structure, the coherence of the whole . . . to the Talmudic rabbi, the most interesting aspect of reality is the human and the societal: the village, the home, the individual. Talmudic Judaism, because of its stress on what and how one eats and drinks, has been called a religion of pots and pans. And so it is, if not that alone, for its raw materials are the irreducible atoms of concrete life.

The Talmud thus represents the climax of the process of interpreting the written Torah. Over time, it has come to be seen as a kind of law code, whose main thrust is practical direction. Initially, however, the many instances of case-law and decisions found in the Talmud were more theoretical than practical. It seems that it was the argument that mattered most, both to the Amoraim themselves and to the editors. The fact that whole sections of it related to Temple worship, whilst the Temple was, in fact, destroyed centuries before the Talmud was compiled, demonstrates this. Study of the sacrificial system was, by the time of the Amoraim, thoroughly academic. Even where the subject-matter of the Talmud is severely practical, the discussion is often conducted in an academic way, as if the stages of the argument are of more significance than its conclusion. Even where Rabbis are named, it is not important whether their arguments are real or imaginary. What matters is their methods, as they ask the meanings of words and phrases, compare one set of laws with another and find the underlying principles of each.

Legal traditions (*halakhah*) and narrative traditions (*aggadah*)

At the same time as the Mishnah was being expounded, so was scripture itself, resulting in the *midrashim* (works of biblical commentary) mentioned in Chapter 2. Rabbinic literature may, therefore, be classified into mishnah and midrash. There is, however, a second way of classifying rabbinic literature – according to its literary genre. The written Torah itself includes both legal material and narrative material. As the oral Torah developed, the traditions also took the form of both law and story.

Halakhah

The name given to the legal traditions is *halakhah*. This is usually taken to derive from the Hebrew verb 'to go' or 'to walk'. Hence *halakhah* means 'the way'. The English rendering of 'Law' is inadequate for two reasons. First, halakhah includes everything that regulates human conduct, far more than would be dealt with, say, in an English court of law. Secondly, it is descriptive as well as prescriptive. It describes 'the way' things are done by God's people, using the form: 'One does this; one does not do that', rather than the imperative: 'Do this; do not do that!' Through halakhah (plural *halakhot*), the Rabbis try to guide the Jewish people to live life, form society, and serve God in the ways they think right. The laws are presented with a look to the future. Thus, even if they are not entirely practical (as the laws of the fifth order of the Mishnah which dealt with Temple purities when by 200 CE the Temple had been in ruins for more than a century) they describe how in an ideal world things are to be done.

Aggadah

The name given to the narrative traditions is *aggadah*. From the Hebrew verb 'to tell', aggadah is essentially story. It still expresses the main themes of Jewish religion, but in the form of legendary or historical encouragement and enthusiasm. Aggadah also includes science, folk-wisdom, and the theoretical subjects of theology and ethics as they have a bearing on behaviour. In the Talmud, most of the material is halakhic, though some aggadic material is included. Nearly all midrash, on the other hand, is aggadic, though a little is halakhic. The imaginative nature of aggadah can be seen in the way in which a number of second century Rabbis interpret the phrase 'the spirit of God' in Genesis 1:2. One takes it to mean 'wind', another 'Adam' and another 'Messiah'. All three interpretations are included with no attempt to adjudicate. The test of their 'rightness' lies entirely in their poetic force. Thus aggadah is important for providing what lies behind the practice, not in the sense of formal doctrine, such as theological belief behind Christian practice, but in terms of vitality and inspiration. Sometimes the story is lengthy, but three very brief talmudic extracts (as found in *A Rabbinic Anthology*, ed. C.G. Montefiore and H. Loewe, Meridian Books, 1963) may give some idea:

Rabbi Hanina ben Idi said: Why are the words of the Torah likened unto water, as it is written, 'Ho, every one that thirsts, come ye to the waters'(Isaiah 55:1)? In order to indicate that just as water leaves high places and goes to low places, so the words of the Torah leave him who is haughty, and stay with him who is humble.

(Taanit 7a)

The Emperor asked Rabbi Joshua ben Hananiah, 'What gives your Sabbath-meat such an aroma?' He replied, 'We have a spice called Sabbath, which is put in the cooking of the meat, and this gives it its aroma.' The Emperor said, 'Give me some of this spice.' He replied, 'For him who keeps the Sabbath, the spice works, for him who does not keep it, it does not work.'

(Shabbat 119a)

Why was man created on Friday: So that, if he become overbearing, one can say to him, The gnat was created before you.

(Sanhedrin 38a)

The *Geonim*

It is halakhah, the legal tradition, which provides the chain from antiquity to the present. As a living tradition, it is subject to a continuous process of adaptation in response to the changing needs of real people. Where study is made of topics which seem to have little direct relevance to contemporary life, its purpose is to see how the original laws can be applied. Links with the ideal world of the Talmud continue to be forged. The list below indicates the titles given to those passing on the tradition from age to age:

Soferim	*200–0 BCE*
Tannaim	*0–220 CE*
Amoraim	*220–c. 500 CE*
Savoraim	*500–c. 650 CE*
Geonim	*650–1050 CE*

The last of these, the *Geonim* (plural of *Gaon*, 'excellency'), headed the leading rabbinic academies in Babylonia. The most famous gaon of the academy at Sura was Saadiah in the tenth century. As rabbis from many countries sent to the Geonim with questions about talmudic rulings, a system of answers, *responsa*, developed. These written replies to questions were usually collected and published by either the authors themselves or by their disciples. The process of halakhic questioning continues far beyond the Geonic period in Babylonia. Significant respondents include Israel Isserlein of Austria (1390–1460), Ezekiel Landau of Bohemia (1713–93), Joseph Saul Nathanson of the Ukraine (1808–75), and Benzion Uziel of Palestine (1880–1945).

Law codes

It is the very vastness of this sea of rabbinic literature which led, especially in the Middle Ages, to halakhah being codified. Not only the size of the Talmud but also its structure makes it difficult to find one's way around. In spite of the names of the orders and tractates, references to a particular topic are found scattered throughout the Talmud. As Louis Jacobs says (*The Structure and Form of the Babylonian Talmud*, CUP, 1991), its form is not logical but literary. Details are included at the point where they will create maximum effect rather than in neat sequence, rather as information appears in a play or a novel. The dangers of such summaries of complex case law are obvious, notably that of replacing a living tradition with a dead codification. Four codes, in particular, have nonetheless exercised an influence, as people needed to know the result of rabbinic discussion rather than the details of the discussion itself. The first is an eleventh-century collection by Rabbi Isaac Alfasi, who was known by the acronym Rif. This paved the way for the thirteenth-century work of Maimonides. His *Mishneh Torah* ('Repetition of the Torah'), assured Spanish Jews: 'henceforth anyone who first reads the Written Torah and then this book will know the entire Oral Torah.' In the fourteenth century came Rabbi Jacob ben Asher's *Arbaah Turim*. Meaning 'Four Rows', this code presented the subject matter of the halakhah under four headings: daily life and rituals; religious regulations such as food laws; relations between the sexes; civil and criminal law.

This four-fold classification was adopted in the last and by far the most influential halakhic code, the *Shulhan Arukh* ('Prepared Table'). This sixteenth-century code was produced by Rabbi

Joseph Caro who, like Rif and Maimonides, lived for a time in Spain. Expelled from there, he settled in Palestine at Safed, a major centre of Jewish learning. The Shulhan Arukh was accepted by most Sefardi Jews and later by the Ashkenazim, once the Polish scholar, Rabbi Moses Isserles, had added notes to it. These notes, covering Ashkenazi practice, were known as the *Mappah*, the 'Tablecloth' for the Prepared Table.

The many subjects covered in the Shulhan Arukh include prohibition against resorting to non-Jewish courts; laws about visiting the sick; and laws about the salting of meat, as in the following examples (translated by Philip S. Alexander):

> *Even if the plaintiff possess a document in which it is written that he may summon the defendant under gentile law – he is still not permitted to summon him before the gentile courts . . . It is a religious duty to visit the sick. Relatives and friends may call immediately, and strangers after three days. If, however, a man falls ill suddenly, both parties may call on him immediately . . . One should not visit those suffering from diseases of the bowels, or of the eyes, or from headaches. So too, anyone gravely ill, to whom conversation would be injurious, must not be visited personally, but one may call at an outer room and make inquiries, and ascertain whether the invalid needs his room swept and sprinkled, or any similar service performed for him. And one should take an interest in his affliction and pray for him . . . In the case of those suffering from diseases of the bowels, the law is that a man must not nurse a woman, but a woman may nurse a man . . . The salt should not be as fine-grained as flour, so that it should not dissolve immediately on the meat and fail to draw out the blood. Nor should it be very coarse, for then it would fall off the meat. Rather it should be medium-sized, like the salt used for cooking; and it should be dry, so that it may be sprinkled easily.*

04

orthodox Judaism

In this chapter you will learn:

- about the continuity between Orthodoxy and rabbinic Judaism
- how Orthodoxy came to define itself at a time of emancipation and enlightenment
- about the origins and development of Hasidism.

Orthodoxy and belief

We know that in the first century CE there was a variety of Jewish sects or movements. Nonetheless, it was the developing rabbinic Judaism which proved to be so formative. Not all would accept the degree of continuity between the Pharisees and the later rabbis outlined in Chapter 3, but few would deny that it was the Judaism which rested on the authority of the written Torah (Bible) and of the oral Torah (Talmud) which had the ingredients to survive the destruction of the Second Temple. This survival was to continue right through the Middle Ages until the modern period which many date from the French Revolution in 1789. From this time onwards, it begins to become impossible to speak of the Jewish faith as if all its adherents believe fundamentally the same. Labels for different types of Judaism begin to be needed.

Defining 'Orthodox'

It is often said that the label 'Orthodox' is misleading since it means 'right belief'. Acknowledging that a variety of beliefs is reflected in rabbinic Judaism, the term 'Orthoprax' might be better. Judaism, so the argument runs, is concerned with 'right practice', with what people do rather than what they believe. For those trying to understand Judaism as it manifests itself in varied form today (especially but not exclusively those on the outside), this argument can be overstated.

It is true that those who today are termed 'Orthodox' seldom use the term of themselves, preferring to describe themselves 'observant'. (Reform Jews coined 'Orthodox' originally as a disparaging term, rather like Anglicans coined the term 'Methodist' for Protestants they judged to be over-methodical in their devotional life.) But this in itself rests on a belief. The belief is that they are observing the Torah (Jewish Law) as it originates in the Bible and is developed in the Talmud. To this extent, they require no label to differentiate them from other Jews, since they are Jews following the chain of tradition. As we noted in Chapter 1 and shall see in later chapters, there are Jews who observe certain festivals and who avoid prohibited food, such as pork, in order to express a sense of identity with the Jewish people rather than because they believe these things to have been commanded by God. Nonetheless, it is hard to imagine why those Jews who observe all possible mitzvot (obligations), often at considerable inconvenience and expense, should do so without a conviction that they are thus commanded as Jews. Logical connections between belief and behaviour can be exaggerated but they can also be underestimated. The facts that not all with Orthodox affiliation are completely observant and that Jewishness comes through biology (halakhically, through the mother) do not destroy the basic link between faith and practice.

The importance of belief

This *Teach Yourself* volume seeks to understand what Judaism is. Merely describing the practices to be expected of various religious groupings, but without any exploration of what lies behind these practices, affords little understanding of the religion. Nor does simply giving the history of the Jewish people and of expressions of Judaism, vital though the historical element is. We are here concerned to ask what practices might be expected of someone who says: 'I am Jewish' in a particular time and place. If belief is not a significant differentiating factor in Judaism (as some maintain), theoretically this religion above all religions should be free from divisions, since differences of belief are what tend to cause internal division. This is explored by Jonathan Sacks, Chief Rabbi of the United Hebrew Congregations of the Commonwealth, in his book *One People?* (Littman, 1993). He resists the term 'denominations', especially as applied to the Orthodox, since, he maintains, the nature of Judaism does not permit recognition of rival versions. He quotes Samson Raphael Hirsch who, as we shall see, is a crucial figure in the development of what is now regarded as Orthodoxy: 'Judaism does not recognize any variants. It knows of no mosaic, prophetic or rabbinic, and of no orthodox or progressive Judaism. It either is Judaism or it is not.' The fact is, however, that what does divide Jews into different religious groupings is belief. There is, on the matter of the authority of the Bible and the binding nature of halakhah, a genuine theological difference between the Orthodox and all others, hence the term 'non-Orthodox' Jews. There are other writers, some it may be said with far less careful scholarship and realistic attention to the views of the different Jewish persuasions than Sacks exemplifies, who feel that it is high time to consider means of unifying a dwindling yet divided faith community. This author is certainly in no position to pass judgement on different types of Judaism or to suggest or predict ways forward. She does, however, sense a deep difference in approach between them which does ultimately depend on belief. Judaism may not fall into the equivalent categories of Roman Catholic, Protestant, and Orthodox in Christianity but there are surely parallels. At the risk of gross oversimplification, it can be claimed that the Christian differences go back to respective beliefs about authority – of scripture and tradition. What these different movements do springs from what they believe. Various sub-groups have sprung up according to convictions about how things should be done. (Methodism was not initially intended as a separate denomination from Anglicanism any more than Reform Judaism initially set out to leave behind Orthodoxy.) Fortunately, Judaism has a long way to go before it rivals Christianity in its number of sub-groupings. And yet, the gulf between Orthodox and non-Orthodox Jews is deeper than that between most Christian denominations. The challenges which led to these different approaches to belief and practice need to be examined.

Continuity and discontinuity

There is a sense in which Orthodox Judaism as we see it in the world today is the same as that described in the previous chapter. After all, it was of the essence of rabbinic Judaism to evolve to meet new situations. In the eighteenth century, however, the newness of the situation was unprecedented. It was in response to this that a new or neo-Orthodoxy developed. Ironically, the challenge came in the form of political emancipation for Jews. It plunged them into a crisis of identity which, it may be said, has yet to find resolution.

Between 600 and 1800 CE, Jewish identity was found in being 'Israel', a holy people. A return from *galut* ('exile') to the land was to be looked forward to (indeed, this applied way beyond 1800). Meanwhile, Jews had to accept political subordination to the peoples in whose lands they lived. Whether in Christian or in Muslim countries, a sanctified life must be pursued in accordance with the standards of belief and practice defined in the Torah, written and oral. It was clear what the Jewish people had to do, who they were, and where they were going.

After the French Revolution and the Napoleonic Wars, Jews in western Europe were given the right to vote and other freedoms that had been denied to them. With the American Constitution and its Bill of Rights in 1787 and a decree of the National Assembly of France in 1791 all people became citizens. Such acceptance into full national life was a novel experience for Jews.

They had been a distinctive people in the food they ate, the clothes they wore, and even the languages they spoke. In northern and eastern Europe they spoke Yiddish, a German dialect with elements of Hebrew, Polish, and Russian. Around the Mediterranean they spoke Ladino, a kind of Spanish. Essentially, they were distinguished by being a religion, a faith different from the majority faith of respective countries and periods.

Modern Orthodoxy

The modern period gave Jews the freedom not to be distinctive, not to be different in education and in occupation from their fellow-citizens. It opened up whole areas of life which formerly had not featured in the application of the Torah. Thus the question arose whether there was a system which could mediate between rabbinic Judaism in its received form and the requirements of living a life integrated into modern circumstance. The central issue became how to balance the competing demands of tradition and modernity.

It was in response to this that the range of systems which now come under the headings of Orthodoxy and non-Orthodoxy emerged. In the following chapter, we shall look at the more radical responses. Here, we consider the response of what we may call 'modern Orthodoxy'. Unlike that which came to be called Reform Judaism, Orthodoxy's response focused not on emancipation but on the chain of tradition. A belief in God's revelation, in the detailed authority of law and custom, and the consequent unwillingness to change any detail of public worship or strict observance, led the nineteenth-century formulation of Orthodoxy to claim full continuity with Judaism as unified and undivided by systems. Its adherents maintained that they were carrying forward the tradition in an unbroken relationship with the past. And yet there was a discontinuity, one forced by rival answers and systems which required the 'traditionalists' to be more self-conscious and more selective. The Judaism which was articulated in this period rested on a new world-view and addressed a different 'Israel' from that of rabbinic Judaism. Its ideal was Torah together with secular learning. A mishnaic saying recommending the study of 'Torah combined with a worldly occupation' (Avot 2:2) became the slogan of Samson Raphael Hirsch. He expounded the phrase as indicating the compatibility of the secular world and culture with Jewish learning.

In 1836, Hirsch published his *Nineteen Letters on Judaism* in which he was critical both of highly secularized schools such as the Philantropin in Frankfurt and of traditional *hadarim* (Jewish religion schools). The former lacked 'the education of the heart' whilst the latter taught 'uncomprehended Judaism as a mechanical habit . . . and without its spirit'. Hirsch advocated a synthesis of the knowledge offered by secular and religious disciplines saying: 'It is the Jewish view that truth, like God its source, is one and indivisible, and that therefore knowledge of it can be only one and indivisible' (in *Judaism Eternal*). The synthesis which Hirsch envisaged largely did not come about, but he did provide an alternative answer to the identity crisis of Jews in nineteenth-century Germany to that coming from the more radical reformers. He offered a way of living in the two worlds which confronted Jews entering the modern period. They could occupy the secular, public world and the private, Jewish world in which the halakhah applied as it always had. In this, Hirsch was firmly a traditionalist. So was he also in the area of biblical study. It is striking that his endorsement of reason in philosophy and science did not extend to biblical criticism which he saw as a mistake. He was resisting the very different versions of Judaism which were emerging in the modern world as he claimed:

> *Orthodox Judaism believes in the divine authenticity of the Bible, and knows nothing of the various authors of the Pentateuch, nor of Pseudo-Isaiah, nor of Maccabean songs under the name of David, nor of Solomon's Ecclesiastes from the time of the Second Temple, and so forth.*

Sweeping statements are too often made about Orthodoxy and the Bible which require some examination if contrasts with non-Orthodoxy are to be accurately portrayed. The accusation that Orthodox Jews are 'fundamentalists' is not helpful, chiefly because the word is used pejoratively and without definition. 'Fundamentalism' carries a range of meanings but the suggestion that Orthodox Jews disregard questions about the language and style of the biblical books (sometimes called low biblical criticism) is simply not true. On historical questions, however (sometimes referred to as higher criticism), the Orthodox attitude to the Bible, particularly the Pentateuch, requires comment.

Orthodox Judaism and the Bible

In the Talmud there is a passage where the Rabbis discuss the order and authorship of the biblical books (Bava Batra 14b–15a). Because of the importance of the Bible in Judaism one might have expected far more extensive treatment of the subject. It would seem that what mattered to the Rabbis was that the books were inspired, albeit with varying degrees of inspiration (as we saw in Chapter 2). Who precisely wrote them was not a matter of any great interest. It was accepted by all that Moses wrote the Pentateuch (the first five books). The only debate between believers and heretics was whether it was 'from Heaven', that is, had God as its real author. The sort of biblical criticism which later emerged was not begun by the Rabbis of the Talmud. The notion of different strands of Pentateuchal writing simply did not arise.

It has been argued, however (notably by the leading Masorti (Conservative) scholar, Louis Jacobs – see Chapter 5), that this does not necessarily imply that God gave to Moses the whole of the Pentateuch, including accounts of events yet to take place. This, according to Jacobs, is to go beyond what the Rabbis actually claimed. That 'Moses received the Torah on Sinai' (Avot 1:1) means rather that the laws and doctrines contained in the written and oral Torah were given at Sinai. This is itself a big claim and one which non-Orthodox Jews do not accept. But it is not simply a matter of non-Orthodox Jews approaching the Bible with philosophical and linguistic skills to help them in interpretation whilst Orthodox Jews retreat into some fundamentalist backwater, as is clear from the work of important figures.

Biblical criticism

We have already mentioned the Saadiah Gaon. He not only translated the Bible into Arabic but also wrote commentaries on a number of biblical books which displayed a deep interest in the workings of the Hebrew language. Rashi's biblical commentaries, often to be found in printed editions of the Hebrew Bible alongside the text, exercised a great influence. Supercommentaries were also written on them, rather like the supercommentaries on Rashi's commentary on the Talmud, as we saw in the previous chapter. A pioneer of biblical criticism was the Spanish scholar, Abraham Ibn Ezra (1089–1164). He claimed that some of the psalms may not have been by David and even that the whole of the final chapter of Deuteronomy was added by Joshua. (Others believe that this applies only to the last eight verses which tell of Moses' death.) Ibn Ezra was also the first critic to suggest that there might be more than one author behind the book of Isaiah. This would explain not only differences in style but also the fact that the first 39 chapters reflect largely the pre-exilic period in Jewish history, 40–55 the exilic period, and 56–66 the post-exilic period. This development of Ibn Ezra's view is generally accepted by biblical scholars today. Whether it is accepted by most Orthodox Jews, however, is another matter. More crucially, Orthodoxy resists any suggestion that the whole Pentateuch was not given to Moses on Sinai. It does not make the distinction, deemed important by the non-Orthodox, between dictation and revelation generally. Orthodox belief is that Moses received the Pentateuch in some non-physical way. There inevitably follows a resistance to biblical criticism of the Pentateuch. That such criticism may become destructive of the Jewish faith is evident in the work of Baruch Spinoza (1632–77). One of the founding fathers of the rational enlightenment, Spinoza had a great influence on western ideas generally, if not on his own Portuguese community in Amsterdam. Questions about biblical authorship led to his denying the whole idea of revelation. Human reason and not God was at work in the Bible. Other major figures in Jewish thought were to engage in this debate, notably Moses Mendelssohn (1729–1786), who sought to make the Bible accessible to modern readers by publishing a German translation together with a commentary of scholarly Jewish exegesis. Mendelssohn is regarded as very much the founding father of the *Haskalah* (the Jewish 'Enlightenment'). This, however, did not lead Mendelssohn, a most observant Jew, in the direction of biblical criticism.

Some, especially the Conservative movement (see Chapter 5) which broke with Orthodoxy on this very issue, feel that the logic of 'enlightened' thought means that the Pentateuch must have been received over many centuries. In a much publicised article in 1995, any Jew who denied that Moses received the Torah directly from God on Sinai was described by Britain's Chief Rabbi as having 'severed links with the faith of his ancestors'. Reform and Liberal retaliated, rightly or wrongly, that the Chief Rabbi's definition of Jewish belief would exclude at least 90 per cent of Anglo-Jewry. In this figure, they were including many Jews with Orthodox synagogue affiliation. It must be remembered, however, that under the umbrella of

Orthodoxy come many who, in both belief and practice, differ from their fellow-Orthodox. There is, however, an Orthodox perspective which finds any accommodation to the modern world whatsoever to be incompatible with the Jewish faith. From this (so-called 'Ultra-Orthodox') standpoint, modern Orthodoxy, whether represented by nineteenth century Hirsch or twenty-first century Sacks, is seen not as too traditional but as not traditional enough.

Ultra-Orthodoxy

'Ultra-Orthodox' is another label which is used by some Jews to denote those of a different (and, it is often implied, mistaken) stance. Certainly, those to whom the term is applied would not describe themselves as such. They are simply observant or traditional. Indeed, one difficulty with the terms for different Jewish movements is that the members of the different movements all see themselves as expressing the essence of what Judaism is. So, as we shall see in the next chapter, the Reform movement stresses the evolutionary nature of halakhic Judaism and claims to be in line with it. Those we are here considering under the heading of 'Ultra-Orthodoxy' demonstrate better than any other Jewish grouping the inadequacy not only of labels but of giving out, by these labels, mistaken impressions and information to those seeking to understand them.

Hasidism

In the first place, Ultra-Orthodoxy is not a homogeneous group. There are two major strands. The first is the Lithuanian tradition which stresses talmudic study in the yeshivah (or academy as described in Chapter 8). The second also stresses the Torah but in combination with what might be described as a mystical approach. This movement is known as 'Hasidism' (often transliterated Chasidism), from the Hebrew *hasid* ('pious', plural *hasidim*). The term 'hasid' had been used of devout Jews who in the second century BCE resisted opposition to their faith, but the Hasidic movement was one not so much of resistance but of revival. Its setting was eastern Europe in the eighteenth century CE, especially Poland and Lithuania and its appeal was to the oppressed Jewish peasants in these lands. It was revivalist in that it sought to deepen devotion, to offer an intimacy with the divine, through joyous expression, especially song and dance.

(Some Hasidic melodies are profoundly moving and it is remarkable how even the slow ones rouse the desire to dance.) Their rabbis, known as *rebbes*, were charismatic figures who denigrated scholarship that lacked spirituality. The first, and thus the founder of the movement, was Rabbi Israel ben Eliezer. Given the title *Baal Shem Tov* ('Master of the Good Name', the name being that of God), he was known by the acronym 'the Besht'. He was a popular healer and his leadership passed to a succession of holy men known as *zaddikim* ('righteous ones', singular *zaddik*). Each zaddik carried authority by virtue of his closeness to God.

This marked a distinct shift from the traditional leadership of the rabbis whose authority lay solely in their scholarship. There consequently grew up a counter-movement, whose members were called the *Mitnagdim* ('opponents'). Its leader was Elijah ben Solomon Zalman of the Lithuanian city of Vilnius who, because of his great learning, was afforded the title (the Vilna) Gaon. He also was a master of the mystical writings of the *Kabbalah* ('Tradition') but he read it differently from the Hasidim, who drew on other sources of inspiration besides learning. Mysticism is not an easily accessible topic and is certainly not essential to a book which is designed to explain the thinking behind the main expressions of Jewish life today. Nonetheless, different forms of it have long influenced Jewish movements and individuals, and not only in Ultra-Orthodoxy.

Hasidic Jews expect their rabbis to be men of transcendent spiritual attainment, from which source they derive their inspiration as leaders. From this mystical tradition, however, they are to derive a way of living which is for the ordinary Jew and not just the leader. The revivalist element of eighteenth-century Hasidism is seen clearly in the unusual missionary outreach of a particular Hasidic group, known as Lubavitcher (from the Russian town of Lubavitch) or Habad (from the Hebrew words for 'wisdom, understanding, and knowledge') Hasidim. The Lubavitch movement stresses both Talmud and Kabbalah. It is unusual in its contact with the outside world, particularly in its educational centres and programmes. Eventually too in eastern Europe, a compromise was found between the Hasidim who emphasized mystical books and practices such as ecstasy, visions, and miracles and the Mitnagdim who emphasized rabbinic learning and piety. The breadth of Judaism and its capacity to absorb new emphases and expressions is thus demonstrated by the Hasidic movement which has proved to have the power to inspire study and observance of the Torah. A movement of considerable originality in the eighteenth century – regarded even as heretical – Hasidism has come by the twentieth century to constitute a bulwark of Orthodoxy. It is represented in large numbers in Agudat Israel, for example, one of the most influential and important organizations within contemporary Orthodoxy encompassing Jews right across the Orthodox spectrum, including the Lithuanian community.

Orthodox affiliation today

Considering the long pedigree of Orthodox Judaism, it is perhaps surprising how small a percentage are affiliated to it in the country with the largest Jewish population in the world, namely the United States. The figure is 9 per cent, though it is growing into a steady stream, especially of young people moving away from their more radical home backgrounds. The second largest centre of Judaism, namely Israel, is unique in the complexity of its immigration. Specific attention will need to be given to it in Chapter 17. Suffice it to say here that, although Orthodoxy has considerable power in Israel, it does not represent the majority of the Jewish population. In Britain the figure is nearer to what one would expect, with approaching half of British Jews being affiliated to the United Synagogue. (The figure given by the Board of Deputies of British Jews in 2002 was 57,000 households.) This is a federation of Ashkenazi synagogues in London, established in 1870 and authorised by Act of Parliament. It appoints the Chief Rabbi and maintains the London *Bet Din* (Jewish Law Court), the importance of which will be discussed in Chapter 9. It is claimed that another 25 per cent of British Jews call themselves Orthodox, some being affiliated to Orthodox synagogues other than those belonging to the United Synagogue. (For instance, in 2002, 6,500 households belonged to the Union of Orthodox congregations and 3,000 to Sefardi congregations.). But it has to be remembered that this 'Orthodoxy' covers a very wide spectrum of observance. Some would describe themselves as Orthodox simply in the sense of not being Reform or because their family is or was Orthodox. (It should also be noted that 25 per cent of British Jews are not synagogue members.) This sometimes puzzles non-Jews making a genuine attempt to understand. They are told that Orthodox Jews will not mix meat and milk dishes together or drive to the synagogue on the Sabbath and then they find those who do. Are they the exception or are they mistaken in calling themselves Orthodox? The best assumption to make so far as not giving offence is concerned is that Orthodox Jews do take seriously the observances outlined in the various chapters of this book.

Ultra-Orthodox

Ultra-Orthodox groups represent a small but noticeable minority. Hasidism was carried to the west by the waves of emigration from the 1880s onward and to the United States and Israel (then Palestine) in the aftermath of World War II. Major Hasidic centres (in the 1930s there were several million Hasidim in eastern Europe) were all but wiped out during the Holocaust. In whatever country, they live in very tightly-knit communities, generally excluding the outside world. There is a sizable Hasidic community in Stamford Hill, North London. Together with Lithuanian Orthodox, they exist, for instance, in parts of Manchester, New York and in the area of Jerusalem called 'Meah Shearim'. The Jewish community of Gateshead (Newcastle) proudly boasts its Lithuanian roots.

When newspapers or television present a report about a Jewish matter they often show a picture of a hasid (the fact that the Hasidim do not approve of photographs of themselves does not stop them from being highly photogenic!), whose black garb (continued from medieval Polish society) and earlocks (in obedience to Leviticus 19:27 'You shall not round off the hair on your temples or mar the edges of your beard') show clearly that he is Jewish. This often applies even when the viewpoint being represented is one at odds with Hasidism, as when they were shown in connection with the establishment of an eruv in north-west London (see Chapter 12). When it comes to practices which non-Jews find difficult to understand, it is the Ultra-Orthodox communities which are likely to be to the fore, simply because they are very observant and in ways which reflect a different age. Their rigorous laws of modesty (derived from the Law Codes), for instance, forbid a man to be alone with any woman except his wife. Even mildly intimate behaviour (such as holding hands) with your wife is considered immodest when other people are present. To ask any other woman even to shake hands is also immodest. A refusal of an Ultra-Orthodox man to shake hands with a woman might be construed as rudeness or rejection by anyone not used to this degree and manner of observance, but it is in no way personal and, as explained, would obtain with any woman except his wife.

05

non-orthodox Judaism

In this chapter you will learn:

- about the development of a movement attempting to re-form Judaism
- about the way in which key differences of belief are seen in the respective roles of women
- about other non-Orthodox movements: Conservative and Liberal.

Reform Judaism and points of departure

It is not always sensible to define something – be it a word, a phrase, an outlook, a movement – by what it is not. Reform Judaism, however, can best be so defined, at least initially. In the opening chapter of a book subtitled *A Guide to Reform Judaism Today*, Rabbi Jonathan Romain writes:

> *The defining characteristic of Reform Judaism is its attitude to the Revelation at Mount Sinai. Something very special occurred, not just to Moses but to the whole community of Israel.*

> (*Faith and Practice*, RSGB, 1991)

After stressing the importance of the covenant which emerged, Romain continues:

> *The book describing that event is held by the Orthodox to have been dictated by God, and to contain the exact and unchanging words of God. Its laws are considered immutable, and decisions relating to new situations at any time in the future must conform to it.*

As we saw in the previous chapter, it is others who tend to use the word 'dictated' when saying what Orthodox Jews believe. They themselves are concerned not with the method of reception but with the conviction that the Torah, as given to Moses, was directly and divinely inspired in a way beyond normal human experience. All subsequent decisions must, therefore, be judged against the first principles there contained. The Reform position as expressed by Romain is that the Torah 'was inspired by God but written down by humans according to their understanding of God's will'. It is:

> *the testimony of a formative experience . . . a continual source book, filled with inspirational passages and practical guidelines . . .*

> *However, it is still a human book . . . open to challenge and revision, and subject to becoming outdated in parts.*

The beginnings of the Reform Movement in Germany

As Romain seeks to differentiate between Orthodoxy and Reform the points at issue emerge as: was the Torah given to Moses on Sinai or over time to a number of people and are its laws obligatory for all time or are they guidelines which may become outdated?

Reform Judaism began in central Europe in the late eighteenth and early nineteenth centuries. It did not set out to be a new religious movement, but it became one as traditional Jewish beliefs and practices came in for reassessment. The need for such reassessment was posed by the intellectual and political freedoms granted to all, including Jews. As we saw in the previous chapter, such emancipated Jews were required to work out what it meant to be both Jewish and full citizens of the countries in which they lived. They needed to define their identity as Jews against the backdrop of other faiths and secularism. Assimilation, not being distinctively Jewish at all, became a temptation and it was to meet this and to offer a faith which positively embraced the whole of life and thought that certain figures began to re-form Judaism. The first was Israel Jacobson in Germany who updated both ideas and practice. The chief idea was the one already stated, that the Torah is only the word of God as interpreted by human beings. Since they can make mistakes, it follows that each generation must test concepts of God in the light of new knowledge and understanding. To keep Judaism ever contemporary (as the reformers maintained, and still maintain, was the aim of rabbinic Judaism), practices which no longer serve any helpful purpose may be rejected. According to the halakhah, for instance, a man descended from the old priestly families of ancient Israel, a *cohen* ('priest') may not marry a divorced woman (Leviticus 21:7). Reform's view on this is that cohens in modern life no longer carry out priestly functions and so should not be singled out from other Jewish men when it comes to whom they may marry. Reform also doubts whether it can be taken for granted, after all the centuries since the fall of the Second Temple in 70 CE, that anyone living now is of priestly stock. Further they feel that reminders of Israelite society's division into Priests, Levites, and Israelites are inappropriate expressions of Judaism in today's society. They cite cases which they consider unfair and illogical. It is not that they are not concerned with halakhic rulings, for Reform considers these an important starting-point, but they believe that laws which sprang from one time *may* not be appropriate in a quite different time. They are, therefore, 'outdated' and rather than be modified they should be thoroughly discarded. Reform applies this principle to certain ritual laws, such as those involving ritual purity (as with the cohen). The moral laws are judged to be binding.

Other founding members of the German movement for reform expressed the possibility, still held by Reform today, that such differentiation between what was binding and what was not could be reconciled with tradition. Abraham Geiger (1810–1874) writes in *Judaism and its History*:

> *Tradition is the developing power which continues in Judaism as an invisible agent . . . Tradition is the animating soul in Judaism . . .*

> *Tradition, like revelation, is a spiritual energy that ever continues to work, a higher power that does not proceed from man, but is an emanation from the Divine Spirit . . .*

Geiger's fellow-reformer, Samuel Holdheim, however, went in a far more radical direction, being prepared to abandon all the mitzvot (obligations).

Other areas of change in early Reform Judaism included public worship. They felt that wavering Jews might be more drawn to services if they bore more resemblance to some contemporary Christian services. So prayers were said in German rather than in Hebrew and organ music was introduced together with mixed choirs. Edifying sermons were included, liturgical references to re-establishing sacrifice were expunged from the traditional prayer book, and the whole service was injected with a greater sense of decorum. Since Reform began, there have been many changes on the liturgical front with some abandoned elements later being reintroduced.

Reform in the United States

In the second half of the nineteenth century, the more radical wing of Reform came to predominate, especially in the United States. Its views were expressed at a meeting of Reform rabbis in Pittsburgh in 1885. In the statement there produced, known as the Pittsburgh Platform, Jews are no longer seen as 'a holy nation' leading a way of life altogether different from that of 'other nations':

We recognise in the Mosaic legislation a system of training the Jewish people for its mission during its national life in Palestine, and today we accept as binding only the moral laws, and maintain only such ceremonies as elevate and sanctify our lives ... We hold that all such Mosaic and rabbinical laws as regulate diet, priestly purity, and dress originated in ages and under the influence of ideas altogether foreign to our present mental and spiritual state ... Their observance in our days is apt rather to obstruct than to further modern spiritual elevation . . . We consider ourselves no longer a nation, but a religious community, and therefore expect neither a return to Palestine, nor a sacrificial worship under the sons of Aaron, nor the restoration of any of the laws concerning the Jewish state.

By 1937, a new statement of 'Guiding Principles of Reform Judaism' had been produced in the United States. Under the influence of some strongly traditional Jews arriving from eastern Europe in the 1890s, many American Jews felt that the Pittsburgh Platform had gone too far. The new statement, produced by Reform rabbis meeting in Columbus (and therefore called the Columbus Platform), took a far more positive view of traditional symbols, ceremonies and above all the mitzvot. The hostility to attempts to establish a Jewish homeland in Palestine was also removed.

A further meeting of Reform rabbis, this time in San Francisco, illustrates the continued move to recover aspects of liturgy and observance which were found to have continuing value. Recognized was a need for 'the use of Hebrew, together with the vernacular, in our worship and instruction'. Responsibilities included:

creating a Jewish home centered on family . . .; lifelong study; private prayer and public worship; keeping the Sabbath and the holy days.

This San Francisco Platform, coming in 1976, constituted the significant 'Centenary Perspective of American Reform Rabbis'. Reform Judaism in America had always had a committee whose answers to questions were rooted in the halakhah (the Responsa Committee). The importance of this, but also its tensions with more modern approaches, is reflected in the 1976 statement:

Within each area of Jewish observance, Reform Jews are called upon to confront the claims of Jewish tradition, however differently perceived, and to exercise their individual autonomy, choosing and creating on the basis of commitment and knowledge.

The Reform movement became very strong among American Jews – and has stayed so. Those who emigrated from Germany in the nineteenth century found that life and attitudes of the 'New World' seemed to go well with the 'New Judaism'. Reform rabbis with western European backgrounds were able to mediate between the more radical, such as Kaufmann Kohler whose views had prevailed at the Pittsburgh meeting, and those who insisted that Reform was a renewal of Judaism rather than a severing. Chief among these mediators was Isaac Mayer Wise who created the major institutions of Reform: the Union of American Hebrew Congregations in 1873, the Hebrew Union College for training rabbis in 1875, and in the same year a rabbinical association. More recently, rabbis with a clear Zionist philosophy (such as Stephen Wise, 1874–1949), an intense knowledge of traditional liturgy (such as A.Z. Idelsohn, 1882–1938) and halakhic proficiency (such as Solomon Freehof, 1892–1990) have enabled a better integration of tradition and change than in the more defensive days of Reform. An equal role was afforded to women and the first woman rabbi was ordained in 1972. Yet there was still a serious attempt to provide 'something for everyone'. For example, a choir to lead the singing was offered as an alternative or addition to a cantor rather than as a replacement. Today 13 per cent of American Jews are Reform, making the majority of Reform Jews who, worldwide, number well over a million.

Reform in Britain

In Britain, practicalities came first and ideological formulations later. Indeed, British Reform started almost by accident and it was some time before it went in the same direction as its German counterpart. The first step was taken by some members of Bevis Marks, the oldest Sefardi synagogue in Britain, in London's East End. Having moved to live in the West End, they wanted a synagogue there, but the East End community opposed this, fearing the loss of financial support from the wealthier West End families. Some members went ahead with their plans, breaking away from Bevis Marks and forming an independent congregation in 1840. They were joined by some Ashkenazi families and called themselves the 'West London Synagogue of British Jews', opening a synagogue in 1842. With their independence, they took the opportunity to make minor reforms in the synagogue service. A prayer book (the first edition of *Forms of Prayer* – see Chapter 10) was published in 1841–2. That they were feeling their way theologically can be seen in the fact that its first minister, the Reverend D. W. Marks, declared that only the written Torah was binding and the oral Torah lacked authority, whilst later Reform rabbis said that parts of the Bible were obsolete and aspects of rabbinic literature were enduring. Continued discussion over the halakhah in Reform is seen by adherents as a strength and by opponents as a confusion. The move in the traditional direction has continued in the second half of the twentieth century. This is particularly true in Britain where Reform is closer to what in America is Conservative Judaism (see below). It constitutes about 17 per cent of synagogue-affiliated Jews in Britain. (Eight per cent belong to the Liberal movement which is the more radical of the two main non-Orthodox groupings in Britain.) They belong to the Reform Synagogues of Great Britain (RSGB), the title now given to an association formed in 1941.

A vital departure from Orthodoxy

We shall see in all the later chapters of this book specific points where there are differences between Orthodox and Reform Judaism. Different practices emerge in rites of passage, food laws, education, worship, observance of the Sabbath and other festivals. But one particular area which has vital practical implications is to be looked at now, since it provides important clues to the major points of departure from Orthodoxy. Reform Judaism began as an attempt to show that Jewish belief and practice were suited to modern times and one of the biggest changes in modern times has been in the role of women. Unlike other changes in the ordering of society which occurred at the outset of Reform, this one is still going on. The matter can hardly be described as 'settled'. There is considerable debate over the principles involved, not least in a number of the world's major religions.

It would not be altogether helpful to define various Christian denominations solely in terms of their views on the role of women. For one thing, even within denominations there are still different attitudes, notably towards women in the Anglican priesthood. For another, the role of women is not expressed as a tenet of faith, though particular attitudes to the authority of scripture and to tradition do lie behind the respective Christian views. Reform Judaism, however, takes a particular stance on the role of women, making equality a guiding principle. Again in Romain's opening pages defining Reform, we read;

> ... women are regarded as the religious equal of men, entitled to the same privileges and liable for the same responsibilities, whether at synagogue, at home or in public. Reform Judaism therefore attempts the daunting task of bringing modern conditions and perceptions within the parameters of Jewish life, so that one can be both religious and realistic.

Just how Reform tries to do this provides a comparison with Orthodox Judaism which is highly instructive of the most important differences between the two movements.

Determining the role of women in Judaism

Though a whole area in itself, the role of women in Judaism is here being explored to exemplify the main points of departure of non-Orthodoxy from Orthodoxy. It is impossible for anyone to be neutral when approaching this subject. Whether one is male or female, old or young, Jewish or non-Jewish, Orthodox or Reform, everyone comes with perceptions of the role a woman should have in the community. When looking specifically at women's role within the Jewish community, we are likely to carry over these perceptions. Today we may apply the term 'sexist' to certain kinds of opinion and behaviour. Though our views on what is sexist and what is not and on a whole range of perceptions and reactions cannot altogether be discarded when we come to consider the role of Jewish women, we might do well to make our aim an understanding of the stances adopted by the different religious groupings. At the risk of caricaturing 'the Jewish woman' (a tendency of plays and television advertisements), we could perhaps offer a profile of an Orthodox Jewish woman in Britain, an Ultra-Orthodox Jewish woman in Britain and a Reform Jewish woman in Britain.

Three 'Jewish Women'

Mrs Middle (of-the-road) Orthodox lives in Manchester. She is married and likely to remain so. She has two children who attend local state schools. She sends her children to a Jewish Sunday school but she herself is not a very regular attender at synagogue. She makes a point of attending the Jewish New Year and the Day of Atonement and when members of her immediate or extended family are involved in a special occasion. In synagogue, she sits in the women's gallery from where she can see the men leading the service, including the prayers and, on Sabbath morning and festivals, the reading from the Torah. Her synagogue belongs to the United Synagogue and some of the other women there attend regularly. She keeps to kosher meat at home, but when eating out or with non-Jewish friends she does not worry about food restrictions. She celebrates Passover with a special meal each year. She goes out to work, leads a busy social life, and is involved in a local charity. Being Jewish is important to her and she hopes that her children will marry a Jewish partner, as she did. She would have particular difficulty in accepting a non-Jewish wife for her son, even if she liked her personally. Unless the daughter-in-law converted to Orthodox Judaism (a demanding process), the grandchildren would not be judged Jewish.

Mrs Ultra-Orthodox lives in Stamford Hill and has a large family as do nearly all her Jewish neighbours. Being married and having children is what she regards as by far her most important role, though she also goes out to work. She had a full-time Jewish education and she sends her children to a Jewish school. She prays and studies regularly, adheres to the food laws strictly, and observes the festivals. She keeps the rules of family purity which means no marital intimacy during menstruation and for the week afterwards, followed by bathing in a ritual bath. She covers her hair except when alone with her husband. She is not really worried about any of her children 'marrying out' as they have little social contact with non-Jews. The oldest one, for instance, works for a firm which employs mainly Ultra-Orthodox Jews.

Mrs Reform lives in north-west London. She has two children who go to a state school. She lives some distance from a synagogue but has started to go more regularly since her elder daughter has become more interested. Her younger daughter is less keen and has mainly non-Jewish friends. One in particular looks likely to become her partner. She would prefer her daughter not to 'marry out', though her own sister did, much to their own mother's dismay. She sets aside Friday evening for a special family meal and visits her Jewish relatives back in Liverpool for Passover and the New Year. Her mother belongs to an Orthodox synagogue, but Mrs Reform finds her own services more meaningful. There, many of the prayers are in English rather than Hebrew and she agrees with the way in which the women in her synagogue take an active part in the reading and prayers. She has even heard mention that their next rabbi could well be a woman.

This sort of popular presentation should not be pressed too far, but it does bring to light the main points of difference. They are: status, that is, matters of birth, conversion, marriage, and divorce; public worship, that is, matters of reading the Torah and saying (or singing) the prayers; and family life, that is, matters of raising a family, education, and employment. Many of these require treatment in specific chapters later in this book. For example, some of the public worship matters, such as the language of prayers, will be better considered in the chapters on Prayer and Synagogue. Questions about ritual purity and the role of the Jewish Courts in determining who is a Jew fall more naturally into the chapter on Marriage. A number of interrelated considerations should, however, be raised at this point.

Women reading the Torah

The drive for sexual equality has naturally not been confined to non-Orthodox Judaism. Currently, the question of whether women can become rabbis is exercising the minds of some neo-Orthodox congregations, especially in the USA. The answer will largely depend on how the role of the contemporary rabbinate is perceived. Is it to make decisions on Jewish laws, to function as a teacher and communal leader, or to perform the tasks of a religious functionary? Whether the rabbinical role for a woman is found to be compatible with the halakhah is still being explored. Meanwhile both in America and in Britain, there are small groups of women who want to adhere to halakhic requirements and yet find the male-dominated Orthodox service unsatisfactory. They have, therefore, established services for women only. There was a particular difficulty in Britain when the court of the Chief Rabbi intervened to stop two services which had been approved by an Orthodox rabbi at his synagogue in north-west London. The difficulty lay in the fact that the women wanted to read from the *sefer Torah* ('Torah scroll'). Such a public reading, with the attendant blessings, requires a quorum which in Orthodoxy is 10 men. The media at the time had a field-day, as they do with any disputes especially among religious people. So *The Independent* on 25 November 1992 carried the headline: 'Women-only worship splits Orthodox Jews' and quoted another rabbi supporting the ban as saying: 'In my view, this has more to do with feminism than religious fervour, and, as such, must be treated with scepticism.' Unfortunately, the newspaper reports did not explain the sefer Torah difficulty on this occasion, leaving the general reader with the impression that women are not allowed to have their own meetings for prayer. This is obviously not the case, as in an Ultra-Orthodox seminary women hold prayer services alone.

Such meetings are now part of the British structure, those in synagogues under the aegis of the Chief Rabbi scrupulously following the halakhah by omitting the few elements of the liturgy that require a quorum. In a few American centres, the reading of the Torah is included, but the lack of an overall authority for American Orthodoxy makes it easier for individual rabbis to sanction new departures than in Britain. There is division of opinion among Orthodox Jews about how far some of these issues, including women only reading the sefer Torah and even women leading prayer in public, are based on sound halakhic usage and how far simply on custom.

A development in Britain has been the 'Jewish Women's Network' which is intended as a forum for dialogue between Jewish women of every description. As one of its Reform members, Rabbi Sheila Shulman, put it at the network's inception in 1993: 'There will be change if women begin to want real change', but, she added: 'I don't know how elastic Orthodox Judaism can be.' Time will tell whether women's prayer groups are a dangerous aberration, possibly leading, rather ironically, to totally segregated worship or a universally accepted means of spiritual inspiration. The discontent among Orthodox Jewish women is certainly attracting attention from the British Chief Rabbi, as he considers the national review which he commissioned when he assumed office and which reported in 1994. Many voiced their criticisms of, among other things: family orientation which, they said, excludes unmarried women, single parents, and widows; women's participation in synagogue life being largely confined to catering; and an Orthodox woman being regarded as still married if her husband refuses her a religious divorce, even if she has been granted a civil one (see Chapter 9).

Exemption from positive time-based mitzvot

The matter of whether women can count in a quorum or lead prayers is another area where it is not always clear whether it is custom or halakhah which is preventing change. Though the Bible presents such strong women as Miriam, Deborah, and Esther, biblical society was clearly patriarchal. The woman was created to be man's helper and she was to obey him (Genesis 3:16). Rules about her role are not given let alone defined, but by the time the Torah was being discussed it was assumed that her main role lay in raising a family rather than in any public sphere. She was not expected to do anything which might interfere with the responsibilities of motherhood. She was, therefore, exempt from positive mitzvot (obligations) which had to be carried out at a specific time of day in a public place. Time-based mitzvot which could be carried out at home (such as fasting on the Day of Atonement and eating unleavened bread at Passover) were obligatory for women as were all negative mitzvot (Kiddushin 1:7). The main time-bound positive mitzvah from which women were exempt was the obligation to pray in the evening, the morning, and the afternoon. Though a man could pray at home, it was judged to be better to pray with a *minyan* ('quorum'), the smallest communal unit. (The Rabbis took the words: 'The glory of a king is a multitude of people' (Proverbs 14:28) to mean that the more people there were gathered for prayer, the greater the homage paid to God.) A minyan was judged to be 10 males over the age of 13 (Berakhot 21b). Men, therefore, had this obligation, since they were not prevented from fulfilling it by home responsibilities. Certain clothing also had to be worn by men at specific prayer times, but again women were exempt (Kiddushin 34a).

These are the rules which still govern Orthodox practice. A woman may pray in a synagogue at specific times, but she is not obliged to. Because she is not obliged, she may not count in a minyan of those who are obliged, nor may she lead others who are fulfilling their obligation. The talmudic principle is that only a person who is himself obligated to perform a mitzvah may perform that mitzvah on behalf of someone else (Berakhot 20b). There are also laws of modesty which some cite against women leading the prayers. The thought is that a woman's voice and appearance might distract a man from his prayers. Considering 'the dignity of the community' (Megillah 23a) is also what lies behind women not being allowed to read from the Torah scroll – even when there is a minyan present, though interestingly this same talmudic passage makes plain that a woman is eligible to read. Being a rabbi or a cantor is thus, at present, ruled out in Orthodox Judaism. From the non-Orthodox viewpoint, new circumstances dictate that customs or even laws for which reasons were firmly based in a past patriarchal society must be abandoned. Each Reform synagogue is autonomous in deciding its practices. In many, but by no means all, women lead the prayers and read from the Torah. Women are counted in a minyan (judged to be desirable but not essential in Reform) and wearing such garments as a prayer shawl is optional practice for them as it is for Reform men. (It is, however, an expectation in Reform that men wear the prayer shawl and some argue that the logic of equality means that this should be matched by the same expectation for women.) There is no balcony or area for women to sit separately from men. Since 1975 in Britain, women have become rabbis, though there was at first some fear of internal dissension about this.

Reform Jews also question (as do some Orthodox Jews) whether, in fact, in Second Temple Judaism women played no part in public worship. That this was so in the Temple itself is not debated. Women clearly were not priests. Indeed, they could not get anywhere near where sacrifices were offered, being confined to the outer court, which lay beyond both the men's court and the priests' court. There is evidence, however, that in the synagogue women were treated more equally than later, when they were seated separately from men and that they took a larger part in the actual service. So, maintains Hyam Maccoby: 'Only a growth in prudishness and concern for decorum led to these changes in the synagogue, as they did in the Christian churches . . .' (*Judaism in the First Century*, Sheldon Press, 1989.) Stefan Reif, examining Hebrew prayer (see Chapter 10), draws attention also to medieval texts which indicate that women could take upon themselves mitzvot from which they were exempt (such as wearing specific items during prayer), counting in a minyan, and not only reading from the Torah but also reciting the blessing.

The public role of women

It is, however, anachronistic simply to label Orthodox practice 'sexist'. Its assumptions may be regarded as 'sexist' by those who do not share them, but in its origins the differentiation between the public role of the man and the private role of the woman, both of them religious roles, was not designed to express any notion of female inferiority. Nor does it centre on whether women should go out to work. The average Ultra-Orthodox woman, as we have indicated, does so, though she is not obliged to and is unlikely to when her children are young. Moreover, there is a proud tradition from rabbinic times of the woman being the bread-winner, enabling the man to study. The crux of the matter lies in the Jewish emphasis on marriage and procreation. If understood as rabbinic duties, then they are the most important role for a woman. If an altogether different starting-point is adopted, which rests on men and women having open to them not only equal religious roles but identical ones, then the Orthodox position is misguided.

The real tension is for Orthodox women who respect not only the halakhah but also the practice ('the way their parents did it'), yet who feel deprived of an involvement in synagogue life which they feel would enhance and not detract from any more private role that they may have. They are no longer satisfied with the argument that, if anything, the woman's religious role in Judaism is greater than the man's because the home is where Jewish values are transmitted and where many observances are carried out. The dilemma is a real one and one which at key points is not limited to Jewish women. It involves the very issue of time and priorities which the ancient Rabbis perhaps perceived with their exemption of women from positive time-bound mitzvot. If the home is the vital source of Jewish learning, is even Jewish identity threatened by women taking on other public responsibilities? Some believe that it is. So Blu Greenberg who recognizes the different positions of women who have a young family and those who have not:

> Maintaining the exemption for mothers of young ... will achieve several things: halakhically, it will be more continuous with the past and it will allay oft-voiced fears that tefillah [prayer] would interfere with family tasks. More important, it will turn the categorical gender exemption from something negative for women, as it is now, to something more positive. It will make a subtle yet powerful statement about the holiness of raising a family, which for a few crucial years can take precedence over the mitzvah of prayer.

> (On Women and Judaism, Jewish Publication Society of America, 1981).

And H.H. Donin:

> It is the woman who usually determines the spiritual character of the home. It is the mother who is most often called upon to answer her children's daily questions. It is the extent of the mother's faith, the strength of her values and beliefs, that plays the dominant role in shaping the spiritual character of the next generation.

(To Raise A Jewish Child, Basic Books, 1977)

The last paragraph quoted, however, might lead others to the very opposite conclusion. Reform feels that it has the answer by allowing each woman to decide how best her faith, and the faith of her family if she has one, may be strengthened.

Conservative Judaism

A breakaway from Reform

The difficulty of balancing the demands of tradition and modernity is exemplified in Conservative Judaism, not least in its views on women's position in the synagogue. Conservative Judaism may be said to have a foot in both Orthodox and Reform camps, affirming the Orthodox position on observing the halakhah and the Reform view on the importance of critical scholarship and belief. It began as a breakaway from the emergent Reform movement in Germany when, in 1845, Rabbi Zacharias Frankel insisted that Hebrew be the language of the liturgy. In 1854, Frankel became the first head of the Jewish Theological Seminary of Breslau. A similar reaction to radical Reform occurred in the USA and the Jewish Theological Seminary of America was established in 1886. Appointed its president in 1902 was Solomon Schechter (1848–1915). Under his leadership, Conservative Judaism became an umbrella for a wide range of traditional Jewish opinion. He resisted any break with accepted halakhah and with the prayer book of neo-Orthodoxy. The seminary was thus able to train rabbis to serve both Orthodox and Conservative congregations.

A breakaway from Conservatism

This situation changed, however, when one of the seminary teachers, Mordecai Kaplan, began treating all halakhah as if it were simply *minhag* ('custom') and presenting Judaism as an evolving religious civilisation rather than a supernaturally revealed religion. In his *Guide to Jewish Ritual*, Kaplan taught that group survival and individual expression should control ritual and not vice versa. A great advocate of equality between the sexes, he created the *Bat Mitzvah* ceremony (see Chapter 8). Between 1945 and 1963, a range of prayer books was produced which eliminated such concepts as a chosen people and a personal Messiah. Their 1994 prayer book does not refer to God but rather to the 'Compassionate One', the 'Infinite', or the 'Eternal'. This movement is known as Reconstructionism and it is estimated to make up between 1 and 2 per cent of the Jewish community in the USA, where it is quite active and has a Reconstructionist organization of congregations and a rabbinical college.

Further tensions in Conservative Judaism

In the face of this development, Conservative Judaism ultimately produced in 1946 a sabbath and festival prayer book. The basic text remained the Hebrew version of modern Ashkenazi Orthodoxy, but there were significant changes made to prayers such as those requesting the restoration of Temple sacrifice and the male negative blessings of God for 'not making me a Gentile . . . a slave . . . a woman.' As the movement generally gained confidence and became distinct from both Orthodoxy and Reform, it worked out its own form of halakhah, as reflected in new documents for religious ceremonies, such as marriage, and the permitting of driving to the synagogue on the Sabbath.

Neither left nor right had been entirely happy with the synthesis expressed in the new prayer book, but it was the re-evaluation of the role of women which dominated American Conservatism in the 1980s and the decision taken in 1983 to train women rabbis in the Jewish Theological Seminary and their subsequent ordination which led to a defection by a more traditional minority.

Similar tensions existed in Britain in the last quarter of the twentieth century. The name given to the movement of 'traditionalist' Conservatives in the USA and in Israel is *Masorti* ('tradition'). The Masorti movement now has eight British synagogues (and a number of communities, for example, in Leeds), but the first was established in a blaze of controversy. The conflict was, and still is, a theological one (which confirms the importance of differences in belief between Orthodoxy and all other Jewish religious groups). It concerned the precise authority of the written Torah. Rabbi Louis Jacobs was rejected for the principalship of Jews' College (the Orthodox rabbinical college in London), where he was already lecturing, and later from the United Synagogue rabbinate. The 'Jacobs Affair' stemmed from his publishing a book, *We have Reason to Believe* (1957), in which he said:

> The Torah did not drop down as a package from heaven, but is an ongoing relationship with the people of Israel. It is a product of many generations of reflection on what is meant by God's word.

Jacobs himself found this belief to be quite compatible with his Orthodox position but, when expelled, he founded the New London Synagogue where he has remained rabbi. The British Masorti movement has not yet ordained women rabbis. At the New London Synagogue, the men and women sit separately, unlike in Conservatism. The latter is now the largest grouping of American Jews numbering 23 per cent. Its United Synagogue is an association of over 800 congregations.

Liberal Judaism

About 25 per cent of synagogue-affiliated Jews in Britain belong to what is sometimes called Progressive Judaism. This includes not only Reform who number about 17 per cent but also Liberal Jews who constitute the remaining eight per cent. The Liberal movement started in 1902 as an off-shoot of Reform and is altogether more radical. It corresponds more closely to American Reform and the more radical wing of German Reform. ('Liberal' rather confusingly denotes the less radical wing of Reform in Germany.) Its organisation, the Union of Liberal and Progressive Synagogues (ULPS), grew out of the Jewish Religious Union founded by Lily Montagu and Claude Montefiore in 1902. In 1912, the words 'for the advancement of Liberal Judaism' were added to the title of the Jewish Religious Union. All this reveals a move away from Reform.

The Liberal movement's first prayer book preferred English to Hebrew and expressed a distinctly anti-Zionist outlook. The spiritual leader of the British Liberal movement between the two world wars was Rabbi Dr Israel Mattuck. By 1956, a college had been founded by the Reform Synagogues of Great Britain in

London to train rabbis and teachers. From 1964 onwards it has been sponsored jointly by RSGB and ULPS. It is named after Leo Baeck (1873–1956), a leader of German Jewry who settled in England after World War II. Liberal Judaism has itself modified, especially on Zionism, but it remains thoroughly non-halakhic, as seen, for instance, in its view that Jewishness passes through either parent and not just the mother. It continues to stress a universal age of peace rather than a more centrally Jewish Messianic Age. Each of the 28 congregations belonging to the ULPS is self-governing and, within each congregation, Liberal Judaism recommends individual decision as the best chance of promoting, purifying, strengthening, and preserving Judaism in the modern world. Nonetheless, it offers general principles and a practical programme which members are then free to accept, modify, or reject. As the most modern and the most radical of the religious Jewish responses to emancipation, Liberal Judaism believes strongly in egalitarianism and boasts some women rabbis of note, including the writer and broadcaster, Julia Neuberger.

06

food laws

In this chapter you will learn:

- the purpose of the food laws
- about the rules governing what is kosher
- how the food laws are observed.

The source and purpose of the food laws

Nothing illustrates better the origins and development of Judaism than the Jewish laws about food. The roots of these laws are in the Hebrew Bible, their amplification is found in the Talmud, and the levels at which they are observed reflect the main stances of the different movements in Judaism. It can be said that observance of traditional food laws is a key indicator of a Jew's overall observance of the halakhah (the rabbinic elaboration of the biblical rules) and his or her general attitude to being distinctively Jewish.

The name given to these laws is *kashrut*, from the word *kasher*. In the Bible and the Talmud, the Hebrew word *kasher* is used to mean 'right' or 'fit'. It can be used of right behaviour and of a person behaving properly. It can be applied to something correctly prepared, to a Torah scroll, for example. Kasher (or *kosher* as it has come into English via its Ashkenazi pronunciation) is now used of food when it is fit to be eaten. The sole criterion for whether or not the food is judged fit is not hygiene but whether or not the Torah permits it. The usual meaning of kosher today is then: food permitted to be eaten.

Its opposite, forbidden food, is said to be *trefah* ('torn'). 'Trefah' was originally used of an animal attacked and killed by a predator, but the term was extended by rabbinic tradition to include any animal afflicted with a potentially fatal wound or physical defect, even if it had not been 'torn' by a wild beast. Such animals cannot be fit for consumption even if slaughtered correctly.

Coming from the Bible, through the Talmud, and into the law codes, Judaism has a whole system of laws dealing with food. Most of these laws come in one or both of two biblical passages: Leviticus 11 and Deuteronomy 14. Central to the first of these are the words which appear many times in the Torah: 'For I am the LORD your God; sanctify yourselves therefore, and be holy, for I am holy.' And an early rabbinic comment on the second says: 'Sanctify yourself with things that are permitted to you' (Sifrei Deuteronomy 14:21).

Holiness

It is here that we find the purpose of the food laws. This is to discipline the Jewish people towards holiness. Whatever concerns of health and hygiene may now be detected in them, the sole purpose of kashrut as stated in the Torah is to express the holiness of the covenant people. For Jews the general state of holiness is a mitzvah and specific commands are ways of expressing the holiness of obedience. Obedience to the complex pattern of mitzvot seen in the food laws is not required of all people but it is, according to the Torah, required of the people of God. By such obedience, they become holy, set apart for the service of God (Exodus 19:3–6).

The ways in which kashrut may distinguish Jews as a people will be discussed below when we consider the attitudes adopted by the Orthodox and non-Orthodox respectively. Meanwhile, there is the notion behind these laws that by exercising discipline in satisfying hunger, the most basic of all human appetites, people may cultivate a particular attitude to life. They remind themselves that they eat to live, not live to eat. The Jewish philosopher, Maimonides, writes that the food laws help: 'train us to master our appetites; accustom us to restrain our desires; and to avoid considering the pleasure of eating and drinking as the goal of man's existence.' Kashrut is, therefore, about not always having what you like when you like. It starts with eating, elevating it into a means of distinctiveness. We see the consecrated nature of eating at many points in Jewish life. In the blessings both before and after a meal and in actions reminiscent of ancient priestly duties (for example, the washing of hands and dipping the special Sabbath bread in salt), the meal table becomes a sanctified place. The Talmud says: 'A man's table is like the altar' (Hagigah 27a). In the vital act of eating, Jews can demonstrate their belief in God and their commitment to his demands at the most fundamental level of their existence.

Deciding what is kosher

The ancient people of Israel is instructed:

> *I am the LORD your God; I have separated you from the peoples. You shall therefore make a distinction between the clean animal and the unclean, and between the unclean bird and the clean; you shall not bring abomination on yourselves by animal or by bird or by anything with which the ground teems, which I have set apart for you to hold unclean.*

(Leviticus 20:24–5)

Everything that is not trefah (unclean or, better, unfit) is kosher (clean, or better, fit). To know what can be eaten, a Jew must, therefore, find out what is declared trefah. According to the list in Leviticus 11, this includes virtually every insect. Some locusts were forbidden (verse 22), but since it is not clear which type was permitted, the rabbinic authorities forbade every kind of locust and, by extension, all insects. Vegetables (all of which are permitted) must, therefore, be washed carefully to ensure that they are free of insects.

The required characteristics of poultry, fish, and meat

Verses 13–19 name many birds as unfit (compare Deuteronomy 14:11–18). Again, however, it is hard to be sure just which birds these are, since not all the Hebrew names can be translated with certainty. It is not clear what makes certain poultry forbidden. Some suggest that it may be their association with cruelty, as those named appear to be birds of prey. To look for a reason for these birds being unclean is, however, to miss the point of the food laws. The Torah is not interested in giving a reason. The food laws fall into the category of hukim (mitzvot whose reason cannot be known with any certainty). In practice, Jews tend to eat only birds traditionally recognized as kosher, such as duck, goose, chicken, and turkey.

When it comes to fish, those which are forbidden are clearly identified. They lack fins and scales (Leviticus 11:10, Deuteronomy 14:10). To be kosher, fish must have both characteristics. Further clarity is given in the halakhah, where it is stated that the scales must be easily removable, thus ruling out a fish like sturgeon. Shellfish are never eaten by any observant Jew.

Animals also must have two characteristics to be kosher. They must chew the cud and have cloven (completely parted) hoofs. Perhaps because it is specifically mentioned as lacking one of these characteristics (verse 7; compare Deuteronomy 14:8), the pig is particularly forbidden. The suggestion is sometimes made that this has something to do with cleanliness, but this is not so. As the Jewish writer, Herman Wouk, amusingly puts it, you could have a pig raised in an incubator on antibiotics, bathed daily, slaughtered in a hospital operating room and its carcass sterilized by ultra-violet rays and the pork chops would not be kosher. Hygiene is not the point; ceremonial cleanliness is. The pig is not unclean in itself (a chicken is by nature hardly more clean), but is unclean to the people of Israel. The discipline is for them.

In the Middle Ages there was, in fact, some discussion about whether animals which chew the cud and have cloven hoofs (and fish with fins and scales) are kosher because of these characteristics or whether these characteristics are only indications that the animals and fish are kosher. But it is simply not possible to know, since the Torah does not say why some creatures are kosher and some are not. As already seen, the food laws, whatever their origin, are to be obeyed simply because obeying them promotes holy living. Not eating pork, like some other food laws, has acquired a special significance because of times in Jewish history when keeping this particular law has cost Jews their lives. In the second century BCE, for example, Antiochus IV threatened death to those Jews who refused orders to eat pork. Animal and bird by-products, such as milk and eggs, can be used only if they come from a kosher species. Camel milk and ostrich eggs are, therefore, not kosher.

There are further rules about animals. Animals that have died of natural causes (Deuteronomy 14:21) or animals that have been killed by other animals (Exodus 22:31) – and by extension have any serious defect such as perforation of the lungs – may not be eaten. Certain parts, even of a permitted animal, are prohibited. One of these is the sciatic nerve. Either this is carefully removed, a complicated procedure known as porging, or the whole hindquarter is avoided. This is in memory of a story in Genesis 32:22–32 in which Jacob wrestles with a mysterious stranger and is injured in the nerve of his thigh. (The story is important for its telling of how the patriarch, Jacob, is renamed 'Israel'.) Another prohibition is of suet, the hard fat formed below the diaphragm. Prohibited fats are those specified for sacrifice in Leviticus 7:1–4, 22–25. Separating these from edible fats is a complex business in kosher butchery.

Removing blood

Also prohibited is blood, because, as Deuteronomy 12:23 puts it: 'the blood is the life'. Since the life of the flesh is in the blood (Leviticus 17:11), the blood is too sacred to be eaten. Even a bloodspot in an egg renders the egg trefah. So far as meat is concerned, as much blood as possible has to be removed. This involves two processes. The first is the Jewish method of slaughtering animals, *shehitah*. This means 'killing' (in the prescribed manner). Shehitah is designed to kill the animal with the minimum amount of pain and to drain the meat of blood. There are many detailed rules and so only a skilled professional slaughterer, a *shohet*, can kill the animal and this under inspection. The shohet, operating at the butcher's shop or slaughter-house, must know the laws thoroughly and have been examined on this and his dexterity. If any regulation is not observed, the meat is called 'torn' and cannot be eaten. The death stroke must be across the neck with a finely sharpened knife. There must be no notch in the knife that might tear the animal's flesh while it is being killed and cause unnecessary pain. The animal's foodpipe and windpipe must be severed cleanly. The bleeding is profuse, but the animal does not bleed to death, as is sometimes objected. The carotid arteries and jugular veins are instantly severed, cutting off the blood supply to the brain. The animal, therefore, loses consciousness before it can feel anything. When shehitah is condemned as cruel to animals, Jews produce scientific evidence that this form of death is as merciful as any that people can visit on animals, and far more merciful than most.

The second process is to remove the remaining blood by kashering (making fit). Nowadays this is usually the responsibility of the butcher or distributor rather than the consumer. The specific process is known as 'salting', as the meat is covered with salt to extract the blood. The meat is first soaked in tepid water for half an hour in order to soften the texture and to help the salt extract the blood. It is then placed on a draining board, scattered with coarse salt, and left for an hour, before being thoroughly rinsed. The details of the laws for salting come in the law code, the Shulhan Arukh.

Separation of meat and milk

There is another aspect of kashrut to which the Shulhan Arukh devotes much space as it tries to expound the biblical teaching. This is the bizarre biblical injunction: 'You shall not boil a kid in its mother's milk.' 'Who would want to?' you might well ask. The prohibition appears three times in the Torah (Exodus 23:19; 34:26; Deuteronomy 14:21). Whatever the practice to which it originally referred, rabbinic tradition, filling 28 pages of the Talmud (e.g. Hullin 115b), has it that a kid in its mother's milk is given as an example of mixing meat and milk. Three prohibitions follow from this: meat and milk may not be boiled together, meat and milk may not be eaten together, and no benefit may be derived from such a mixture.

The consequent separation of meat and milk dishes in cooking makes heavy demands on the person in the kitchen. Having separate utensils, cutlery, crockery, washing-up bowls, dish-clothes, and teatowels is taken for granted in an Orthodox household. Such dual equipment includes the kitchen sink, with one sink for meat (often, along with all its accessories, colour-coded red) and another for milk (colour-coded blue). It was, no doubt, the absorbent nature of pottery, from which most dishes were made in early times, that led the Rabbis of the Talmud to prohibit using the same utensils for meat and dairy foods. Orthodox Jews believe, however, that the intention of the law was to keep separate sets of dishes, whether made of non-absorbent glass or pyrex or of absorbent materials, and so dairy and meat utensils are not used interchangeably. If metal pots and pans are unknowingly used for the wrong item or inadvertently come into contact with non-kosher food, they can and must be made kosher (kashered) with boiling water. The kashering process causes the offending matter to be exuded. Items made of absorbent materials, such as earthenware or plastic, cannot be kashered.

Meat is such a common ingredient that it soon becomes apparent why an observant Jew finds it so difficult to eat in a non-Jewish home or in a Jewish home where kashrut is not kept. Not only can meat and milk items not be mixed in the preparation of a meal, but they cannot be eaten straight after each other. Thirty minutes must be allowed between milk and meat and a much longer time, often three hours (though this varies between one and six hours according to locality or family tradition), between meat and milk dishes, since meat takes longer than milk to digest. Foods such as fish, that contain neither meat nor milk, are known as *parev* or *parve*, a yiddish word for 'neutral'. They can be eaten with either milk or meat.

Further rules at Passover

During the festival of Passover, there are special dietary rules. Then, and only then, any product that involves anything which is *hametz* ('leavened', literally 'sour' or 'fermented') is forbidden. (Separate utensils and appliances are used. Alternatively, those that have absorbed such a product must be kashered, if they can be, for Passover.) Alcoholic drinks derived from a leavened grain product (e.g. whisky) are not permitted. At other times, the kashrut of wine depends not on its source but on who handles it.

Many Orthodox Jews will not use wine if a non-Jew has been involved at any stage from picking the grape to bottling the wine. This goes back to talmudic times when wine used in connection with idolatrous worship was absolutely forbidden to Jews. Later this prohibition was extended to all wine touched by non-Jews. (If the wine has been boiled in the process of manufacture, it is no longer deemed sacramental and the prohibition does not apply.)

Levels of observance

Orthodox

Many Jews observe the laws of kashrut in their entirety and with exact care. The Orthodox position is that the traditional halakhah is binding. What may be eaten is governed by the many regulations derived from the Bible and by the rabbinic elaborations of the biblical rules. If this entails great effort, expense, and non-assimilation into non-Jewish society, then this after all serves the purpose of all these dietary laws. They are a reminder of distinctiveness. They require discrimination, recognizing that the body and food are given by God who calls for holiness in his people.

Recent studies in America and elsewhere have revealed that standards of observance among adherents of all the various non-Orthodox movements are not particularly high and are continuing to decline. This is perhaps surprising when it is remembered that kashrut, along with Sabbath observance, is the area which has a most direct bearing on the life of most Jews and which is widely regarded as constituting the backbone of Jewish life. America, having the largest Jewish community in the world and being the best documented, helps us to see the theoretical positions of the respective groups. Different responses on kashrut illustrate particularly well the difficulty in deciding, once the traditional belief that halakhah is binding has been rejected, how much scope is to be allowed to the individual (or small community) in determining what is a 'Jewish' life.

Reform

In the early days of Reform Judaism, its leaders took the view that food laws are devoid of rationale and harmful to good relations between Jews and non-Jews. Geiger and Holdheim in Germany and, even more so, Kohler in America took this negative view. The distinction made was not between Mosaic and rabbinic laws, but between different types of laws. Whilst the moral laws were considered binding, ceremonial laws had as their purpose to enhance and sanctify life. If they failed to do that, they should be abandoned. The most radical statement on the matter came in the Pittsburgh Platform, the decisions of the rabbinical conference of 1885 (as quoted in Chapter 5) which suggests that kashrut may, in fact, be an obstacle to 'spiritual elevation'. The Columbus Platform of 1937 took a more positive view of halakhah in general and a move even further in this direction is to be found in the latest comprehensive declaration of American Reform Rabbis, the Centenary Perspective of 1976.

In practice today, many Reform Jews do keep at least some of the traditional rules (and many Orthodox Jews ignore some of them), but, from the Orthodox position, there is no rationale for Reform practice. It is a matter of personal preference. The impression given by leading Reform teachers remains that kashrut is not vital and can too easily become an impediment to true religious feeling.

It is easy to see why it is assumed that Reform Judaism adopts a negative approach to kashrut. This assumption can be challenged, however. Certainly there remains among Reform Jews today a wariness about attaching importance to the meticulous observance of dietary laws as sufficient in itself. Only when they are a reminder of the values demanded by Judaism and are accompanied by ethical behaviour do they serve their purpose. There is also concern about divisiveness caused by disagreement between kashrut authorities. In the USA, any rabbi may decide. In Britain, there are two main authorities: the Chief Rabbi's court and the Union of Orthodox Hebrew congregations which has recently produced a list in an attempt to eliminate discrepancies. Kosher butchers, bakers, and restaurants (usually serving only meat or only dairy foods) must all display a licence from a rabbinic board. This takes responsibility for ensuring that everything is done properly.

Kosher food in shops can be recognized by the seal of several Orthodox rabbinical bodies that vouch for kashrut. The buyer should look for the Hebrew for 'kosher' or for a seal or label (*hekhser*) on the packet or tin. K and U (the symbol of the Union of Orthodox Hebrew Congregations) are the most popular. A wide range of kosher products is available today in supermarkets, usually manufactured in Israel or the USA.

Of particular importance to Reform is the distinction that is made between private and communal life. Unlike Orthodoxy, Reform makes a distinction between different aspects of kashrut. Kashrut should be observed not because they are given by God to Moses, but because they may encourage self-discipline and a sense of Jewish identity. They might also have a hygienic value. It is, however, for each household to decide the degree of observance which best serves these purposes. It is not necessarily all or nothing. There are, therefore, wide variations according to the families concerned. Some Reform Jews keep kashrut completely and some partially. The latter maintain that the laws they keep are biblical, such as abstaining from eating milk and meat products together, whilst those they regard as unnecessary 'additions' are largely the post-biblical interpretations of kashrut, such as detailed regulations for separate crockery and utensils. Since this was not the original objection when Reform began and since Reform does not specify the particular aspects that should be kept, it may be argued that this position, a very common one, has evolved largely from the desire to facilitate relations with non-Jews. Certainly, eating with non-Jewish friends or in public restaurants becomes much easier. Fish or vegetarian meals can simply be requested.

Whatever each Reform Jew's individual view on the value of the food laws, there are certain minimum standards. Foods specifically forbidden in the Bible are discouraged, especially pork, abstinence from which constitutes a law universally recognised and sanctified by history from the time of the Maccabees to that of Hitler. Eating only meat purchased from a kosher butcher where the animal will have been killed and cleaned in the prescribed way is also expected. Such butchers exist in areas of high Jewish settlement. Elsewhere, some Reform synagogues run their own 'kosher shop', stocking fresh or frozen products aiding the observance of kashrut. (Quite a distance may have to be travelled by Jews living where there are few other Jews.) The Reform Synagogues of Great Britain and the Assembly of Rabbis (the professional body to which all British Reform Rabbis belong) fully supports the Board of Deputies in its public defence of shehitah. This was seen particularly in 1987 when there were attempts to make shehitah illegal.

Standards of observance at a synagogue or synagogue-organized event are designed to be as inclusive as possible. The idea is to enable most Jews to participate without qualms and to avoid division between Jews with different views. Some Reform synagogues, for example, permit fish or vegetarian meals only, whilst others ensure that any meat which is served is kosher.

Reform tends to consider much Orthodox observance unnecessary, rejecting, for instance, alcohol prohibitions and the need for special supervision and labelling of items at Passover which are already totally free of leaven. However, there is an area where, in recent times, Reform thinking moves in the direction of extending the biblical restrictions. Some Reform Jews abstain from animals bred under methods of modern technological farming, such as battery hens. Their argument is that, by contradicting Judaism's insistence on the humane treatment of animals, including those to be killed for food (see Leviticus 22:28; Deuteronomy 5:14, 22:6–7; Proverbs 12:10), these foods are what could be described as morally trefah.

Different viewpoints

Orthodox Jews reject any distinction between biblical laws and their later interpretation which, to their mind, forms a 'fence around the Torah' to prevent the biblical ordinances from being violated. They also believe that making eating out easier weakens Jewish identity. Strictly traditional Jews will not eat in non-Jewish homes or allow non-kosher food in their own. There are gradations, however, in modern observance, and some Orthodox Jews will eat dairy or vegetarian food outside the home under certain circumstances. Some Reform Jews also have doubts about what might be construed as one set of rules for eating at home and another for elsewhere. Whilst others may press a distinction between the Jewishness of one's home and the secular world outside, they fear the charge of inconsistency, even hypocrisy, and the risk of confusing their own children. From the point of view of a non-Jew proposing to entertain Jewish guests, it is sensible to avoid serving meat and shellfish. In view of the wide range of expressions of kashrut, it is best to ask Jewish guests what they can eat and drink.

Conservative Judaism occupies an intermediate position (between Orthodox norms and Reform radicalism) on kashrut, as on much else. Since it allows each person to judge whether each of the regulations enhances or detracts from his or her spiritual development, it may be judged to be nearer to Reform. The result can be a thoroughgoing adherence to the traditional halakhah or a more selective approach. Liberal Jews also stress the individual's judgement on whether the laws help cultivate a truly religious existence. Reconstructionists, on the other hand, may well subordinate their personal preferences to the idea of 'Jewish civilisation' and so keep at least some of the food laws because of the place which they have traditionally occupied in corporate Jewish life. This sense of a common bond is, as we have seen, one purpose of kashrut which most Jews endorse.

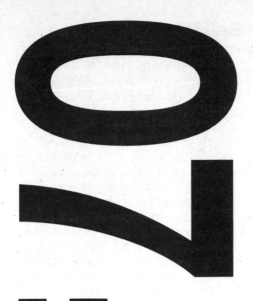

07

life and death matters

In this chapter you will learn:

- how important beliefs are expressed in birth and death ceremonies
- about the importance of circumcision
- what Jews believe about the after-life.

Expressions of belief

Lying behind the fundamental practices of a religion are fundamental beliefs. We turn at this point to the two most vital
moments in the life of a Jew and the rites of passage associated
with them. Whilst there are, of course, many variations in
custom from area to area and age to age, birth and death rituals
are expressions of profound beliefs which lie at the heart of
Judaism. Chief among them are a belief in the importance of
having children, in the sanctity of human life, in the fallibility yet
potential of individuals to live as God intends, in the equality of
all members of the covenant people, and in the reality of both
death and an after-life. Jews today differ on some aspects of
expression and, to a lesser degree, in the precise formulation of
the beliefs. However, these areas of debate – such as exactly
when life begins and when it ends, what form the after-life takes
– raise matters which for centuries have characterised the
questioning and evolving faith of Judaism. What people really
believe shows itself at critical moments.

Foremost among these for family and friends are the arrival of
a new life and the departure of an existing one. Many attendant
decisions, sharpened by twentieth-century developments in
medical technology and ethics, also reflect key beliefs. Whilst it
is not possible to say simply: 'Jews don't agree with cremation'
or 'Jews don't practise birth control' (for many do), it is possible
to outline both Orthodox practice and belief and the areas
where non-Orthodox Jews differ. More important for the non-
Jew is not the description of the practice but a grasp of what
informs it so that, whatever one's own views on these matters
(which are always sensitive and often controversial), misinfor-
mation and misunderstanding do not muddy the waters. In the
USA, there is the 'Jewish Patient's Bill of Rights', a document to
help the patient or family resist undue pressure to conform and
to help the medical team avoid giving offence to those in their
care. It is a pity that a similarly practical guide is not available
in Britain.

The importance of having children

The very first mitzvah (obligation) in the Torah is: 'Be fruitful
and multiply' (Genesis 1:28; compare Genesis 9:1). The need to
perpetuate life for the survival of the religion is clearly
recognized, not least when the Jewish population in most

countries of the world is declining. Hasidic communities feel this particularly acutely. But from ancient times the sense of both the obligation and the blessing of children has been strong. We see in biblical and rabbinic writings the way in which children are regarded as a gift and the deprivation of them a serious misfortune (e.g. Genesis 16:1). The crucial point in Judaism, however, is the increase not merely in Jewish numbers but in people recognizing a certain relationship to God, obeying him, and thus bringing about his rule on earth.

Circumcision

The supreme expression of this belief is found in the practice of circumcision. The Hebrew term for this, *brit milah* ('covenant of circumcision'), itself conveys the key concept. The 'brit' referred to (and often the ceremony is called simply a 'brit' or in the Ashkenazi pronunciation a 'bris') is the covenant between God and Abraham. Genesis 17:9–14 enjoins this covenant 'in the flesh' for all males on the eighth day after birth. (Leviticus 12:3 also states this requirement.) The importance attached to the timing is seen in the fact that circumcision takes place on the eighth day even if this coincides with the Sabbath or even the Day of Atonement. Only if the baby's health is in any doubt is the brit postponed.

The Bible provides no reason for the timing nor for circumcision itself as the mark of God's covenant with the descendants of Abraham. Many suggestions have been made for why the removal of the foreskin is an appropriate sign of loyalty to God. Some stress the link with creating the next generation. Others emphasize the uselessness of the foreskin and see its removal as a sign of a man's co-operating with God to perfect himself and serve God with every organ of his body.

Whatever the explanations offered later, the antiquity of the obligation itself is not in doubt, nor the zeal with which Jews have kept it over the ages. 1 Maccabees 1:60–61, for instance, testifies to the way in which Jews were martyred rather than forego circumcision as commanded by those hoping to destroy Judaism. It remains a requirement for any male wishing to convert to Judaism (see Chapter 9). The act does not, however, make anyone Jewish. It simply marks the commitment to the religion. Anyone born of a Jewish mother is halakhically (legally) Jewish, regardless of whether he has been circumcised. Anyone unable to be circumcised (because, for instance, of haemophilia) is no less Jewish. Circumcision for Jews is, then, a wholly religious rite. Arguing for its desirability on hygienic grounds, as if Abraham had extraordinary knowledge of dangers attendant on not being circumcised, is to look in the wrong direction. It is known that ancient Egyptians and others practised circumcision and it has been estimated that one seventh of the world's current population practises it, including Moslems as a sign of submission to Allah. For a Jew its peculiar significance is that of belonging to the covenant people.

The ceremony is accordingly communal. Between the ninth and nineteenth centuries CE, it was often held in the synagogue. Today the preferred place is the home, but a minyan (ten adult men required for public prayer in Orthodoxy) should ideally be present. A private circumcision performed by a surgeon in hospital with none of the prescribed prayers is judged by Orthodox and non-Orthodox alike to empty the brit of its religious significance. Where family and friends gather as part of the covenant people, the whole event has about it, even to a non-Jewish observer, a ring of great antiquity and devotion. Though there are some radical Reform Jews who do not practise circumcision, maintaining that spiritual obedience can be expressed without an external sign, it is striking that it is judged by most Jews to be a vitally important expression of their Jewishness.

The person who performs a ritual circumcision is a *mohel*. He is a trained expert both in the physical technique and in the religious ritual. The operation is swift, as the foreskin of the penis is snipped, its inner lining removed, and a dressing put on to stop the bleeding. Godparents and other relatives are often present, though the mother may find the occasion too distressing to attend. The father blesses God for circumcision, by which sons 'enter into the covenant of Abraham our father'.

Another feature of the ceremony is the placing of a baby briefly on a special chair before handing him to the *sandek* (a central figure who has the honour of holding the baby on his lap). This 'throne of Elijah' is a reminder of the prophet's role in recalling the ancient Israelites to their covenant responsibilities. (See, e.g. 1 Kings 18; 19; Malachi 3:1; 4:5–6.) It is also the occasion on which the baby boy is given his Hebrew name during one of the prayers: Our God and God of our fathers, preserve this child to his father and to his mother, and let his name be called in Israel —— the son of ——. (This name, Jacob Ben Samuel, for

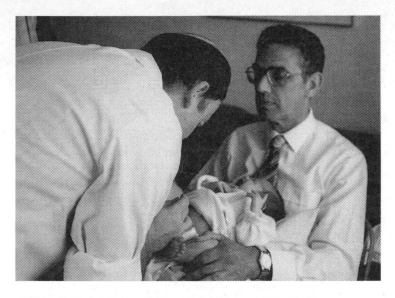

at this brit, the baby's grandfather acts as the *sandek* ('holder')

instance, was the only name of a Jew until the eighteenth century when certain governments, for example, Poland, started to require family names. Even then, many simply adopted their fathers' first names as their surnames as in Jacobs or Samuelson.) Sefardi Jews often choose the name of a living relative whilst Ashkenazi Jews give the name of a deceased relative or biblical hero. The person's Hebrew name is used in religious contexts such as when getting married or being called up to read the Torah.

Girls

Girls are given their Hebrew name (e.g. Hannah Bat Miriam) in the synagogue on the Sabbath following the birth, on which occasion the father is called up to read the Torah. Some Reform Jews hold an equivalent ceremony to brit milah in which God is blessed for the 'covenant of life' rather than the 'covenant of circumcision'. Some also hold a ceremony of baby blessing in the synagogue some weeks after the birth. This is often held for boys too, in addition to their circumcision. The aim is to involve the wider community in a more relaxed celebration of the birth.

Pidyon Ha-Ben

A further ceremony for an Orthodox couple if their first baby is a son is *Pidyon Ha-Ben* ('redemption of the son'). This recalls the special religious status of first-born sons in biblical times. Unless they belonged to the family of a priest (a cohen), they had to be 'bought back' from priestly service by their fathers. So the first-born (literally 'opening the womb' as in Exodus 13:2 and so not by Caesarian section) is bought back unless the father is a cohen or a Levite or the mother is the daughter of a cohen or a Levite. Reform Judaism rarely performs this ceremony, having abolished the role of a cohen and maintaining that it discriminates against the other children in the family.

The sanctity of human life

A belief in the sacredness of each individual life is demonstrated in Jewish attitudes to contraception, abortion, euthanasia, suicide, autopsy, and, in recent times, transplants and genetic engineering. According to the halakhah, contraceptive devices cannot be used except where there is a serious threat to the health of the mother. Even then, the marital act should be as normal as possible, so Jewish law grades methods of contraception from the least to the most objectionable, starting with oral contraceptives (early forms of which are discussed in rabbinic literature) which are considered not to interfere with the natural process of insemination (as in the 'spilling of seed' in Genesis 38:9–10) and ending with the condom or withdrawal which clearly do interfere with this process. Vasectomy is regarded as a mutilation of the body and is not permitted, though sterilization for women is sometimes allowed if there is a danger to life (Shabbat 110b–111a). Reform leaves all family planning matters, including whether to have children at all (unlike the minimum requirement stated in Yevamot 61b as a son and a daughter), entirely to the couple concerned.

In vitro fertilization is generally approved if sperm and egg have been taken from the married Jewish partners. Artificial insemination by an anonymous donor could mean that incest unwittingly occurs. According to the Mishnah, abortion is not only permitted but mandatory if the mother's life is in danger (Ohalot 7:6), the full life taking precedence over the potential life of the foetus. Responsa (legal answers) on abortion continue in recent times, especially in the USA where Conservative Judaism predominates. Conservatism is concerned to be halakhically correct but it accepts some procedures rejected by Orthodox (e.g. most sorts of contraception). The State of Israel passed an Abortion Law in 1977, for the circumstances of rape, incest, serious deformity, and pregnancy in minors. The Orthodox opposed this rather like the Roman Catholic Church opposes such a law in the Irish Republic. Sperm banks and experiments on embryos are forbidden, as is organ donation if there is more than a 50 per cent chance of the donor or the recipient dying. There is an objection to heart transplants if the organ is taken from someone who may be judged not to have reached the boundaries of death. Jewish tradition maintains that the cessation of the vital functions of both heart and lungs constitutes death. But the possibility of keeping these organs alive even after the brain is dead (judged, by the observant Jew, not to indicate death) and the matter of just what may be attached to keep a body alive have led to questions which are answered differently by the various branches of Judaism. Orthodoxy does not permit any organ transplant unless there is a specific recipient who would die without receiving the organ immediately. Reform permits the preservation of organs for future use and not only life-saving transplants but also ones which can improve the quality of life, such as corneal transplants. (Corneal transplants are also permitted by Orthodoxy because blindness is a danger to life.) On this and on other crucial issues there is considerable debate among Jews, as among other faith communities, in the light of new knowledge and skill.

Death ceremonies

The way in which the body is treated after death very clearly reflects a belief not only in the sanctity of human life but also in the equal worth and mutual responsibility of each member of the covenant people. Precise guidelines vary. In Orthodoxy, for example, the body is never left alone before the funeral and autopsy is regarded as desecration of the body, though it is permitted when the law of the land requires it. The body is prepared for burial by a group, appointed by each congregation, of men to attend to men and of women to attend to women. This voluntary organization is known as a *hevra kaddishah* ('sacred society') and belonging to it is regarded as a privilege afforded only to the most highly respected. This group may also have stayed with the dying person. After death, a purification rite is carried out. This involves a thorough bathing and cleaning of the corpse which is then wrapped in the plainest white garments, including a *kittel*, a smock-like garment worn by Jewish men on the Day of Atonement. This *taharah* (ritual washing of the corpse) is in addition to any normal washing which might have been done. It can take place in the home or in the mortuary, but it expresses a spiritual cleansing and Orthodox Jews strictly forbid non-Jews to 'lay out' a body in a hospital or chapel. In most communities, a prayer shawl is also placed round a man's shoulders. One of its fringes is cut to indicate that the dead are not subject to the mitzvot (see Chapter 10).

As a mark of respect, the funeral should take place as soon as possible after the time of death, though not on the Sabbath or on the first and last days of festivals. The ceremony is held in a hall in the cemetery grounds and stresses both the merits of the person who has died and a trust in God's justice. Then everyone fulfils the mitzvah of escorting the body to the grave. Orthodox Jews believe that human beings must return to the dust (Genesis 3:19) and so do not permit cremation. There is also the belief that the body, having decomposed and returned naturally to the earth, will be physically resurrected in the Messianic Age. In biblical times, the body was buried in direct contact with the soil and this is still the practice in Israel. Usually today, however, the body lies in a wooden coffin but this must be plain and covered with a black sheet rather than expensively designed or adorned in a way which may draw attention to someone's wealth or lack of it. Flowers are not customary at any Jewish funeral. Reform belief is that a continuation of the soul after death is independent of the condition of the body. This permits not only post-mortem examinations and organ transplants but also cremation. The liturgy at a cremation service is the same as at a burial. Christian symbols may need removing from some crematoria. (It is not permitted to bury a Jew in a non-Jewish cemetery.) Having lost the grave as a focus for grief, Reform Jews may later bury the ashes in a cemetery and erect a tombstone. Scattering the ashes is discouraged. Just before or soon after the funeral, Orthodox mourners keep the custom of formally tearing their clothes as a sign of deep grief. Some Reform Jews also find this an outlet for emotion.

Grief and hope

Mourning the reality of death and asserting belief in an after-life are inextricably linked in Judaism. The Jewish cemetery is itself called *Bet Olam* ('House of Eternity') or *Bet Ha-Hayyim* ('the House of Life'). Though these names might originally have been euphemisms, they also express the Jewish belief that death is not the end. The same belief lies behind a common greeting to the recently bereaved: 'I wish you long life.' This is not to deny their sadness but to assert that life (both that of the dead and that of the living) goes on. The most powerful expression of this attitude is found in the prayer known as the *Kaddish* (the Aramaic for 'holy' or 'sanctified'). This prayer, in different forms, is always offered in Jewish worship throughout the world, but, when mourning a death, it acquires particular force. For the mourners' Kaddish focuses not on the dead (who are not even mentioned) but on God's name which the world should hallow. Its opening words, based on Ezekiel 38:23, 'Magnified and sanctified be his great Name in the world which he hath created according to his will', affirm the faith of the mourners. They declare a belief that even when God's rule may seem least evident in their own lives it nonetheless operates. The prayer is for continued and increasing faithfulness that God's kingdom with its promise of resurrection may fully come. Children are obliged to recite the prayer at the funeral of a parent and daily for 11 months following. When there are no children, Kaddish is recited by other relatives or someone engaged for the specific purpose. The hevra kaddishah has a particular role in supporting the mourners in their grief.

The end of the funeral marks the beginning of a formal mourning period. In a remarkably open and healthy way, the first stage of mourning is one of great intensity. It lasts seven days and is known, therefore, as *shiva* ('seven'). The mourners 'sit shiva', that is, they sit on low stools to symbolise their grief and generally withdraw from public obligations. They may leave their home only on the Sabbath (and between the death and the burial cannot count in the minyan). They do not join the synagogue congregation until after the joyful welcome of the Sabbath on the Friday evening (see Chapter 12). It is judged that they would find this particularly hard. Neglecting physical appearance, men do not shave or cut their hair. Meals, especially the first one, are brought by members of the community who also form a minyan to recite prayers in the home.

Though differing circumstances and temperaments mean that people experience bereavement in different ways and over different periods of time, Jewish mourning rites are designed to encourage a gradual return to normal life whilst giving structure and support to people coming to terms with their loss. Following shiva there is a further period of *sheloshim* ('30' days), as in the mourning for Moses described in Deuteronomy 34:8. During sheloshim, the mourner returns to work, but is restricted from visiting places of entertainment. Religious festivals are, however, observed. In the case of someone mourning a parent, the restrictions of sheloshim continue for a full year after the funeral. At the end of the year, the 'child' observes *Yahrzeit* (a Yiddish term for 'anniversary'). This is the final ritual of mourning. It is a day of reflection and repentance and some Jews, therefore, observe it as a fast. On the eve of Yahrzeit many light a candle which burns for 24 hours. They may attend synagogue and recite Kaddish as they will each year on the anniversary of the death. On Yahrzeit, a small stone is left on the tombstone, perhaps as a further expression of remembering a parent by maintaining the grave. On the last day of the Pilgrim Festivals and on the Day of Atonement the departed are also recalled in *Yizkor* ('memorial service').

At some point before the first Yahrzeit, there is often a stone-setting ceremony which relatives and friends attend. Tombstones are not erected at the time of burial but between four and 12 months afterwards. They can be horizontal (Sefardi practice) or

being buried on the west-facing slope of the Mount of Olives has special significance, especially for those who believe that the Golden Gate in the eastern wall of Jerusalem will be miraculously unblocked when the dead are raised from their graves

vertical (Ashkenazi practice). The stone-setting may be accompanied by a short service designed to address the need of the mourners at this stage, but this is not to be regarded as a second funeral. Part of a Reform prayer for this occasion asks that when mourners see the stone they may be reminded 'not only of the dead but also of You, God of everlasting life.' It continues: 'In their sorrow, You are with them . . .Teach them that death is swallowed up forever in eternal life.' The Orthodox funeral service similarly affirms that one day God will conquer death itself, quoting Isaiah 25:8: 'He maketh death to vanish in life eternal; and the Lord God wipeth away tears from off all faces . . .'

For the most part Judaism encourages a concentration on this life rather than on the next. The prospect of death is not one to be feared but to be kept in mind as incentive to daily faithfulness. So the Mishnah urges people to repent one day before their death and speaks of this world as 'an ante-chamber to the world to come' in which preparation should be made (Avot 4:17). That the after-life is something to be looked forward to is, however, expressed in the same passage, as it says that: 'better is one hour of blissfulness of spirit in the world to come than the whole life of this world.' Such a belief arrived late in Judaism. The Bible gives a predominantly gloomy picture of everyone (whether good or bad, slave or king) going at death to *sheol* ('pit'), a shady underworld where people are cut off even from God (see Job 7:9 and Psalm 88). This could hardly be described as 'life'. 'Living on' was envisaged only in communal terms, that is, in the descendants of the people of Israel. In the Second Temple period, we see the Sadducean group denying any idea of individual resurrection, whilst the Pharisaic group regards it as an essential of faith. They see it as the corollary of belief in a loving God who gives human life for people to learn what it is to obey him.

Orthodox Jews follow the Pharisaic teaching. Yet, they acknowledge that a physical resurrection 'does not necessarily imply identity with the material composing the body when alive' (Rabbi Hertz in his commentary in the *Authorised Daily Prayer Book*). It is rather: 'the sum-total of all our deeds and thoughts, habits and character . . . There is for the soul in the World-to-come identity of personality with the soul in the earthly life.' There is clearly difficulty in Judaism, as there is in Christianity, in wording a belief in the 'world to come' (in Hebrew *Olam Ha-Ba*), a fundamentally new order (coming after the Messianic Age which is conceived in essentially earthly terms). Descriptions of the precise nature of this after-life are to be recognized, says

Louis Jacobs, as: 'pure speculation about a state unlike anything we can experience in this life, but which people have tried to describe as best they can with the language they have.' Ideas of heaven and hell, of resurrection of the body and immortality of the soul have fed into Jewish concepts from Hebrew and Greek thought and from Jewish and Christian developments. There is a wide range of opinion among present-day Jews. The fundamental belief rests, however, on living now and 'forever' in ways which God intends.

08

Jewish education

In this chapter you will learn:

- about the ways in which children are taught their faith
- about the obligations Jews take on as they become adults
- about Jewish schools and later Jewish Studies.

The importance of education

Jewish literature abounds in references to the supreme importance of study. In a religion centred on the Torah (in the Bible and in rabbinic writings and codes) this emphasis on religious learning is not difficult to explain. The practice of the religion with all its mitzvot (obligations) requires, in the first place, knowledge. Further, the motivation for practising the religion requires an understanding of its purpose. There is the need to cultivate a sense of inspiration, of devotion, of spirituality. This is what lies behind the thought that study is itself a devotional act. Indeed, it is considered to be more vital than prayer in that it offers the student contact with the God who is the inspiration of the sacred texts. The Talmud says that the study of the Torah is greater than the rebuilding of the Temple (Megillah 16b) and that, while a house of prayer may be converted into a house of study, a house of study – being the more sacred – may not be converted into a house of prayer (Megillah 27a). Of the many references to the devotional value of study in Mishnah Pirke Avot (e.g. 1:6, 15; 2:4–6, 8; 3:6; 5:22) the most striking is in 3:3: '. . . if two sit together and interchange words of Torah, the Divine Presence abides between them.' Another famous Mishnah passage, cited and elaborated in the prayer book, says that the study of the Torah is equal to all the following: 'honouring father and mother, deeds of loving-kindness, making peace between a man and his fellow' (Peah 1:1).

Nurturing faith

It has long been recognized that the starting-point for learning the faith is the home. So the people of Israel were bidden:

> Keep these words that I am commanding you today in your heart. Recite them to your children and talk about them when you are at home and when you are away, when you lie down and when you rise. Bind them as a sign on your hand, fix them as an emblem on the doorposts of your house and on your gates.
>
> (Deuteronomy 6:6–9)

Physical reminders of the Torah (see tefillin and mezuzah in Chapter 10) together with parental instruction are here enjoined. Whilst higher education in Jewish studies is only for some, enough education to equip each Jew to belong to 'a priestly kingdom and a holy nation' is for all, though at times females have been restricted. It is remarkable that as early as Pharisaic times steps were taken to supplement the home education in the faith by establishing a network of schools, orphan and poor children being educated at the expense of the community. According to Bava Batra 20b–21a, elementary education was instituted for boys of six or seven by the High Priest Joshua Ben Gamla (c.64–5 CE). The elementary school was followed by the 'advanced school', the *Bet Midrash* ('house of study') which was housed near or in the synagogue. In the Middle Ages the term *Talmud Torah* came to be used of the elementary school. A Talmud Torah for girls was reportedly established in Rome in the fifteenth century but it took four centuries before Jewish schooling for girls became fully established.

Parents and children

The ways in which subsequent generations have tried to provide this more formal Jewish education will be considered shortly as we turn to what is provided in the synagogue and in Jewish day schools. That the very survival of the Jewish community depends on the effective transmission of the faith remains as true as ever it was and the role of the family in this transmission remains vital. Usually a minority group, Jews have always recognized that it is their responsibility to educate, in the sense of instruct, their children religiously. They do not expect others to do it for them. By contrast, Christians are sometimes reluctant to acknowledge the ineffectiveness of Christian nurture if this is left to the state schools. It is not the task of Religious Education in such schools to inculcate a particular commitment. The days when it was assumed in Britain that the subject should promote Christian belief and practice are long gone. Religious Instruction was taken to be instruction in Christianity, the religion of what was then the vast majority in Britain. Some parents seem reluctant to accept the logic of the position that if they genuinely want their children not just to know about the Christian faith but also to follow it then the home and the church are where this should be communicated.

Continuously declining numbers in an already small Jewish community of about 285,000 in Britain have led to particular initiatives recently to strengthen the home's capacity to educate religiously. Orthodox, Ultra-Orthodox, and Reform are all concerned with what Jonathan Sacks has entitled 'Jewish continuity'. The Reform movement, in particular, has developed programmes of what it calls 'Jewish family education'. The necessity for this stems not only from the fact that the Jewish death rate is outstripping the Jewish birth rate but also from the general impact of an increasingly secular approach to life. The USA, finding many parents wanting to pass on the Jewish religious heritage to their children but lacking a knowledge of it themselves, pioneered such programmes in the 1980s. To equip teachers and provide resources, the first Bureau of Jewish Education was founded in New York in 1910 and now every major US city has such an organization. In a publication from the Greater Los Angeles bureau, the sociologist Samuel Heilman writes:

> Despite all the pressures and realities that appear to be undermining the family, Jews are still by and large living within family units . . . Even many uncommitted Jews want to be actively Jewish, but they either do not know how to go about doing so, or they have few available options for Jewish expression . . . Jewish commitment rises and falls with changes in family status.

Britain followed suit in the 1990s, notably at the Centre for Jewish Education at the headquarters for Reform Judaism, the Sternberg Centre. This centre's programmes try to be non-threatening and non-lecturing as they teach parents alongside their children. Sometimes it is basic Hebrew that they need and sometimes it is the relearning of skills and meanings pertaining to festivals. The programmes offer experiential learning to the family as together they light the candles for Friday night dinner (as Sabbath begins) or celebrate the Passover meal, or build a tabernacle for the Festival of Tabernacles. Whilst there has always been Jewish adult education, limited numbers have bought into it and there is perceived to be a growing separation between the child's education at synagogue and the home as the ultimate conveyor of Jewish identity. Extensive programmes for adult, as distinct from family, education remain, largely in north-west London at the Sternberg Centre, at the Spiro Institute for the Study of Jewish History and Culture, and at Yakar, an independent Orthodox centre. Many synagogues provide some opportunity for adult education, often in the form of a *shiur* ('religion class') where Jewish texts are studied.

In the synagogue

Coming of age

Much of the Jewish education which takes place is preparing children to take on as adults the obligations of the Jewish religion. In Orthodox Judaism this age of 'religious majority' is 12 for girls and 13 for boys. The Talmud states 13 as the age 'for the fulfilment of the commandments' (Avot 5:24), such as observing the full fast day on the Day of Atonement (Ketubah 50a). From the day when he is 13 according to the Jewish calendar (see Chapter 13), a Jewish boy becomes *Bar Mitzvah* ('son of the commandment', combining an Aramaic and a Hebrew word). Judged to mature earlier, a girl on her twelfth birthday automatically becomes *Bat Mitzvah* ('daughter of the commandment'). Reform Judaism in its early days disliked both the differentiation between boys and girls and the way in which becoming bar or bat mitzvah often seemed to be an end rather than a beginning as children fell away from their Jewish studies once they reached this age. It also felt that the ages set in talmudic times when people started employment much younger than they do today had become inappropriate. It, therefore, abandoned any formal marking of this age in favour of a confirmation at 15 or 16. The ceremony was often held at the Festival of Shavuot (see Chapter 14) since what was being confirmed was loyalty to the covenant at Sinai, the focus of this festival. More commonly today, Reform communities offer the option of a Bar or Bat Mitzvah ceremony, both at 13, provided the candidate gives a written pledge to continue in religious education until confirmation is reached. There is then sometimes a *Ben* (Hebrew for 'son') or *Bat Torah* ceremony where the candidate takes the whole of the morning service on the Sabbath or on Shavuot. Whatever is learnt afterwards, the aim pre-Bar or Bat Mitzvah is to provide sufficient understanding of the language of worship and observance to enable the individual to participate fully in Jewish life.

Reform Judaism, stressing equality between the sexes, considers all the commandments to be equally incumbent on girls as on boys. The following declaration (worded here in its female form) from the Reform Prayer Book expresses the purpose of the celebration at 13:

In the presence of my teachers, the leaders and the members of this holy congregation, I now prepare to take upon myself the duties which are binding on all the family of Israel. I ask their help in the years that lie ahead to strengthen my loyalty and devotion so that I may grow in charity and good deeds. I think also of those who have gone before me, who through all the troubles of the world preserved this heritage of holiness and goodness, so that I should enter into it now.

May I be a true Batmitzvah, a daughter of the commandment, taking my place in the community of Israel, accepting its responsibilities, rejoicing in its blessing. May I be a witness to the living God and His goodness, and the tradition that lives within me.

I remember all those who have helped me reach this time. I give thanks for the love and care of my family, the patience and instruction of my teachers, and the support and companionship of my friends.

In the Torah I have read the word of God. With your help may I go on to fulfil it in my life. Amen.

Whether in Orthodox or non-Orthodox synagogues, attendance at a religion school held at the synagogue is required for some years. Most schools start with classes for five-year-olds, usually held two or three evenings a week after school and/or on a Sunday morning. (Liberal congregations may hold them on a Saturday morning to facilitate attendance at the synagogue by the whole family in one journey.) The Orthodox term for these 'Sunday schools' is *hadarim* (singular *heder*). A heder is literally a 'room'. (Before Jewish emancipation, a heder was a small Jewish 'school' with a small number of pupils, fitting into one room, studying religious texts. They could progress from class to class receiving at least this formal education before employment.) Each heder is divided into classes for different age groups with activities ranging from the basics of the Hebrew alphabet and prayers to detailed study of the Humash (the Pentateuch) and the Talmud. In some London Orthodox hadarim, a syllabus is followed with set examinations.

Taking on the obligations of an adult

In the period preceding the Bar or Bat Mitzvah, there is a greater concentration on reading Hebrew and on the obligations of the faith. Both these are vital for the candidates to participate fully in the ceremony which recognizes their new status. It must be stressed that the ceremony does not in itself alter anything. Indeed, at least for boys in Orthodoxy, it is not a separate ceremony but the ordinary Sabbath morning service falling immediately after the boy turns 13. Non-Jews tend to speak of Jewish boys 'having a Bar Mitzvah', but they do not so much 'have' it as 'become' it, that is, they become subject to all the mitzvot of the covenant community. The service then marks the time when a boy becomes Bar Mitzvah. If a Jewish boy does not participate in this service, he is still Bar Mitzvah once he is 13. A Bar Mitzvah celebration may well be held in the hall after the service. There may be a further celebratory dinner with family and friends, but there is a concern among the leaders of Jewish communities that this does not become so lavish that its preparation overwhelms the preparation for the service itself. Party or no party, the significance of the age of 13 lies in the admittance to Jewish adulthood. The parents, as stated by the father in the synagogue, are freed 'from the responsibility for this child'.

In an Orthodox service, adulthood is marked by the boy's taking part in a service in which the Torah is read. Though usually the Sabbath service, it can be a Monday, Thursday, or a festival (see Chapter 11). If he is able and if this is the tradition of his synagogue, he will read the Torah portion for that day. Alternatively, he may recite the blessings before or after the reading or he may read the appointed passage from the Prophets following the Torah reading. Reform practice is largely the same in this regard, though the boy might also give a talk about the passage read. This being called up to read the Torah is part of the celebration of a girl's Bat Mitzvah, though not generally in Orthodoxy where women do not lead a congregation in worship or count in a minyan (see Chapter 4). Nor do they put on tefillin worn by adult males for weekday morning prayers (see Chapter 10). The usual Orthodox practice is to have a special ceremony in the synagogue on the Sunday afternoon for all the girls who have turned 12 in the previous year. This is called a *Bat Hayil* ('daughter of worth', as in the reference to 'a woman of worth' in Proverbs 31:10). Family, friends, and congregation gather to hear each Bat Hayil read in Hebrew a passage of her choice perhaps with comment. There continues to be discussion in Orthodox circles over whether a Bat Mitzvah celebration is more appropriate and in Reform and Liberal circles over whether more emphasis should be put on confirmation rather than on a Bat or a Bar Mitzvah. All communities are concerned not only to reflect the approach of their respective traditions but also to discourage any sense of Jewish education being complete by the ages of 12 or 13.

In school

Today, 50 per cent of the 45,000 Jewish children of school age in Britain attend non-Jewish schools and so are dependent on the synagogue for their Jewish religious education. The other 50 per cent, however, attend a Jewish school. In some Latin American and Muslim countries, the figure is over 90 per cent. The global figure is about 40 per cent of eligible students, aged 3–17. In the USA, there are several types of Jewish schools, representing definite affiliations – be they Orthodox, Reform, or Conservative. In Britain, the choice is less wide. There are several Ultra-Orthodox schools, for example the Lubavitch School (Primary and Secondary) in Stamford Hill, and there is one (but so far only one) non-Orthodox school, at the Sternberg Centre. This school, the Akiva, is a co-educational school for children from 5 to 11 with hopes to extend to 12 to 16-year-olds in due course. It is 'under the auspices of the Reform and Liberal Jewish movements and is open to all those who identify with the Jewish community.' It aims to foster a positive identity with Judaism, its culture, and the Jewish community. Its curriculum covers the full range of primary school subjects in which 'secular studies and Jewish living and learning are not kept separate but are brought together.' The vast majority of Jewish schools in Britain, however, are under the auspices of the United Synagogue from whose Board of Education they receive a grant. One such Orthodox school is the Michael Sobell Sinai School in Middlesex. Here too the full primary curriculum is covered but Jewish education, usually called *Limmudei Kodesh* ('religious studies') occupies about 25 per cent of the timetable, again integrated into each day rather than as a separate element. It has open enrolment and is non-selective in terms of both ability and Jewish observance. Some children come from extremely observant families whilst for others the school offers their only specifically Jewish education. The school has a mixture of Jewish and non-Jewish teachers with no obligation on them to teach Jewish Studies. Over 80 per cent of children go on from the Michael Sobell Sinai School to Jewish secondary schools. Those in favour of separate religious schools see this as a demonstration of the need for and the success of Jewish primary schools. Those against see it as demonstrating the difficulty of slotting back from segregation into integration. Whether Jewish children ultimately have a better sense of their identity in an environment where religious observance is facilitated by such things as the provision of kosher meals at lunchtime is the fundamental question at issue.

The best-known and the oldest Jewish school in Britain is the Jews' Free School founded in London in 1817. At the end of the nineteenth century, it was the largest elementary school in Europe. Other cities with a large Jewish population also have Jewish secondary schools, for example, the King David High School in Liverpool. All of them stress high academic standards but they also provide a Jewish curriculum in the form of Bible, Talmud, and Hebrew – both modern and classical.

In higher education (academy, seminary, and college)

Each year, boys from the Lubavitch School in Stamford Hill go straight to a rabbinic academy where they stay for an average of five years. Some, though not most of them, will progress through all the different stages to complete rabbinical training. The name for such an academy is *yeshivah* (plural *yeshivot*). From the Hebrew *yashav* ('to sit'), the term connotes the sitting of young men as they study tomes of the Talmud. Though some study alone, most work in pairs in what is called the *havruta* ('companionship') system. Such talmudic studies constitute the main focus of yeshivah life. The other subjects studied are Jewish philosophy, ethics, law codes and commentaries. At the root of all these is the Bible, as was discussed in Chapter 2. There mention was made of Rashi and Ibn Ezra as great biblical commentators, but there were many others, notably Rashi's grandson, Rashbam (an acronym for Rabbi Samuel ben Meier) in the eleventh and twelfth centuries and the Sefardi scholar, Nahmanides (an acronym for Rabbi Moses ben Nahman) in the twelfth and thirteenth centuries. Principles for interpreting the Bible are sometimes traced back to tannaitic times (see Chapter 3). Rashi and Ibn Ezra largely confined themselves to the plain meaning of the text, whereas Nahmanides showed equal interest in readings which were more interpretative. The plain sense, he maintained, is important yet major value lies in how it has come to be applied in Jewish life. During the Emancipation, yeshivot all but disappeared from western Europe (as did the heder), but they persisted in eastern Europe, some of them existing to this day, having survived the death-blow dealt by the Holocaust (for example, one in Volozhin, Lithuania, founded in 1803). Russian (and then Nazi) persecution resulted in some transfer of traditional scholarship to the USA and western Europe, for example the Gateshead yeshivah, founded in 1927. Modern seminaries and universities were founded on neo-Orthodox lines in the late nineteenth century, notably New York's Yeshiva University in 1886.

The equivalent educational institution for girls is the seminary. There the range of subjects is wider and the course of study far more structured than in the yeshivah. Though the havruta system is also used, generally the approach is similar to that of a university with lectures, written assignments, and research projects. Many follow a three-year course, whilst others stay for one or two years.

The chief higher education college for mainstream Orthodoxy in Britain is the London School of Jewish Studies. Again some students will train as rabbis, whilst others may attend for shorter courses. The College also trains *hazanim* ('cantors', singular *hazan*). Reform and Liberal rabbis are trained at the Leo Baeck College from where they can serve either Reform or Liberal communities. The five year course is heavily textual and includes Bible, Talmud, Philosophy, History, Practical Ethics and Counselling. There is a fourth year placement and the final year is spent with a congregation but with a dissertation being written. In the USA (and also in Israel) there has been a growth in traditional yeshivot in recent years, but most Jewish higher education institutions are primarily for the training of rabbis, for example, the Reform Hebrew Union College (founded in Cincinnati in 1875).

Jewish Studies

Jewish Studies can also be pursued in many universities and colleges around the world. In Britain, these often fall within the orbit of Religious Studies, as at Manchester University which, in the Department of Religions and Theology, established in 1995 a Chair in Modern Jewish Studies and which has another Professor who is expert in post-biblical Jewish literature. Sometimes there is just one course within a department, for example on Holocaust Theology as in Bristol University's Religious Studies or on the Third Reich as in Leicester University's History Degree. Many universities and colleges have staff with expertise in Hebrew Bible and Dead Sea Scroll Studies, such as Edinburgh University's Divinity Faculty, and Departments of Middle Eastern Studies provide textual courses, on Talmud, for example, at Manchester University. Degree courses in Jewish Studies continue to increase. Oxford University offers such a BA, as well as its long-established Hebrew BA.

Specific centres further Jewish Studies, including the Oxford Centre for Hebrew and Jewish Studies, and Cambridge University's Taylor-Schechter Genizah Research Unit established in 1974. The latter is the outcome of the discovery of an extensive collection of fragments in Cairo, from biblical times and many later periods in Jewish history, by Solomon Schechter (founder of Conservative Judaism). He was appointed Reader in Rabbinics at Cambridge University in 1892 and Professor of Hebrew at University College London in 1899, and many eminent scholars have followed Schechter's work. The fragments shed light on the development of Jewish law, philosophy, and poetry and on religious, social and economic activity (including children's education) in Near Eastern Jewish communities between the seventh and thirteenth centuries. Significant language studies also issue from these discoveries. (The fragments are also studied on microfilm in other research centres such as the Yeshiva University in the USA and the Hebrew University in Israel.) Since the Holocaust, these two countries have become the major centres of Jewish education. Israel provides vital materials and personnel for schools in small Diaspora communities and offers educational trips lasting from several months to a year. Whilst some involved in these studies will be Jewish, it is clear that what is provided by these institutions does not assume or specifically cultivate the commitment to Jewish belief and practice which lie behind what we have generally considered in this chapter as 'Jewish education'. Some institutions do, however, have a dual approach. So the Leo Baeck College not only trains Jewish rabbis and teachers but also offers a BA and an MA in Jewish Studies. The latter includes rabbinic literature and Jewish history and thought.

09

marriage

In this chapter you will learn:

- about Jewish views of sex, marriage, and divorce
- about the Jewish wedding ceremony
- about conversion to Judaism.

Sex and marriage in Judaism

We have already seen at many points (particularly in Chapter 5), the great importance attached to marriage in Judaism. It is rated highly on two counts. First, it can provide emotional and spiritual fulfilment in the form of support and companionship. The written Torah decrees that 'man should not be alone' (Genesis 2:18) but should cherish a woman in an intimate relationship (Genesis 2:24). The oral Torah says:

> A man who has no wife is doomed to an existence without joy, without blessing, without experiencing life's true goodness, without Torah, without protection and without peace.

(Yevamot 62b)

Secondly it can provide physical fulfilment in the form of sexual expression. There is no suggestion in Judaism that the celibate life is specially holy. On the contrary, marriage is seen as the ideal and sex as the most intimate and enjoyable way of deepening a relationship. When Orthodox Judaism speaks of a sexual relationship it means marriage. The Hebrew word for marriage, *Kiddushin* ('sanctification') expresses its special sanctity. Marriage is not only a sacred relationship, but *the* sacred relationship. Questions about the acceptability of homosexual relationships do not arise as they are condemned in the Torah, for example, in Leviticus 18:22; 20:13. Reform Jews wrestle with these questions, however, as do all the major Christian denominations. Whilst Roman Catholic statements are categorically against homosexuality, reports from the other main churches reflect considerable debate. Can a declared homosexual hold office in a church, can he or she be ordained, can a committed relationship between Christian homosexuals be recognized in a church ceremony? Similar questions are debated in the Reform Jewish community in the USA and more recently in Britain. Both Reform and Orthodox agree, however, in their condemnation of infidelity, promiscuity and sexual exploitation. They also agree that in marriage one woman is set apart for one man in faithfulness, loyalty, and mutual respect. Polygamy was not actually forbidden until about 1000CE, but the evidence suggests that monogamy had been the norm in Jewish life for centuries earlier.

The stress on a man's appreciation of his wife is to be found in rabbinic statements, but it is sometimes overlooked by those who find the wording altogether too patriarchal. The perspective of the writer is always male, but even so it is the woman who is seen as the key to a fulfilling life. Some maintain that the Rabbis recognize her as spiritually superior with the wry suggestion that this may be why she is not required to keep so many mitzvot (obligations) as her male counterpart. Hirsch, for example, claims that 'women have greater fervour and faith than men.' Certainly, tradition bids 'be careful about the honour of your wife, for blessing enters the house only because of the wife' (Bava Metzia 59a).

Ritual purity

Whether one is impressed by such injunctions or put off by them divides many Jewish women. Overall, the division of opinion does not fall neatly into Orthodox and non-Orthodox, modern or old-fashioned, feminist or sexist (if these are opposite), as we saw when considering different views of women's role in Chapter 5. Yet, there is one particular area of biblical and talmudic practice which only a few Reform women find helpful and even then for rather different reasons from the traditional ones. This is the area of *niddah* ('separation'). The laws of niddah, which pertain to ritual purity (or family purity), are regarded by some as demeaning to women and by others, including some Reform women, as an expression of Jewish femininity. To understand how this can be it is necessary to consider the thinking behind these laws.

The biblical statements about niddah come in Leviticus (15:19–24; 18:19; 20:18) and the talmudic details in the tractate Niddah (in the order, Tohorot, 'Purities'). Indeed, Niddah is the only mishnaic tractate on 'Purities' to be commented on in the Babylonian Talmud which perhaps illustrates the importance of the subject-matter. The laws of niddah relate to the purity of holy things, especially the Temple. Anything and anyone coming into contact with the Temple must stay pure and this entails avoiding contact with what are considered defiling substances. So a priest who came into contact with a dead body would have to purify himself before he handled Temple sacrifice and get rid of his defilement. Immediately one moves from this to finding that a menstruating woman is regarded as defiling, the conclusion is too easily reached that sex is regarded by the Rabbis as in some way dirty. Yet nothing could be further from the truth. A married couple was and is encouraged to have intercourse on the

Sabbath as appropriate on a joyful day. A husband is urged to consider his wife's pleasure during intercourse and not to let his work away from home deprive his wife for longer intervals than she was expecting when she married him.

The solution lies in realizing that it is not sex which is seen as defiling the ritual purity but menstrual blood. Other than that Leviticus says so, it is not known why this came to be regarded as one of the defiling substances. The suggestion is that, like the other substances (such as the emission of semen outside a woman's body and various diseases such as leprosy), it in some way represents death.

The Rabbis established a minimum of twelve days during which the menstruant woman must not have sexual contact. To those who accept these rules, this time of restraint is regarded positively. It requires couples to find ways other than the physical to express their relationship. It cultivates appreciation, consideration and respect. As Blu Greenberg, a staunch advocate of niddah as a specially female mitzvah, writes:

> . . . it was intended to protect women's selves and sexuality; not bad, considering that society was orientated to the female serving the male, sexually and otherwise. Niddah also provided safeguards against women becoming mere sex objects; even when the law could not change social perceptions, at least it minimised those times when this attitude could be acted upon. (On Women and Judaism)

She continues:

> The laws of niddah continually remind me that I am a Jew and niddah reinforces that deep inner contentment with a Jewish way of life. Acceptance of the mitzvah, then, is the base: attendant sensations of community, 'Jewish womanhood' and 'chain to tradition' are the embellishments.

It is interesting that the number who, from a range of religious perspectives, are finding something similar in niddah seems to be increasing. A sense of identity and holiness for Jewish women is experienced by some instead of a sense of degrading out-datedness which the observance suggests to others.

The *mikveh*

That we know that there is an increasing number rests on the statistics of women who now visit a *mikveh* ('a gathering' of water) on a monthly basis. This is the cleansing process for a married woman after menstruation (and just before marriage and after childbirth). For ritual cleansing, the water has to have been gathered naturally to form 'living waters'. A stream, river, pond, lake, or ocean constitutes a mikveh, but most women use a specially constructed indoor pool where a certain proportion of the water is rain water. There is a bathroom attached in which she prepares herself for the mikveh, removing all clothing, rings, and any other items which might prevent the pure water from reaching every part of the body. After washing in the normal way, she enters the mikveh and is immersed completely in it, reciting the appropriate blessing. The practice is called *tevilah* ('immersion').

Such spiritual cleansing is also practised at other times in Judaism and not just by women. A few very pious men immerse themselves in a mikveh before the Sabbath and annual festivals. More men do this just before the Day of Atonement when the aim of the whole day is to remove anything which stops people from being 'at one' with God by coming between them. Tevilah is also a ritual requirement for someone at the end of the process of converting to the Jewish faith (see below).

A Jewish wedding

The *hupah*

A Jewish wedding always takes place under a *hupah* (canopy). This symbolizes the sacred space of the marital home. As the ceremony begins, the bride, escorted by either her parents or both mothers (or sometimes by her father), joins the bridegroom who is already under the hupah. They stand facing the rabbi or official who is conducting this part of the ceremony. Forming a square, the fathers of the couple stand on the groom's left and the mothers on the bride's right. At its simplest the hupah can be a *tallit* ('prayer shawl') held above the couple's heads by four friends of the groom. It can, however, be more structured and elaborately decorated, particularly with flowers which line the four supporting poles. Simple or elaborate, a hupah can be in the open air or, as is more usual, in a synagogue.

Vows

There may be some variations in the ceremony but it generally takes the following form. First, the initial blessings are recited – over wine as both partners drink from a cup as a symbol of shared joy and over marriage itself. There is then the giving of the ring. In most congregations this is done by the groom placing a wedding ring on the forefinger of the right hand where it can be displayed most clearly to the two witnesses. (The ring is later transferred to the finger usual in the country of the wedding.) This is the crucial moment as the groom says the words: 'Behold, thou art consecrated to me by this ring, according to the Law of Moses and of Israel.' These words are important legally and religiously. They constitute the vows of Jewish marriage, though in some Liberal ceremonies in Britain both the man and the woman recite the English words: 'With this ring, I thee wed . . .', borrowed from the Christian wedding service. Reform weddings usually follow the traditional form, but it is customary for the bride at this point to give the groom a ring whilst making the same declaration of consecration. They are thus set apart from others for each other. A lifelong commitment is implied but Judaism does not believe that people can promise this in vows 'for better or worse . . .'.

The marriage contract

The third element in the ceremony focuses on the marriage contract, the ketubah. The person conducting the wedding reads it out in Aramaic and often gives an English summary. The ketubah is a written marriage settlement stating the practical commitment of the husband to provide for his wife and assuring her of financial protection from her husband's estate in the event of divorce or his death. Sometimes the ketubah is drawn up and signed during the ceremony. In some communities the groom reads and agrees to the ketubah before the ceremony begins. In Reform ceremonies, there is often a simple marriage certificate which both bride and groom sign. The final element is the reciting of seven blessings. Praising God for the creation of all things, of Man, and of man and woman in his image, these blessings deliberately invoke the bliss of the garden of Eden. Not only the story of creation, but also the history of Israel and its future hopes are echoed. The whole ceremony is designed to sanctify the ordinary, to transform this particular couple as their love embodies God's creation, revelation, and redemption in the here and now. These eloquent blessings are recited again at the end of the wedding reception. Traditionally, they are also recited at the end of a celebratory meal held in a different home for each of the seven nights following the wedding. The Jewish wedding feast is a jubilant occasion with much joy and dancing.

The marriage ceremony was originally in two parts, with about a year between. The first part, the betrothal, took place in the bride's home. There the couple became legally bound to each other but did not live together. This first part now constitutes the initial blessings. The second part, the actual marriage, used to be when the bride entered the hupah. There the ring would be given, the contract read, and the seven blessings recited.

Other features of the wedding celebration

Other features that often accompany a Jewish marriage ceremony include fasting beforehand in preparation for a solemn occasion (usually in Orthodox congregations) and the breaking of a wine glass as the groom stamps on it to shouts of *Mazel tov* ('Congratulations', literally 'Good Luck'). In Orthodoxy the breaking glass is a reminder of the destruction of the Temple, whilst in Reform it is a more general reminder of life's fragility and sadness. Jeremiah 33:10–11 is read which has a similar theme of interwoven joy and sorrow as it calls to mind the restoration, redemption, and return of the Israelite people after the exile, the prophet counselling renewed hope with the enemy at the gate of Jerusalem. Sometimes the couple are left in a private room for a brief period immediately after the ceremony, this signifying their new status as man and wife.

Jewish weddings can take place on any day except the Sabbath and festivals. These days are special occasions in themselves and legal transactions are not allowed on them. Most Jewish weddings take place on a Sunday, usually in the afternoon enabling those travelling from a distance to start out after the Sabbath restrictions have ended. A choir, organ music, even a video are all permitted in synagogues at a wedding. Periods of mourning – personal and national – are avoided by Orthodox Jews when selecting a wedding date. Fasting is for many part of such mourning. In Britain a Jewish religious wedding is also a legal transaction and no civil ceremony is required. A rabbi usually officiates, though it can be any observant Jew sufficiently familiar with the requirements.

Marriages between Jews and non-Jews

Marrying 'out of the faith'

There used to be Jewish match-makers whose business it was to introduce people they considered suitable bearing in mind their religious observance. Apart from in very traditional circles, this is no longer how most Jews meet their partners. For all except Ultra-Orthodox Jews, employment and social life are likely to be in a thoroughly assimilated society. The consequences of this when it comes to marriage give rise to much concern in the Jewish community. In the USA over 50 per cent of Jews now marry non-Jews and the British rate approaches this at the beginning of the twenty-first century. In an age which stresses (or at least claims to stress) individual freedom and tolerance between people both of different denominational groupings within a religion and of different religions altogether, Jewish opposition to intermarriage may take some understanding. The term which is sometimes used for such marriage expresses the main cause for concern. 'Out-marriage' means marrying out of the faith and it is the Jewish faith, with so much of its expression in the life of the home, which is perceived to be at stake. To understand the depth of feeling requires a consideration of the historical and cultural background. In former generations, marrying a non-Jew meant taking leave of your family, community, and faith. You could not be neutral and so a Jew who married a Christian was making the most powerful gesture of rejection. On the part of the family there was often a sense of failure as the child totally disappeared from the scene. Today there is a neutral society, yet the emotional charge remains, compounded by the historical experience of Christian hostility towards Jews. This dismay at intermarriage applies even if the parents are not observant religiously.

Consequent decline in Jewish population and observance

The fears have also to be set in the context of other figures indicating a steady decline in Jewish life. In 1991 it was estimated that the annual Jewish birth rate of the previous decade was roughly two-thirds the death-rate, that a third of Jewish marriages end in divorce, that nearly 20 per cent of Jewish children experience the breakdown of their parents' marriages, and that only half the Jews who marry do so in a synagogue. That the decline is continuing and moreover sharpening is confirmed by the Director of the Chief Rabbi's Marriage Authorization Office, Rabbi Dr Julian Shindler ('Marriage Trends in Anglo-Jewry' in *Le'ela: A Journal of Judaism Today*, April 1993). It is not altogether certain how many of the missing half of expected synagogue marriages are because of intermarriage. Some Jews will be living together rather than marrying, others will be marrying a Jewish partner but in a purely civil ceremony, but Shindler believes that intermarriage accounts for by far the greater number. Different parts of Anglo-Jewry recognize the problem, but not all are agreed on the solution.

We have already noted the emphasis on marriage as the relationship in which the Jewish faith can be supremely expressed and on the importance of raising a Jewish family. The Orthodox view is that this can be achieved only when two committed Jewish partners make a solemn promise to set up a Jewish home together. In this there can be no place for a non-Jewish partner. This is a realistic approach since it is hard to see how the demanding commitment to such things as kashrut (food laws) can be kept by a non-Jew. What would be the motivation for all the effort and expense unless the laws were considered important? Furthermore, in this the most profound of relationships, the ideal is that the partners are at one in everything. Yet, if their sense of God is different, they are going to differ at the deepest level. The more their respective faiths matter to them, the more the differences will matter. The same is true of the impact on the children. The more interested the parents are in their respective religions, the more difficult it can be for a child being brought up in both.

When he was Chief Rabbi, Immanuel Jakobovits articulated the Orthodox opposition to any Jew marrying a non-Jew. A crucial factor is the halakhic ruling (reiterated by Jakobovits against an American alternative) that only a child born of a Jewish mother is Jewish. Since more Jewish men than Jewish women 'marry out', very serious difficulties arise. Though some women convert to Judaism (see below) before they marry, most do not. Such a wedding cannot then take place in a synagogue. The Marriage Act of 1949, following earlier legislation, permits the registration of synagogue marriages for 'two persons both professing the Jewish religion'. All synagogues in Britain are bound by this. Nor may any rabbi play any official role in an interfaith marriage.

(Having seen how the ceremony differs from say a Christian one with crucial words spoken 'according to the Law of Moses' rather than 'in the Name of the Father, the Son, and the Holy Spirit', it is not difficult to see why such a ceremony is judged impossible. The Torah and the Holy Trinity are surely difficult to merge with any real sense.) In the USA, such participation is forbidden for Orthodox, Conservative, and Reconstructionist rabbis and discouraged for Reform.

Reform Judaism and intermarriage

Certain moves have been made by British Reform rabbis in recent years as a constructive approach to the realities of the situation. Wary of being perceived as encouraging intermarriage, the instigator of these moves, Rabbi Dr Jonathan Romain, makes plain that he recognizes intermarriage as a threat to the future of Judaism. His working party's report in 1982 states that 'a primary task is to encourage Jew to marry Jew'. Yet he feels that trying to meet the threat must entail practical steps other than simply rejecting the non-Jewish partner and thus the Jewish partner from the life of the synagogue. Once a marriage between a Jew and a non-Jew occurs, certain strategies should, he believes, be adopted to try to keep alive any Jewish links. He has, therefore, instituted seminars for such Jews and (since 1989) their non-Jewish partners in which he aims to strengthen any Jewish elements of their life together. This outreach programme is jointly sponsored by Reform and Liberal Judaism at the Sternberg Centre. The 1990 Annual Conference of the Reform Synagogues of Great Britain welcomed:

> . . . the initiatives that have been directed towards bringing those in mixed-faith relationships back to Jewish life, promoting Jewish identity and education, and offering appropriate care to Jews and their families.

In another attempt to stop intermarriage being the end of the line, British Reform permits children of a Jewish father but a non-Jewish mother to attend religion school at the local synagogue. Though this in no way confers Jewish status on the child, the hope is that such preparation may lay the foundation for later conversion should the child choose this. (Reform cites Ketubot 11a as giving the principle of facilitating conversion for the benefit of the child.) In some cases, the child's conversion does not require the conversion of the mother who, says

Romain, 'may have good reason' for not choosing to convert even though she is happy to support the father in passing on his Jewish heritage and 'bringing up their children as Jews'. Though the honesty of the other's position is laudable, it has to be admitted that very real problems exist here especially in dealings with Orthodox Jews who require each individual to convert in order to become Jewish (see below). Some fear that British Reform is moving towards the position in the USA where any child of a mixed marriage is 'under presumption of Jewish status', a resolution passed at the 1983 Central Conference of American Rabbis. This decision means that there are many who identify as Jews and belong to a synagogue who are not regarded as Jews by the Orthodox and this in the country with the largest Jewish community in the world. Some see this as obstructive by the Orthodox, others as irresponsible by the Reform, and others as indicating the need for a totally different criterion of Jewish identity.

This is patently an area in which feelings run high and in which Orthodox and non-Orthodox responses differ radically. The one perceives itself as preserving Jewish life by adhering strictly to the halakhah. The other espouses the same intention by following the Reform principle of reassessing the essentials of Judaism, by being pragmatic in existing circumstances and being as inclusivist as possible in terms of attendance at synagogue and religion school. When Jonathan Sacks launched the Jewish continuity initiative in 1993, to reach those 'not marrying, marrying out or leaving the community in some other way' was one of his aims. As time goes on, it is hard to see how the different religious groupings of Anglo-Jewry can co-operate in this particular area, as we shall see as we turn now to the whole issue of status. What Jewish continuity is and how best to preserve it are precisely the spheres of disagreement.

The religious court (*Bet Din*) and laws of status

In rabbinic writings, Jews are instructed to deal with disputes in their own religious courts rather than in civil ones. The name for such a rabbinic court is a *Bet Din* (literally 'house of judgement'; plural *Batei Din*). They exist in towns with a sizable Jewish population. In London, there are four Orthodox Batei Din: representing the Sefardi Community, the Union of Orthodox

Hebrew Congregations (Hasidic), the Federation of Synagogues, and the United Synagogue respectively. The last one, called the London Bet Din, is the court of the Chief Rabbi and was established under an Act of Parliament in 1890. Anyone can use a Bet Din, provided both parties in the dispute agree. By an agreement valid under English Law (the Arbitration Acts of 1950 and 1979), once both parties have signed a deed of arbitration, the Bet Din's findings are as binding as in a civil court. The ancient religious responsibility of administering absolute justice (Deuteronomy 16:18–19) is taken very seriously and each court is made up of three highly qualified and experienced rabbis.

Deciding disputed cases takes up only about 20 per cent of the London Bet Din's time. It issues guidance about such matters as the onset of festivals and kashrut – whether individual queries or granting licences to caterers and bakers. Its main task, however, is to deal with questions of personal status, that is, Jewish religious status. These may involve adoption, conversion, or divorce. Each year, it handles the cases of between 300 and 400 non-Jewish people wanting to be admitted to the Jewish faith and supervises the writing and handing over of 170–200 *Gittin* ('certificates of divorce', singular *get*). Each Orthodox Bet Din recognizes the decision of another Bet Din on judicial matters and usually on gittin. So, for example, the London Bet Din is not a court of appeal over the Bet Din in Manchester, Leeds, or Glasgow. (In the USA and in Israel, there is a tendency to constitute an informal court to try to get a divorce certificate, as in the Israeli case described below.)

In Reform Judaism

Halakhically, anyone born of a Jewish mother or who has converted to Judaism is Jewish. (Liberal Judaism recognizes as Jewish a child born of either a Jewish mother or father, as does Reform Judaism in the USA since 1983.) A thorny problem for all Reform Jews, however, is that conversions and also divorces handled by their own Bet Din are not recognized as valid by Orthodox Jews. The Reform Bet Din was established in 1948 since when it has served all communities belonging to the RSGB. It has its seat in north London at the Sternberg Centre for Judaism, the headquarters of the RSGB. Any court-sitting has, like the Orthodox, three *dayanim* (judges, singular *dayan*) who are ordained rabbis, though unlike Orthodoxy they are not full-time on the Bet Din but congregational rabbis who serve on a rota basis. Reform seldom hears civil cases unless they involve a specifically Jewish issue. It prides itself on taking the compassionate interpretation of the halakhah. Whilst still retaining its distinctive perspective, British Reform has felt in recent years that it ought to bring its status procedures as close as possible to those of other Jewish groups. Hence, the necessity of a *get* for someone wishing to remarry in a synagogue was reinstated in the 1940s. In the 1970s, it also fulfilled the traditional requirements for conversion and now greatly regrets that this has not been judged satisfactory by the Orthodox.

Conversion

In the case of converts intending to contract a Jewish marriage, the Jewish partner must be a member of a Reform synagogue before the candidate can be registered with the Reform Bet Din. Orthodoxy accepts very few applicants for conversion, insisting that they be strictly observant and have studied for several years. Nearly always a non-missionary religion, Judaism has long discouraged people from converting. There is a revealing talmudic passage about doubting someone's motives in wanting to join a people so 'scorned, oppressed, humiliated, and made to suffer' (Yevamot 47a–b). Reform stresses, however, the more welcoming parts of the passage which talk about not overburdening someone or being over-meticulous. The usual procedure in Reform is an interview with the local rabbi who explains the three conditions for conversion. The first requirement is a sincere desire to become Jewish, a willingness to subscribe to Jewish beliefs and practices, and a wish to identify with the Jewish community. The initial interview is sometimes followed by a second some time later if the candidate starts from very little awareness of the religion. Converting for the convenience of a Jewish marriage is always a possibility and Reform is wary of this motive though far less so than Orthodox Judaism.

The second requirement is that the candidate attains a competent level of Jewish knowledge to feel at home carrying out Jewish practices and to teach any children. This involves a weekly class about the religion – its beliefs, practices, history and language – held in the local Reform synagogue for the minimum of a year. (A background with a Jewish father but non-Jewish mother sometimes enables the shortening of this course.)

The third condition is the fulfilling of ritual requirements: circumcision for males – performed by a mohel (see Chapter 7).

Both male and female candidates must undergo *tevilah* (immersion in a ritual bath). Liberal Judaism does not require this, nor did Reform until 1977 when it accepted it to harmonize RSGB practice with Judaism worldwide. After extensive discussion, the Assembly of Rabbis made it obligatory in 1980. All Reform synagogues in other European countries and in Israel require tevilah for conversion, as do all Conservative and Orthodox synagogues. (A Liberal convert is nonetheless recognized by Reform as Jewish.) The pre-war Manchester Reform synagogue, for example, had its own mikveh on site and it is not known just when or why British Reform dropped the requirement for converts, but the American Reform and British Liberal movements clearly influenced the decision. The mikveh at the Sternberg Centre was built for converts, though a few wives, especially younger ones, find ritual immersion a helpful expression of being a Jewish woman. It is optional just before marriage in Reform unlike Orthodoxy where it is an obligation. Reform stresses on this occasion not ritual purity but the beginning of a new life.

When all three requirements have been met, the candidate appears for an interview before the Bet Din, finally to establish the necessary knowledge and commitment. If accepted, the convert receives a certificate admitting him or her 'as a proselyte of righteousness'. Children converting with their parents also have to fulfil the main requirements. About 100 adults each year convert to Judaism through the Reform Bet Din, the majority being attached to a Jewish partner. Orthodoxy insists on strict halakhic procedures throughout.

A Jewish divorce

When the rabbis said that 'he who divorces his wife is hated by God' (Gittin 90b), they surely expressed the undesirability of divorce. Yet the fact that they devote so much discussion to the practicalities of it shows that they recognize the reality of marriage breakdown. From the earliest times, the belief that marriage is a lifelong bond, whatever happens, has not been part of the Jewish faith. Deuteronomy 24:1–4 (and 22:13–21, 28–29) states the biblical permission and procedure for divorce. We have noted (in Chapter 3) some of the rabbinic debate about what constitutes 'some indecency' as the ground for divorce, but there is no vow 'till death do us part' presenting obstacles. Even on the 'grounds for divorce' (which include general dissatisfaction between the two parties), Judaism does not apportion blame in the way which still largely dominates British civil divorce law. Indeed, until 1969, someone's fault (a 'matrimonial offence' such as cruelty or adultery) had to be established before there could even be a divorce. The ground of the 'irretrievable breakdown' of the marriage was then admitted, though reforms to try to take the adversarial acrimony out of the divorce process are a long time coming.

The divorce contract

The Jewish divorce process is a formal and final undoing of the marriage process. As the ketubah began the marriage, so the get ends it, both 'in conformity with the rabbis' rulings'. It is significant that five out of the seven mishnaic tractates that pertain to women and family are devoted to the transfer of women with either the formation or the dissolution of the marital bond. The woman is regarded as one unit in the social order of the household in which she is 'holy to a man'. If she leaves this and becomes 'permitted to every man', she does not then become the head of a household with her children. Rather, she returns to her father's household. For all these restrictions of a woman in rabbinic times, she is afforded great honour. If a marriage is ended or invalid, everything is designed to restore the status quo before the transaction, not because women are seen as possessions, but because it is assumed that she is financially dependent upon a man.

In some ways, Judaism was way ahead of its time in recognizing the realities of broken relationships and in seeking to protect the female partner who was dependent. Some would also applaud its seeing marriage as a contract rather than as an indissoluble union or sacrament. Contracts can rightly be ended if their conditions are not satisfactorily fulfilled. Yet on one crucial matter, in the view of most people (including most Jews), Jewish divorce is old-fashioned. This is the way in which the final word in divorce is granted to men. A woman may initiate divorce proceedings, but she cannot be officially released from the marriage without her husband's consent. This has led to cases such as one reported in *The Guardian* (22 February 1993):

> For the past 30 years, Yihya Avraham has been three words away from freedom. Ever since the 80-year-old Israeli was imprisoned in 1963, he has refused to say 'I am willing' – words which would free him, both from prison and from his 52-year marriage.

In Israel, where the only Jewish marriage, divorce, and remarriage is a religious one, the reluctant Mrs Avraham remains, so long as her husband chooses, *agunah* (plural *agunot*, 'anchored') to the vindictive Mr Avraham. The rabbinical court can imprison such a man but it still cannot compel him to give his consent to a divorce. In the instance cited here, the couple married in the Yemen when she was 12 years old and separated as many as 40 years ago. *The Guardian*'s account of the bizarre ending of the marriage is amusing but the sort of situation it reflects less so:

> For two days, the wife kept vigil at the airport. When she finally spotted her husband, the police detained him and he was taken before the ad hoc airport court to face an ultimatum: agree to the divorce, or miss the flight. He took the first option.

Though this is obviously an extreme case, there are many unhappy agunot who want to stay within Orthodoxy and yet want to be free to remarry. Not only Orthodox but also Conservative Judaism has difficulty in finding a solution to the problem of the agunah. Such a woman may, in fact, have a husband who is missing – perhaps from wartime. 'Presumed dead' makes no difference to the situation. Unless she has a divorce certificate, she remains married to the absent husband. The impossibility of simply rescinding such a halakhic law lies in the ancient decision that a rabbinic assembly superior to the one which decreed it is required. There is no contemporary assembly which is deemed greater than the ancient assemblies behind the Talmud. It may be argued that the halakhah is much wider in its possibilities than is acknowledged by the non-Orthodox and that Orthodox authorities could solve many apparently intractable problems should they choose to draw on this wide tradition. The matter of the woman whose husband refuses to divorce her is one such area. There are, in fact, legal avenues for freeing such a woman to remarry. These resemble the Roman Catholic dissolution of a marriage. The process may be regarded as artificial but also as morally justified.

Non-Orthodox Judaism rejects the whole idea of agunah as unethical. Nothing can be gained and everything can be lost by regarding a woman who is judged to be either widowed or divorced according to civil law as still married. Not only the woman suffers from the injustice but also any children who are born from her next civil marriage. In Orthodox terms, they are *mamzerim* (singular *mamzer*, 'offspring of a forbidden union' such as adultery or incest). This 'illegitimacy' in turn drastically limits their own marriage choice. Someone judged to be a mamzer can, according to the Mishnah, marry only another mamzer, a proselyte, or a freed slave. Reform has abolished the whole concept of illegitimacy. A Reform Bet Din can no more compel a partner (male or female, since an eighth century rabbinical decree said that a woman also cannot be forced to divorce) to consent to a get than an Orthodox Bet Din can. However, if all efforts at persuasion fail, it takes upon itself the power to award a get if the couple are already divorced civilly. Liberal Jews do not require a get before remarriage. A couple is accepted at a Reform synagogue if they transfer their membership there, though a get would be required if they had yet to marry and wanted the ceremony to be in the Reform synagogue.

10

prayer

In this chapter you will learn:

- when and why Jews pray
- about the origin and development of Jewish prayers
- about physical aids to prayer.

The point of praying

Vital to Judaism is the conviction that God communicates with human beings. The primary means of this communication is seen as the Torah, both written and oral. Hence, in *talmud Torah* ('Torah study') the Jew is to hear the divine revelation and in some way further it. Closely related to study is *tefillah* ('prayer'). The word possibly derives from the Hebrew root for 'to judge', with the thought that in tefillah people call on God to judge all their thoughts and actions. This may include the notion of self-examination, judging oneself. Other Hebrew words connected with praying also express this emphasis on bringing human life under God's scrutiny and guidance, on being tuned and open to what God requires. *Avodah* ('service') referred in Temple times to public worship. Some stress the sacrificial nature of this 'service', sharply distinguished from prayer (tefillah). Others, notably Samson Raphael Hirsch, maintain that Jewish worship always had prayer hand in hand with sacrifice. 1 Kings 8:27–30 makes plain that Solomon's Temple was dedicated to prayer. Further, *the* service, par excellence, the avodah performed by the High Priest on the Day of Atonement, included not only ritual in the sense of what was done but also liturgy in the sense of what was said. Leviticus 16 was read to the people on that day as indeed it still is. In such passages as Isaiah 1:11–15 from the eighth century BCE we see a condemnation of insincerity in both sacrifice and prayer.

Certainly, when, on the destruction of the Temple, sacrifice was no longer possible there were already in place patterns of prayer designed not to affect or influence God but to achieve the spiritual edification of humanity. Hirsch even traces synagogue prayer right back to the 'Men of the Great Synagogue' in the fifth century BCE. There is much dispute over the antiquity of certain formulas for prayers. Nonetheless, the term *avodah shebalev* ('service of the heart') was used by the Rabbis (e.g. Taanit 2a, cf. Deuteronomy 11:13) to mean 'prayer'. Hence the main prayer book of Liberal Jews was called *Service of the Heart* (1967). Their new prayer book of 1995 is called *Service of the New Heart* continuing the rabbinic phrase with words from Ezekiel 36:26 – 'I will give you a new heart and put a new spirit within you.' (Their prayer book for the High Holy Days is called *Gates of Repentance*.)

Times of prayer

According to the Talmud, it was the Temple services which determined the times for Jewish prayer. Each day, sacrifice was offered in the morning and in the afternoon. So now there is daily prayer, the morning service being known (as was the morning sacrifice) as *shaharit* ('morning') and the afternoon service (like the afternoon sacrifice) as *minhah* ('offering' of flour mingled with oil). A part of the sacrificial service went on into the evening and this extension is reflected in the institution of evening prayer, the term for this service being *maariv* ('evening'). The times are given in the Mishnah:

> The morning Tefillah may be said any time until midday. Rabbi Judah says: Until the fourth hour [i.e. mid-morning]. The afternoon Tefillah may be said any time until sunset. Rabbi Judah says: Until midway through the afternoon. The evening Tefillah has no set time; and the Additional Tefillah may be said any time during the day. Rabbi Judah says: until the seventh hour: [i.e. 1.00 a.m.].

> (Berakhot 4:1)

The 'additional prayer' mentioned here corresponds to the extra sacrificial service on the Sabbath and the High Holy Days. It is, therefore, called *musaf* ('additional'). Musaf often follows the Torah reading in the service of shaharit, giving a morning service of over two hours. Another reason given for the institution of the three main times for prayer is the example of the patriarchs: Abraham (Genesis 19:27), Isaac (Genesis 24:63 where the Hebrew speaks of his 'meditating'), and Jacob (Genesis 28:11).

Kavanah and *devekut*

Set times are meant to detract from neither spontaneity nor sincerity. Two further words connected with prayer indicate the need for concentration and for a sense of God. The first is *kavanah* which can be rendered as 'devotion' or 'direction' or 'intention', the opposite of the lip-service condemned in Isaiah 29:13. Maimonides, who himself contributed to Jewish liturgy, emphasized the importance attached to kavanah in the Talmud. He maintained that prayer without kavanah was no prayer at all and had to be done again with kavanah. A person, he said, 'should empty his mind of all other thoughts and regard himself as if he were standing before the Divine Presence'. Kavanah entails also an awareness of the full meaning of the words chosen for prayer. The Shulhan Arukh similarly states: 'Better a little supplication with kavanah, than a great deal without it.' Hasidic leaders also saw the dangers of public prayers at set times. In the eighteenth century, Rabbi Nahman encouraged his followers to find themselves a secluded place and pour out their thoughts to God. He speaks of the audacity of prayer in the first place. Daring is required, he says, to stand in prayer before 'the greatness of the Creator':

> Prayer is a mystery, directed in its essence towards changing the order of the world. Every star and sphere is fixed in its order, yet man wants to change the order of nature; he asks for miracles. Hence, at the moment of prayer man must lay aside his capacity for shame. If men had shame, they would, God forbid, lose the faith that prayer is answered.

Kavanah can, it is maintained, lead to a state of *devekut*, the second significant word. This can perhaps best be translated 'communion with God'. According to the writings of the Kabbalah (Jewish mysticism), devekut, as the highest spiritual achievement, may be obtained by many more people than those usually classed as mystics. Hasidism goes so far as to say that devekut should be the believer's constant state of mind. Yet in prayer particularly there may be a mystical encounter with the Divine. The founder of Habad Hasidism, Shneur Zalman, speaks of prayer as:

> the foundation of the whole Torah. This means that man knows God, recognising His greatness and His splendour with a serene and whole mind, and an understanding heart. Man should reflect on these ideas until his rational soul is awakened to love God, to cleave to him and to His Torah, and to desire His commandments.

Blessing God

The physical place for prayer can be anywhere at all. Typically in Judaism, it is not the place but the time which is set apart as holy (see on the Sabbath in Chapter 12). We see this very clearly in the paradigmatic prayer of Judaism, the *berakhah* ('blessing'). This is not one particular prayer but a type of prayer. Its importance is indicated by the fact that the plural, *berakhot*, is the name of the first mishnaic tractate, in which rules for prayers are found, as in the extract concerning times above and as in Berakhot 9:1–3:

> If a man saw a place where miracles had been wrought for Israel he should say, 'Blessed is he that wrought miracles for our fathers in this place' . . . If he saw shooting stars, earthquakes, lightnings, thunders and storms he should say, 'Blessed is he whose power and might fill the world' . . . For rain and good tidings he should say, 'Blessed is he, the good and the doer of good.' For bad tidings he should say, 'Blessed is he, the true judge.' If a man built a house or bought new vessels he should say, 'Blessed is he that hath given us life.'

The standard opening of the berakhah is: 'Blessed art Thou, O Lord our God, King of the Universe, who hast . . .' What follows can be, as above, an unusual or new sight, the receiving of news (good or bad), or it may be before eating any kind of food or drink or performing a mitzvah (this applies only to a ritual obligation and not to an ethical one) such as circumcision ('. . . commanded us to make our sons enter into the covenant of Abraham our father'). Two aspects of this phrasing are important. First, it is God who is blessed and not the event, the object, or the mitzvah. Thus God is blessed 'who createst the fruit of the vine' and not the wine itself. Secondly, there is a change of person from the second ('Thou') to the third ('who hast'), as if the world can provide only an indirect experience of the holy God. Through a particular moment, the transcendent and eternal God reveals his presence.

Nowhere is this better captured than in the specific blessing for reaching a juncture in time, which may be rendered: 'Blessed are You, Lord our God, who has kept us in life, has sustained us, and has permitted us to reach this moment.' This blessing takes its name from the Hebrew for 'who has kept us alive', *sheheheyanu*. So on completing a new house and taking possession, a Jew does not bless God for the place but for the moment. Sheheheyanu is offered also at the beginning of all festivals, the emphasis being on the privilege of being alive and able to celebrate a particular time of God's revelation.

Home and synagogue

Though these blessings, and indeed other prayers, may be offered wherever the experience occurs, the synagogue and the home remain the major locations. The prayer books of all the branches of Judaism, therefore, contain a combination of prayers for the synagogue and for the home. Many may be offered in either place. One more usually located in the home is the grace after meals. This appears to be the earliest formal benediction. (The priestly blessing of Numbers 6:22–27 which, as we saw in Chapter 2, seems in essence to date back as far as the seventh century BCE, belongs to a different order of blessing altogether.) More important than its precise date is the way in which the grace after meals provides an insight into the place of prayer in Judaism. In his *Short History*, subtitled *Three Meals, Three Epochs*, Jacob Neusner pays particular attention to this prayer. Whilst not all would accept his entire approach, none would deny the basic premise that the table at which meals are eaten becomes, after the destruction of the Temple, the equivalent of the altar. So in the four parts of this prayer, the participant is moved from the here and now to the time to come, from the meal just eaten to the banquet at the end of history. The words of the middle two paragraphs invoke the entire sacred history of the Jewish people and point towards the final redemption. They include the words:

> *We thank thee, O Lord our God, because thou didst give as an heritage unto our fathers a desirable, good and ample land . . .; as well as for thy covenant which thou hast sealed in our flesh, the Torah which thou hast taught us, thy statutes which thou hast made known unto us, the life, grace and loving kindness which thou hast bestowed upon us, and for the good wherewith thou dost constantly feed and sustain us on every day, in every season, at every hour . . . O our God, our Father, feed us, nourish us, sustain, support and relieve us, and speedily, O Lord our God, grant us relief from all our troubles . . .*

After this, writes Neusner, the concluding paragraph:

> *returns us to the point at which we began: thanks for lunch . . . The diners were hungry and ate, a common-place, entirely secular action, but through the medium of words the experience of hunger and of eating is turned into an encounter with another world of meaning altogether.*

Communal prayers – ancient and modern

The *Shema*

The twin pillars of communal prayer are the Shema and the Amidah. In a recent study of Jewish liturgical history, *Judaism and Hebrew Prayer* (Cambridge University Press, 1993), Stefan Reif holds that the two prayers may well have come into the later rabbinic literature from separate sources and with different traditions about just when they were to be recited. The *Shema* takes its name from the opening word, 'Hear'. The prayer is, in fact, made up of three biblical passages: Deuteronomy 6:4–9; 11:13–21, and Numbers 15:37–41. The first passage (as printed in the Orthodox daily prayer book) begins:

HEAR, O ISRAEL: THE LORD IS OUR GOD, THE LORD IS ONE. (Instead of the Hebrew letters rendered 'LORD' in English translations, a Jew will out of reverence for the name and thus the nature of God say *Adonai* which means 'Lord' or *Ha-Shem*, 'The Name'.) It continues:

> *And thou shalt love the Lord thy God with all thine heart, and with all thy soul, and with all thy might.*

In these opening biblical verses, God addresses Israel, rather than Israel addresses God. Thus it becomes a declaration of faith in what is absolutely central to Judaism: that there is only one God and that he requires whole-hearted obedience from his people. It is essentially a corporate prayer in which the community states its obligations to the God who has revealed his Torah and who has redeemed and who will in the future redeem his people. The Shema forms part of a Jew's morning and evening prayers, whether he is in the synagogue or at home. The opening sentence is recited as the Torah scroll is taken from the ark on the Sabbath and other festivals (see Chapter 11), and at other crucial moments. It is the aim of a devout Jew to die with these words on the lips. It ends a prayer of deathbed confession which ideally is recited by the dying person. If he or she is unable, those present should say it, helping the person to die affirming the Jewish faith.

The *Amidah*

Amidah means 'standing' and the prayer is so-called because the worshipper recites it standing, facing Jerusalem. The prayer comprises a series of berakhot as described above, though with God being blessed at the end rather than at the beginning of each unit. They now number 19, but the original number was 18 giving the prayer the alternative name *Shemoneh esreh* ('18') – *berakhot* ('benedictions') being understood. It is not certain whether the later addition was the twelfth benediction concerning heretics or the fifteenth concerning David.

So basic to Jewish liturgy is the Amidah that it is sometimes simply called the prayer, *Tefillah*. In the time of the Tannaim, there was still controversy over the exact number and contents of the berakhot. Some believe that a skeletal form of the prayer goes back to Temple times. If so, it probably comprises the opening three and the concluding three berakhot. These three are those now said at Sabbath and festival services. On weekdays – morning, afternoon and evening – all 19 are said, moving from praise to petition to thanksgiving. The petitionary section forms the bulk of the prayer, numbering 4–16, and requests that both spiritual and physical needs be met. Such things as wisdom, repentance, healing, worldly comfort, freedom, justice, and final salvation by the Messiah are all requested. The final request is for peace. As in all Jewish prayer, the community makes its requests in the plural, for example, in the sixth berakhah:

> *Forgive us, O our Father, for we have sinned; pardon us, O our King, for we have transgressed; for thou dost pardon and forgive. Blessed art thou, O Lord, who art gracious, and dost abundantly forgive.*

Yet, the petitionary section is prayed silently as each individual prays by and for himself or herself, along with other silent, praying individuals. The collective aspect is then emphasized by the leader repeating the Amidah aloud. As Neusner evocatively puts it:

> *To contemplate the power of these prayers imagine a room full of people, all standing by themselves yet in close proximity, some swaying this way and that, all addressing themselves directly and intimately to God in a whisper or in a low tone. They do not move their feet, for they are now standing before the King of kings, and it is not meet to shift and shuffle. If spoken to, they will not answer. Their attention is fixed upon the words of supplication, praise and gratitude. When they begin, they bend their knees – so too toward the*

end – and at the conclusion they step back and with-draw from the Presence.

(*A Short History of Judaism,* Fortress Press, 1992)

The *Alenu*

There is a third compulsory element (originally concluding just the New Year service but now all services) of obligatory public worship. Taking its name from the opening word, *Alenu* ('It is upon us'), it concerns Israel's role within a world-setting. It draws the community outward to the nations to whom it must witness that God is the only God. Together the Shema, the Amidah, and the Alenu cover the same themes as the grace after meals: creation, revelation, and redemption. Indeed, when taken with the blessings which precede it, the Shema itself includes all three themes.

Psalms

Public prayers are full of biblical passages and phrases. Sometimes whole Psalms are recited. The book of Psalms contains different sorts of prayer such as praise, thanksgiving, lament, and confession. The setting for many of them is the Temple, some referring directly to pilgrimage (e.g. Psalms 42, 122), others to Mount Zion and Jerusalem as the source of inspiration (e.g. Psalms 24,150), and others to various kinds of sacrifices (e.g. Psalms 20:3, 54:6). Some scholars feel able to relate particular Psalms to specific festivals or national occasions such as the enthronement of the king. The precise relationship between types of Psalms and Temple worship, however, is the subject of debate among scholars of the Hebrew Bible. So also is the relationship between communal and individual prayer. Not all would accept the linking of liturgy and ritual assumed earlier in this chapter. A long and complex liturgical history runs from the Bible to what constitute the foundation prayers of Jewish worship today. There is, nonetheless, a weight of opinion, ranging from rabbinic sources to recent biblical scholarship, in favour of interpreting most of the Psalms as part of worship in the first or second Temple. There is also consensus of opinion on the fact that the book of Psalms exercised a major influence and also on the date and location of the first Jewish prayer book as the Babylonian academies of the ninth to the twelfth centuries. Whatever the age and source of each prayer, the compilations of these religious leaders were the earliest forerunners of what became the standard rabbinic prayer book.

Prayer books

The *siddur*

Today, prayers for general use – whether at home or synagogue – are printed in the main prayer book, the *siddur* ('order'). This order of prayer, such as we have noted with the Shema, the Amidah, and the Alenu, serves many purposes. It affirms Jewish faith and historical experiences. It discourages selfish prayer by being communal whilst at the same time recognizing individual concerns. It provides phrases, some of great antiquity, which give a sense of continuity and security. It offers a pattern and a unity for Jews all over the world, regardless of whether each individual at every time and in every place would naturally pray certain prayers or, indeed pray at all, if left to purely personal mood and habit. All worshipping Jews accept the siddur as the vital expression of their hopes and convictions. In Britain, the Orthodox siddur is *The Authorised Daily Prayer Book*, the Reform siddur is *Forms of Prayer for Jewish Worship (Daily, Sabbath, and Occasional Prayers)*, and the Liberal siddur is *Service of the New Heart*.

The *Mahzor*

Prayers for special occasions in the year's cycle (see Chapter 13) are printed in a festival prayer book known as a *mahzor* ('cycle'). A number of examples from the Reform mahzor for the High Holy Days appear in Chapter 15. An example from the Liberal mahzor reads:

> Lord our God, we turn now to You once more to cry out our longing and the longing of all men and women for a beginning of the wholeness we call peace . . . The intelligence You have implanted within us we have applied to the arts of war; with the skill we have from You we make engines of terror and pain.

Some may find the use of modern phrases such as 'engines of terror and pain' offputtingly earthy whilst others find them powerful in their starkness. Some may feel the adoption of inclusive language such as 'all men and women' unnecessary in a religion which assumes community whilst others feel it to be essential if Jews in an avowedly non-sexist society are to pray with any conviction.

The inclusion of prayers – some in the vernacular and some in Hebrew – and the modernizing of the language of some ancient ones are just two of the changes made by Reform and Liberal Judaism in both the festival and the daily prayer books. Other changes fall into three main categories: theological, historical, and structural. (Reif's volume mentioned above gives an excellent survey of modern developments in its last two chapters, with details of all the major prayer books published until 1990.) One of the main areas which the Hamburg movement in the nineteenth century wanted to re-form was liturgy. In particular, they removed or shortened most of the *piyyutim* ('liturgical poems') composed mainly before the thirteenth century, not only because they considered them outdated in language and in thought but also because they made the services so long. Biblical and rabbinic texts dealing with sacrifices were generally omitted and German was used instead of or alongside Hebrew for certain prayers. The alterations were not altogether systematic or consistent, a point made by the 'spiritual father of the Reform movement', Abraham Geiger. He wanted less Hebrew and not even a hint of anything positive about sacrifice. Even more radical were the policies of Samuel Holdheim which included replacing Sabbath with Sunday worship and abolishing head-covering, prayer-shawl, and the sounding of the ram's horn on the Day of Atonement.

As Reform grew in strength, it moved further and further away from traditional versions of the prayer book. In some congregations, even the Shema and the Amidah were severely truncated and the musaf service, with its clear association with sacrifices, was abolished. These radical changes gathered momentum in England, France, Holland and the USA whilst Germany began to become more moderate ('liberal', in German usage). Since the middle of the nineteenth century, however, the move has been steadily towards a synthesis of tradition and modernity. This stems in no small measure from Zacharias Frankel and his 'positive-historical' approach to Judaism. The most recent edition of *Forms of Prayer*, produced by the RSGB, now stands closer to the traditional siddur. The most recent Liberal siddur (1995), also reflects a positive evaluation of some traditional elements. The opposition of Reform and Liberal Jews to Zionism in the first half of the twentieth century has modified in the second half. Both liturgies include items relating to the modern State of Israel, though the Liberal is still hesitant and the Reform too lacks the thorough-going Zionism of modern Orthodoxy.

Some of the theological alterations remain. National and particularist elements were erased by the early reformers as no longer in keeping with modern thinking. Today, some find the traditional wording of the Alenu disparaging of non-Jews and so alter the phrasing, though the essential obligation of the prayer of witnessing to the one God remains the same. Prayers for peace similarly speak of the Jew's role in promoting this throughout the world rather than praying for Israel's peace. The other main omissions are prayers for the restoration of sacrifice – Conservative Judaism, keeping the closest to tradition, puts the approval of sacrifice in the past tense and goes on to pray for a similarly heartfelt devotion, as lay behind the Temple offerings, in the present – a personal Messiah, the resurrection of the dead, though the wording of the Conservative prayer books especially (as in: 'Blessed art Thou, O Lord who callest the dead to life everlasting') admits a wide range of interpretation. Reform says: '. . . who renews life beyond death', though the Hebrew original has been left unchanged.

Reform generally now tries to strike a balance between the traditional Hebrew forms and liturgical reform. Prayers which were repeated several times in one service, especially in Aramaic, a language unknown to most Jews today, are limited to one recitation. (An exception is the Kaddish on the Sabbath. See Chapter 7.) Historical changes include the introduction of prayers commemorating the Holocaust and recalling Israel's more recent history, such as Independence Day. The structure of the Reform siddur differs from the Orthodox one in putting Sabbath prayers first and daily prayers afterwards, recognizing that for most Jews communal prayer occurs on the Sabbath.

Physical reminders

We noted at the outset the need for kavanah (intention) in Jewish prayer. Though customs vary, there are some physical gestures and items of clothing which have been adopted to cultivate the right attitude and atmosphere for prayer. Some of these are particularly potent reminders of the central Jewish beliefs in the unity of God, in the Torah as his revelation, and in the obligations of the Torah as the means of living as 'a holy people'.

Body language

The talmudic rules for the movements referred to in the earlier description of the Amidah are summarized in the main law code, the Shulhan Arukh:

> *One must bow four times during the Amidah: At the beginning and at the end of the first benediction and at the beginning and at the end of the Modim [thanksgiving] prayer. When one says 'Praised' he should bend over until the joints of his spinal column stand out, and also bow his head. Then, before one pronounces the name of the Lord, he should begin slowly to stand erect, according to the verse, 'The Lord lifts up those who are bowed down' (Psalm 146:8). After the recitation of the Amidah, and before the worshipper recites 'May he who ordains the order of the universe bring peace to us and to all Israel', he should bow and take three short steps backward, like a servant taking leave of his master.*

The general idea appears to be that God requires submission but not subservience in human obedience. Rashi comments on Berakhot 34b which requires the High Priest to bow more often than the ordinary person and the king more than the High Priest: 'The greater the person, the greater the need for submission.'

Other physical gestures may include prostration while reciting the Alenu at the New Year Festival and the Day of Atonement (and the Avodah – the account of the Temple service) and the covering of the eyes during the opening verse of the Shema to cut out distractions. Whilst some find being still aids concentration, others prefer a gentle swaying. One of the many explanations offered for this practice is the reference in Psalm 35:10 – 'All my bones shall say, "O LORD, who is like you?"' Some Hasidic groups have, since the days of their founder, the Baal Shem Tov, encouraged vigorous movement as conducive to sensing God's nearness, though this is to be spontaneous rather than at fixed points in prayer.

Yarmulkah

A general expression of reverence is the 'skull-cap', called variously a *yarmulkah* (possibly a contraction of the Yiddish for 'fear of the King', God being conceived as above), a *capel*, or a *kippah*. These are always circular though there is wide variation in size and colour. The origins of this are not known, though many think it began as a means of differentiation from Christian prayer in which men uncover their heads as a mark of respect. Some Jewish men wear a yarmulkah all the time and others when the name of God is spoken as in study and in prayer. Hats worn outdoors are worn by some men in a synagogue and in some communities officials wear top hats. Male visitors to a synagogue may be expected to cover their heads.

Tallit

The garment most associated with prayer is the *tallit* ('shawl'). It is made of white wool, cotton, or silk though never a mixture (prohibited in Leviticus 19:19), with either blue or black horizontal stripes at each end. It can be square or rectangular, but its crucial feature are fringes in each of its four corners. The significance of the *tzitzit* ('fringes') is given in Numbers 15:38–41:

> Speak to the Israelites, and tell them to make fringes on the corners of their garments throughout their generations and to put a blue cord on the fringe at each corner. You have the fringe so that, when you see it, you remember all the commandments of the LORD and do them . . . So you shall . . . do all my commandments and, and you shall be holy to your God. I am the LORD your God, who brought you out of the land of Egypt, to be your God . . .

The tallit is worn by Orthodox men (that is, over the age of 13) during morning prayer at home or in the synagogue. Some, especially the leader, wear it also during evening prayer. It is placed around the shoulders and sometimes over the head (as in the photograph below) in some cases preceded by the following kabbalistic meditation:

> I am here wrapping myself around with a tallit to which tzitzit are attached, in order to carry out the command of my Creator . . . And just as I cover myself with the tallit in this world, so may my soul deserve to be clothed with a beautiful spiritual robe in the World to Come, in the Garden of Eden.

Reform considers the wearing of a tallit to be standard for men (in some communities this means only married men) and optional for women, but some maintain that it should be obligatory for a woman if she takes on the same responsibilities

at his Bar Mitzvah, a boy takes on the adult obligation of wearing tefillin for his daily morning prayers

this scene at the Western Wall in Jerusalem was on a weekday

had it been the Sabbath, the men would not have worn tefillin since, as a festival itself, the Sabbath is considered sufficient sign of the covenant

and privileges as men in the synagogue, such as opening the ark or being called up to read from the Torah. (This was argued, for instance, by Rabbi David Kunin, in *The Journal of Progressive Judaism*, May 1994, calling for Reform to follow what he maintains are halakhic principles on the nature of obligation.) A small tallit (*tallit katan*) is worn by some traditional Jews as an undergarment throughout the day. This garment is also known as an *arba kanfot* ('four-cornered vest'). The vital feature of the tallit katan is also the tzitzit as a reminder of the mitzvot of the covenant people.

Tefillin

The same principle of remembering lies behind the wearing of *tefillin* (sometimes translated 'phylacteries') for morning prayer in the synagogue or at home. In Progressive Judaism, this is open to all over the age of 13, but is not obligatory for any. In Orthodoxy, adult males are obligated to 'lay tefillin', the phrase referring to the way in which tefillin are bound to the body with symbolic winding of the two straps. One is placed on the arm opposite the heart and the other on the forehead in obedience to Deuteronomy 6:4–9; 11:13–21 (the first two portions of the Shema) and Exodus 13:1–10; 13:11–16. These four passages are placed inside the tefillin, on scrolls handwritten by a qualified scribe. The black boxes themselves are made from the skin of kosher animals. Whilst educational organizations produce facsimiles of tefillin for demonstration, it should be noted that the real thing is handled with great reverence.

Mezuzah

The first two of these passages are also on the parchment fixed to the front doorpost (and sometimes to all rooms used for living in) of a Jewish house, in obedience to the passages themselves which command a reminder of the Torah on the doorposts, *mezuzot* (singular, *mezuzah*). The mezuzah is often placed in a case before it is affixed, slanting upwards towards the door, on the right-hand doorpost. The inseparable link between prayer and study of the Torah and the dual importance of home and synagogue for observance of the mitzvot are nowhere more clearly exemplified.

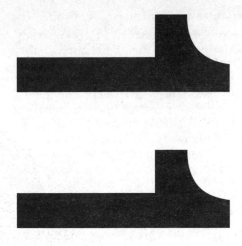

the Synagogue

In this chapter you will learn:

- about the origins and functions of the synagogue
- about the reading of the Torah
- about the role of the Rabbi.

Terms and functions

The synagogue building now serves a range of functions: study, prayer, and general meeting-place for the community. It may house a Bet Midrash (house of study), though, as we saw in Chapter 8, this is often a separate building. The synagogue as *Bet Tefillah* ('a house of prayer') was largely covered in Chapter 10. It must be reiterated, however, that Jews offer prayer privately as well as communally and that communal prayer does not require a synagogue. It should be added that it is far from clear just when and where a synagogue became associated with prayer. The Greek word for 'prayer [house]', *proseuche*, occurs in inscriptions from Egyptian sites in the third century BCE, but until the late first century BCE there is no source which establishes the existence of a specific building for Jewish prayer in either Palestine or Babylon.

The title *Bet Knesset* ('a house of assembly') is the main term for synagogue (apart from the more colloquial 'shul' which is actually the word most commonly used). It is often said not only to sum up its true nature and importance but also to reveal the origins of the institution of synagogue itself. *Knesset* means 'assembly' (as in the name of the Israeli Parliament) and so *Bet Ha-Knesset* is 'the meeting-place' (the 'Ha' simply indicates the definite article in Hebrew). Use of 'Bet Knesset' in the Talmud has a formal ring, suggesting that the gathering was an important occasion rather than just a 'get-together' of the people. How the synagogue developed as a 'community centre' is not clear, but the term 'Bet Knesset' gives the fullest indication of the activities which go on in the modern synagogue. People gather: for study, for prayer and the reading of the Torah, for meetings, clubs, social occasions, and celebrations. No division is made between sacred and secular. The synagogue complex houses all activities.

The origins of the synagogue

Although it is generally accepted that very little can be known with certainty about the synagogue before the first century BCE, the evidence suggests that the forerunner of the modern synagogue was the local assembly-point of Greek-speaking Jews of the Diaspora. Wanting to express a sense of Jewish community, they met for a variety of social and religious activities, including study, prayer, readings from Scripture, and other traditional Jewish customs. It is interesting that the earliest Palestinian inscription to refer to such a meeting-place says nothing of communal prayer. (Theodotus, probably in the first century CE, is here called an 'archisynagogue', a 'synagogue ruler' and the building is for the reading of the Torah, the teaching of the commandments, and for hospitality.) The explanation may well be that, for Jews with access to the Temple, there was no need to create another 'sacred space' and there was moreover a reluctance to do so. There were probably communal buildings (and outdoor locations) where prayer was regularly offered but these lacked the sacred features which later became essential to a synagogue. So it would seem that the term *knesset* corresponds exactly to the original meaning of its Greek equivalent, *sunagoge*, a formal assembly or congregation rather than a building. Perhaps this explains why in the early Christian centuries there was no standard form of physical structure. Indeed, there are very few physical requirements of a synagogue to this day. Those there are revolve around the Torah and its reading (see below).

Some trace the beginnings of the synagogue back to the exile in the sixth century BCE. Deprived of the Temple, it may well be that Jews gathered together for prayer. What the textual evidence more obviously suggests, however, is that Jews gathered in Israel after the exile, with the Temple restored, to hear the reading of the Torah (Nehemiah 8:7–8). One tradition credits Ezra with instituting readings on Monday and Thursday mornings when many people would be gathered for market days and court sessions (Jerusalem Talmud 4:1) and on Sabbath afternoons when shopkeepers would be free to come (Bava Kama 82a). (References dating the public reading of the Torah on certain special occasions to the times of Moses, of Joshua, and Josiah occur in Deuteronomy 31:10.f; Joshua 8:34; and 2 Kings 23:2 respectively.) By the first century CE, both the philosopher Philo and the historian Josephus speak of regular Sabbath readings as an established custom. The centrality of the synagogue for reading Scriptures is well-attested in the New Testament (e.g. Luke 4:16–20 refers specifically to reading and Mark 6:2; Matthew 12:9; Acts 18:4 refer to teaching) whilst there is only one New Testament text (Matthew 6:5) which locates prayer in the synagogue and even this could well be referring to a 'gathering' rather than to a building.

It is after the destruction of the Second Temple in 70 CE that all the various expressions of worship could be brought together in specific buildings in Palestine and it is, therefore, not surprising that from this point onwards the prominence of the synagogue rises steeply. (The Talmud speaks of as many as 394 'houses of assembly' in Jerusalem alone by 70 CE but the number of 'synagogues' in the sense of buildings which housed all worship except sacrifice is likely to have become significant only after this date.) What we now have is an amalgamation of a prayer-house, a study house, and a meeting-place, reminding us of the synagogue's diverse and complex origins as an institution. Yet, the centrality of the Torah remains.

Reading the Torah

Aron Kodesh

A synagogue – whether it is a large and ornate building or a small, plain room – must have two features: an ark for housing the scrolls of the Torah and a desk from which to read them. According to Exodus 25:10–16, the Tabernacle erected in the wilderness housed the two tablets of stone given to Moses at Sinai. These were contained in a wooden box covered with gold, known as *aron kodesh* ('holy ark'). This ark disappeared at the time of the destruction of Solomon's Temple. In talmudic times, the ark was a similar portable chest but since medieval times it has been a cupboard fixed in the east wall of the synagogue. (Sefardi Jews call it a *heikhal* ('sanctuary') rather than aron kodesh.) In it are kept the scrolls of the Torah and it thus forms the focal point of the synagogue. There is usually a beautifully embroidered curtain in front of the ark or just inside the doors. (Some consider this to be reminiscent of the veil before the innermost part of the Temple, the Holy of Holies.) The West London synagogue is famous for its open grille work which enables the scrolls to be seen throughout the service. More usually, this impressive sight comes to view shortly before the Torah is taken out to be read.

Above the ark are often two tablets representing the Ten Commandments and giving the first two words of each commandment (usually with the Hebrew letters for the name of God as found in Exodus 3:14 not written in full out of reverence) and sometimes other sayings such as: 'Know before whom you stand.' There is also a *ner tamid* ('everburning light'), symbolizing the divine presence. Most modern synagogues use an electric light, but a few (including the West London) still have the traditional oil lamp corresponding to the lamp burning continually in the Tabernacle (Exodus 27:20–1), from which the

the beautiful baroque interior
of the Chatham Memorial
Synagogue and the simplicity
of the synagogue at the
Sternberg Centre

ner tamid derives its name. In the synagogue, it seems to be a relatively recent innovation as there are no references to a synagogue ner tamid before the eighteenth century. Light is, however, an ancient symbol of God's presence, as in the Tabernacle and later in the Temple where there was a *menorah* ('candelabrum') as described in Exodus 25:31–40; 37:17–24. Some synagogues also have a menorah (either the standard seven-branched or nine-branched as for the festival of Hanukah) to the right of the ark.

The *bimah*

The other focus of activity is the *bimah* ('platform') from which the Torah is read. This can be quite an extensive platform or a simpler reading-desk. In Orthodox synagogues it is normally in the centre. Maimonides prescribed this position but the *Kesef Mishneh*, a commentary on his code, says that this was simply to improve audibility and in small synagogues the bimah can be placed to one side. (This view was disputed in the later literature.) One of the changes brought about in the Reform movement at the beginning of the nineteenth century was the placing of the bimah directly in front of the ark. The seats are arranged accordingly, so that people face the bimah. In Orthodox synagogues, women always sit separately in either a balcony or an area divided by a screen, following the talmudic view that men must not be distracted from their obligation to pray.

Services for prayer are held in the synagogue daily in the evening, morning, and afternoon. Some of the prayers described in Chapter 10 require a minyan (traditionally 10 adult males). Orthodox and many other Jews consider it an obligation to recite the other prayers on their own if there are insufficient numbers for a synagogue service. On Shabbat and festivals, the reading is at the centre of worship, accompanied by ceremonial leading up to the moment when the Torah scroll is brought out of the aron kodesh.

Portions of the Torah

On each Sabbath morning, one portion of the Torah is read. The length of the *sidra* ('order' or 'section', plural *sidrot*) depends on whether or not the synagogue is Orthodox. Orthodox communities follow the ancient Babylonian practice of reading

the whole of the Torah in one year and so each week cover
several chapters and parts of chapters. (The existing chapter
divisions came into the Bible late and often cut across the sense
of a passage.) Palestinian Jews used to spread the reading over
three years. This triennial cycle has been adopted by Reform
communities, on the ground that a shorter passage helps
concentration and attendant dignity in worship. They also point
out that the Talmud refers to a three-year system in ancient Israel
which preceded the Babylonian custom (Megillah 29b). The
present liturgical calendar in Reform does not include the entire
Torah, considering some passages (such as genealogies as in
Genesis 36 and lists of dermatological ailments as in Leviticus
13) unhelpful in public reading. Most of it is covered, however,
by dividing each *parashah* ('weekly portion', plural *parashiyot* –
the words are used interchangeably with sidra and sidrot) of the
annual cycle into three parts and reading from each part once
every three years. This ensures some correspondence with what
is read each week in all other synagogues worldwide.
(Occasionally, the extra length of festival observance in Orthodoxy outside Israel means that their Torah readings do not
synchronize with those of Reform, as when the festival of Simhat
Torah falls a day later – see Chapters 13 and 14). In all
congregations, the liturgical cycle ends when the last part of
Deuteronomy and the first part of Genesis are read on the
festival of Simhat Torah (see chapter 14).

Haftarah

On Sabbaths, festivals, fasts, and at the afternoon service on the
Day of Atonement, the Torah reading is followed by a reading
from the Prophets (see Chapter 2). It is not known when this
custom began though a mishnaic passage indicates its antiquity
(Megillah 4:1). Since it completes or concludes the Torah, this
reading takes the name *haftarah* ('conclusion', plural *haftarot*).
The haftarah relates to the particular feast or fast (see examples
in Chapters 13–15) or contains a message linked with the sidra
of the day. Thus in the annual cycle, Micah 5:6–6:8 includes a
reference to Balak, the first subject (and therefore the name) of
the sidra in Numbers 22:2–25:9, and the spies of Joshua 22:1–24
parallel the spies sent out by Moses in sidra Numbers 13. The
triennial cycle, with a section from the Prophets for each section
from the Torah, inevitably has a larger number of haftarot. (This
also explains why the choice of haftarah in the Sefardic liturgy,
emanating from the Jews of Spain, sometimes differs from that

of the Ashkenazim, who follow the German liturgy.) This cycle includes not only the Prophets but also a greater selection from the Writings (see Chapter 2) than is traditionally read publicly, such as Job and Daniel. Reform again claims to be echoing talmudic practice here (Shabbat 116b), but a totally new development is their inclusion of a passage from the Apocrypha (see Chapter 2), notably 1 Maccabees 2:1–28 as the haftarah for the second Sabbath during the festival of Hanukah rather than the traditional 1 Kings 7:40–50.

Sefer Torah

In the synagogue service, the haftarah is read from a printed book, but the sidra is always read from a scroll, a *sefer* (plural *sifrei*). After the doors of the ark have been opened, one *sefer Torah* is ceremonially lifted out of the ark and carried in procession directly to the bimah, passing (where the bimah is sited in the centre) through the middle of the congregation who lean forward to touch it with the fringes of their tallit (prayer-shawl) as it passes. This sense of reverence characterizes everything about the sefer Torah, the way it is written, decorated, handled, and read.

The sefer Torah is a parchment scroll on which the first five books of the Bible are written. It is meticulously copied by hand with special pen and ink by a professional *sofer* ('scribe'). The Hebrew consists of consonants only. There is no pointing – the vowel signs beneath the consonants in a printed version (a humash) – no punctuation, and no musical signs above the letters to guide the reader when chanting. It is, therefore, no easy task to read and many who might wish to be called up for the honour of reading lack sufficient skill in Hebrew. In Sefardi communities, a sefer Torah rests on two rollers inside a heavy wooden or metal case which is carved or engraved and decorated in metal or leather. The two halves of the case are hinged and open like a book to display the scroll. The appropriate passage is found by rotating the protruding poles of the rollers and the scroll is fixed on a stand on the bimah in order to be read.

Ashkenazi sifrei Torah are rolled up and the two rollers brought together and tied with a linen binder. They are then wrapped in a silk or velvet mantle over which is hung a silver breastplate often decorated with symbols of the majesty of the Torah such as flowers or crowns. The breastplate represents the one worn by the High Priest in Temple times. A further crown often adorns the top of both the Ashkenazi and Sefardi sefer. Beneath the crown, securing the poles there are sometimes *rimmonim* ('pomegranates'). These silver finials have attached to them dangling bells which chime as the sefer is carried to and from the bimah. As the procession moves right round the congregation after the reading, the sound and sight leaves no one in any doubt about what is central to the service. At the bimah, the sefer is held aloft for everyone to see and then undressed of its symbols. An Ashkenazi sefer is placed horizontally and the reader keeps his (or, in a Progressive synagogue, her) place without direct contact with the text by means of a *yad* ('hand'), a silver or brass pointer.

Language and music

In an Orthodox synagogue, both the Torah and the Prophets are chanted in Hebrew as described above. This may be by someone specially trained or by someone who is marking a special occasion such as the Sabbath before his wedding or the completion of a period of mourning a close relative. The sidra is so long that it is divided into sections and at least seven different people must be called up to the bimah either to read or to recite the blessing before or after or to witness and follow the reading. The term given to this privilege is *aliyah* ('ascent'). The usual Reform practice is for only one person to be given an aliyah and for the sidra to be read rather than chanted. Immediately before or after the Hebrew, a vernacular translation is given. (In some communities, this is provided verse by verse.) The dominant aim is clarity and accessibility whilst retaining the ancient language of the Torah. The haftarah is usually read in the vernacular in Reform synagogues with only the blessing before or after said or sung in Hebrew.

Cantor

Though anyone who is eligible and capable of chanting the Torah (and of leading the prayers) may do so, Orthodox synagogues often employ a professional cantor, a *hazan* (plural *hazanim*). In earlier times, the hazan was an administrative official who attended to the practical needs of the community. Now the hazan's role is chiefly to conduct most of the service. The hazan will be highly trained not only as a singer but also specifically in *hazanut* (Jewish liturgical music). In the USA, for example, the first school for the training of hazanim was the

Hebrew Union College of Sacred Music founded in 1948. British hazanim train at the London School of Jewish Studies.

There is a disquiet about the future of this whole musical tradition and what it can offer Jewish worship. The expense of a hazan is prohibitive for small communities and others are choosing to dispense with his services. Few Reform synagogues, even large ones, employ a cantor. This is partly because more of their service is in the vernacular and so does not require the skill. Reform services are also shorter and may well employ a choir (always mixed) and an organ (situated in a balcony, as the 1870 organ in the West London Synagogue, or behind the ark) to lead the singing. Even without either of these, Reform puts the stress on congregational participation rather than on any solo elements and any leading tends to be done by a rabbi in place of a hazan.

Not only were there singer-musicians in Solomon's Temple (e.g. 1 Chronicles 25), but there were also musical instruments (e.g Psalm 92:2–4). After the destruction of the Temple, certain restrictions were introduced. There are three considerations: the need for restraint when mourning the loss of the Temple, a determination to avoid trying to replicate the Temple in the synagogue, and the fact that musical instruments cannot be played on Shabbat or festivals (see Chapter 12). Some Orthodox synagogues do have an organ but this is primarily for weddings. Reform does not have these restrictions, since its nineteenth-century originators opposed the emphasis on the Temple. (Indeed, in the USA, Reform synagogues are often called 'temples'.)

In synagogues without instruments, all the emphasis falls on the vocal line. Some believe that the simplest and purest form of this goes back at least to the time of Ezra and possibly to the First Temple period. The remarkable unity between the three major different traditions of Jewish liturgical music – Ashkenazi, Sefardi, and Oriental – strongly suggest a common root in Temple chant. Fascinating comparisons have been made (by, for example, Professor Yahezkiel Brown of Tel Aviv University) of Jewish Yemenite chant and Christian Gregorian plainsong. The common characteristic is short phrases combined in a predetermined sequence to form an extended recitative. The phrases are indicated by symbols above or below the Hebrew text in a system known as 'cantillation'. (There are different forms of cantillation of the Torah and of the haftarah.) The system which was perfected in the ninth century CE is still used today. These 'fixed chants' flourished in the Golden Age of Spanish Jewry (900–1400 CE) and when Sefardi Jews were expelled in the late fifteenth century they took their music with them to countries around the Mediterranean, such as Morocco. The hazan is a nineteenth-century development and the organ only came into its own in Jewish worship with the beginnings of the Reform movement. The choir also, with four-part harmony, is a modern introduction to Jewish liturgical music.

Religious leadership

A hazan is a paid employee of the synagogue. Having been trained extensively in Bible, Talmud, and prayer book, he is often afforded the title of 'Reverend'. Engaging also in pastoral work and generally carrying authority on religious matters in the community, the hazan exercises religious leadership. He (or, in Progressive communities, she) has an obligation to lead the community, especially in their worship.

Rabbi

The other paid employee of the synagogue and Judaism's main religious leader is the rabbi. Whilst the hazan needs to be knowledgeable about the Torah and how it should be chanted, the rabbi needs to be expert in all matters relating to it. It is the centrality of the Torah in Judaism which gives the rabbi his central role and he retains this only in so far as he studies and teaches the Torah. The title *rabbi* ('my master') was originally reserved for teachers of the Mishnah. Their paid employment lay not in interpreting the Torah, however, but in quite mundane occupations such as tentmaking or cobbling. Medieval rabbis often had rather more lucrative occupations as doctors or merchants. But, poor or rich, the respect and authority vested in the rabbi derived entirely from his knowledge of the Torah and his ability to give decisions from it to meet the practical needs of Jewish people.

We know that in eastern Europe in the eighteenth century there was conflict between rabbinic leaders and charismatic ones (see Chapter 4). There will always be a certain suspicion in Judaism of anyone whose spiritual leadership is not based on intensive study of the Torah. It is not that charisma, compassion, and all the other qualities which are needed by the modern rabbi are regarded as unimportant or incompatible with expertise in the Torah, but simply that, without the Torah, Judaism (as the religion most people understand it to be) does not exist. The rabbi is not a glorified social worker (though it is hard to imagine a rabbi who is lacking in pastoral skills being able to meet the needs of a community) nor an imaginative interpreter (though this gift might not come amiss) but one whose training seeks to equip him (or her) to lead a community in which the Torah is read, studied, and lived out. The sermon as a feature of the synagogue service is a relatively new method for doing this, though there used to be travelling preachers who expounded biblical or rabbinic texts. There are differing views in Judaism (as there are in Christianity) about the effectiveness of the spoken word, especially delivered at any length, in giving instruction and inspiration to an age increasingly dominated by visual and often brief modes of communication. Yet if anyone should be able to relate divine revelation to the human situation, it is the Jewish rabbi since this is the ancient and ongoing task of this religion.

In Progressive synagogues, there is even greater emphasis put on the sermon and the rabbi is likely to lead the rest of the service as well. Recognition of the need for skilled handling of serious personal difficulties, likely to be found in any congregation, is leading to many Reform rabbis taking further training in psychotherapy or other forms of counselling. The task of giving guidance on ethical and ritual questions remains one where the rabbi is considered the spiritual expert and some rabbis gather together examples of questions and answers to form a published body of Reform responsa. Involvement in social events and membership of the synagogue council are also part of the Reform rabbi's role, these organizational tasks not usually being expected of the Orthodox rabbi. The wider community would also expect to see the Reform rabbi as someone representing Jewish beliefs and practices on local committees. Though the model of the Christian cleric has obviously exercised an influence on Reform perceptions, the lengthy training at rabbinical college still centres on the Torah. It is the college which finally awards rabbis their *smikhah* ('ordination') from which their authority derives. Though not accepted by Orthodox authorities, a Reform smikhah from the Leo Baeck College is recognized worldwide by Conservative, Liberal, and other Reform communities. On matters of custom, such as how much of the service is in Hebrew, each rabbi is independent of central control and there is much greater variation between Reform synagogues than there is between Orthodox synagogues. On matters of status, however, the Bet Din makes all decisions (see Chapter 9) and Reform rabbis are subject to certain rulings from their membership of the Assembly of Rabbis. In Britain, for example, they may not officiate at a mixed-faith marriage (see Chapter 9).

Chief Rabbi

The central authority for the United Synagogue in Britain derives from the office of the Chief Rabbi. Appointed by the government as a spokesman for British Jewry, the Chief Rabbi is intended to represent all synagogue affiliations, but this role is becoming increasingly fragile. The furore over Rabbi Jonathan Sacks' statement early in 1995 that anyone who does not accept that the Torah was given in its entirety by God to Moses has 'severed links with the faith of his ancestors' further exposed the difficulty. His education and training are those of a modern Orthodox rabbi. That many of his rabbis are inspired by right-wing Orthodoxy forms one horn of his dilemma. To the left of the United Synagogue, Masorti (Conservative), Reform, and Liberal rabbis are simply unable to accept his definition of Judaism. Caught on the other horn of the dilemma, Dr Sacks' approach excludes at least 25 per cent (and probably many more) of British Jews. As the Liberal rabbi, David Goldberg, is quoted as saying: 'The way things are going, this could be the last Chief Rabbi who is accepted as the nominal spokesman for all of Anglo-Jewry' (*The Independent*, 14 January 1995).

Few other countries have a Chief Rabbinate. Israel's originated in the days of the British Mandate when the mandatory authority regarded the settlement as a religious rather than a political entity and consequently was willing to speak only to a religious authority. In France, Poland, and South Africa, the function is primarily one of representing the Jewish community to the secular authorities.

12

the Sabbath

In this chapter you will learn:

- about the origins and purpose of a day of rest
- how Jews over the ages have defined work prohibited on Shabbat
- about the ceremonies of Shabbat.

A sense of time out

That people need a respite from the routine of work is not a Jewish discovery. Even those referred to, by themselves or others, as 'workaholics' tend to admit that there is benefit to be had from 'time off'. In England, in recent years, there has been considerable discussion about the desirability of Sunday trading. This has revolved particularly around questions of work, leisure, and worship. Should those who choose to engage in Christian worship on Sunday have the right to determine whether or not others shop on this day? Will pressure be put on small businesses and employees to work on a day when they would prefer to be free to worship or to do other things? When the term 'Sabbath' appears in any discussion, it tends to have a negative ring and to be associated with 'kill-joys' who want to restrict people from doing what they enjoy. The Sabbath conjures up in people's minds images of the sombre, supposedly joyless, Sunday of the Calvinists. How far the Christian Sunday (the day chosen by the early Christians in celebration of Jesus' resurrection whilst Saturday remained as the Jewish holy day) has benefited from what it has borrowed from the restrictions of the Jewish Sabbath is open to debate. What is certain, however, is that to gain any sense of the spirit and purpose of the Jewish Sabbath we need to depart from this negative image.

Defining *Shabbat*

'Rest', which is how the Hebrew word *Shabbat* is often translated, is indeed a feature of the seventh day of the Jewish week, but the way in which this 'rest' is perceived, its nature and function, is far removed from an oppressive imposition of boredom. *Shabbat*, which is related to the Hebrew verb for 'to cease', is a word which cannot be truly translated ('Sabbath' simply renders the Hebrew *Shabbat*) as there is no equivalent word in any other tradition or culture. The unique element in Judaism's 'day of rest' is not so much 'time off' in the sense of 'time off work' as 'time out' in the sense of 'time out of time'. The idea is that a routine change of pace, organized and focused in particular ways, can give the whole of human existence an extra dimension.

We may gain some appreciation of this when we consider the vital role which Shabbat has played in sustaining the Jewish faith. When the Ethiopian Jews, *Falashas*, were harassed by nineteenth-century missionaries to name the Saviour of the Jews, they answered: 'The Saviour of the Jews is the Sabbath.' In the twentieth century, the philosopher Ahad Ha-Am said: 'Far more than Israel has kept the Sabbath, it is the Sabbath that has kept Israel.' It is not just that the setting aside of this day has marked Jews as a group, distinguishable from Muslims setting aside Friday or Christians setting aside Sunday. It is that Shabbat combines the three main themes of the Jewish religion: creation, revelation, and redemption, in a way that Jews everywhere can observe in practical terms.

God the Creator

The crucial biblical passage, which gives us the key to Shabbat, comes at the climax of the creation story in Genesis 1:1–2:4. Genesis 2:1–3 reads:

> *Thus the heavens and the earth were finished, and all their multitude. And on the seventh day God finished the work that he had done, and he rested on the seventh day from all the work that he had done. So God blessed the seventh day and hallowed it, because on it God rested from all the work that he had done in creation.*

Shabbat is then the celebration of God's complete and perfect creation. On this day, Jews are to remember particularly that God is creator and they his creatures. The remainder of the week they may share in his creative activity, but, on this day, they must imitate the creator and rest. By so doing, the intention is, they may reflect on their God-given powers and so make the right use of them. As Judah Halevi puts it:

> *The observance of the Sabbath is itself an acknowledge-ment of His omnipotence, and at the same time an acknowledgement of the creation by the divine word.* (*in* Kuzari)

Holy time

The sanctification of Shabbat by God's resting lies behind the command to 'remember the sabbath day' and 'keep it holy' as it comes in Exodus 20:8. Much is made in Jewish writing of the fact that the Bible connects holiness far more with time than with space. The Hebrew for 'holy', *kaddosh*, applies in the first instance to God himself. He is holy in the sense of being mysteriously set apart from the material world and its limitations. Yet God is available to his people by what he sets apart or sanctifies. God is accessible in holy books (e.g. the Talmud), in holy places (e.g. the ark of the covenant), and supremely in his mitzvot (commands). Before performing any mitzvah, the berakhah (blessing) is recited: 'Blessed art thou, O Lord our God, King of the Universe, who hast hallowed us by thy commandments.' But, as the contemporary American religious philosopher, Abraham Heschel, points out, the first holy object in the history of the world was not a mountain or an altar but a time. In his prose-poem, *The Sabbath*, he writes:

> *Judaism teaches us to be attached to holiness in time, to be attached to sacred events, to learn how to consecrate sanctuaries that emerge from the magnificent stream of a year. The Sabbaths are our great cathedrals; and our Holy of Holies is a shrine that neither the Romans nor the Germans were able to burn . . . the Day of Atonement . . . The meaning of the Sabbath is to celebrate time rather than space; Six days a week we live under the tyranny of things of space; on the Sabbath we try to become attuned to holiness in time. It is a day on which we are called upon to share in what is eternal in time, to turn from the results of creation to the mystery of creation; from the world of creation to the creation of the world.*

All the observances and the liturgy of Shabbat are designed to capture this sense of 'holy time', time which is part of present existence and yet is beyond it. Shabbat is the only one of the holy days to be ordained in the Ten Commandments. Two versions of these commandments exist in the Torah. It is from the Exodus version, just quoted, that the Rabbis of the Talmud derive what may be described as the positive ways of keeping Shabbat. The opening word, 'Remember', speaks, they say, to the emotions, and so the Jew must celebrate in positive ways. As Rabbi Judah the Pious (a saintly figure of medieval Germany) writes in his *Book of the Pious*:

> *One should bathe on Sabbath eve and dress in his best clothes and arrange for an oneg shabbat ('joy of the Sabbath') celebration, and read those things which are suitable for the Sabbath day.*

But from the other version of the Ten Commandments the rabbis derive what may be described as the negative side of keeping

Shabbat, chiefly in not working. In Deuteronomy 5:12–15 we find Shabbat again as the fourth commandment but linked not with creation but with redemption. The freedom to rest was given to the Israelites by God's redeeming them from slavery in Egypt. The opening word of this version is 'observe' and from this comes the injunction to protect with great care this holy time, hedging it about with what came to be detailed concrete regulations (e.g. Shavuot 20b).

Thus Shabbat is perceived as God's gift to Israel, a sign of his special covenant with them and of revelation, the means of living with a sense of God as creator. It is described as offering Jews 'a foretaste of the world to come', a way of experiencing the delights of the final redemption, of already living in God's Kingdom. This profusion of themes is expressed in the prayers for Shabbat as recited, for example, over wine, in the additional service, in the afternoon service, and in this extract from the morning liturgy, instituting Shabbat:

> . . . thou didst not bestow it, O Lord our God, unto the other nations of the earth, nor didst thou, O our King, make it the heritage of those who worship idols, nor do the unrighteous dwell in its rest; but unto thy people Israel thou didst give it in love, unto the seed of Jacob whom thou didst choose. The people that sanctify the seventh day, even all of them shall be satiated and delighted with thy goodness, seeing that thou didst find pleasure in the seventh day, and didst hallow it; thou didst call it the most desirable of days, in remembrance of the creation.

Resting from work in the Bible, the Talmud, and Orthodox Judaism

The purpose of Shabbat is clear, but the question arises, as it must have done in ancient times: how is this to be achieved? It is hard to know at what point in Jewish history this day became an important one for worship. What we do know from numerous biblical texts (e.g. Exodus 31:14; Leviticus 16:29, 31; Jeremiah 17:22) is that, from ancient times, the characteristic way of making Shabbat was to refrain from work. (The Hebrew root still carries the sense of stopping work.) The question inevitably follows; what precisely constitutes 'work'? The answers given to this by the Rabbis of the Mishnah and Talmud and the ways in which these answers are interpreted first by Orthodox and then by non-Orthodox Jews have important practical implications.

The Bible gives very few explicit prohibitions about Shabbat. Exodus 16:29 states: 'each of you stay where you are; do not leave your place on the seventh day' whilst Exodus 35:3 states; 'You shall kindle no fire in all your dwellings on the sabbath day.' The previous verse states the death penalty for 'whoever does any work' on Shabbat. It is to the whole of this passage that the Rabbis turned when they came to establish the laws applying to the work restrictions of Shabbat. God, they believed, left it to human beings to complete his creation by building a *mishkan*, a 'sanctuary' or 'tabernacle', and it is this creative activity which is described in Exodus 35.

Building the tabernacle

Mishkan is hard to render in English. It comes from the Hebrew root 'to dwell' and it denotes the transportable tent of meeting, the focus of God's presence dwelling with the Israelites in the wilderness. This became the pattern for the Temple built later in Jerusalem. The second half of the book of Exodus is devoted to a description of the mishkan and a summary of its details is given in Exodus 31:1–11. Significantly, this is followed by one of the major biblical references to Shabbat (verses 12–17). This linkage between the mishkan and Shabbat appears not only here but also in Exodus 35 itself and in Leviticus 19:30 and 26:2 where the command is given: 'You shall keep my sabbaths and reverence my sanctuary.' The Talmud follows this by seeing a connection between God's sanctuary in space and God's sanctuary in time. Creative work (in Hebrew *melakhah*, plural *melakhot*) is defined as anything involved in building the mishkan (Shabbat 49b). The Rabbis arrived at seven basic categories of prohibited work, subdividing them into a total of 39 prohibitions:

1 growing and preparing food (11 prohibitions)
2 making clothing (13 prohibitions)
3 leatherwork and writing (nine prohibitions)
4 providing shelter (two prohibitions)
5 creating and extinguishing fire (two prohibitions)
6 completing work (one prohibition)
7 transporting goods (one prohibition)

Any activity related to these 39 categories of work was also prohibited (Shabbat 7:2).

In trying to understand the variations in modern Jewish observance, we need to go back to the fundamental difference between Orthodoxy and non-Orthodoxy. Indeed, Sabbath-observance gives one of the clearest indicators of where any Jew is on the religious spectrum. Rather than risk infringing the traditional halakhah (legal requirements), an Orthodox Jew avoids any act which might, however remotely, correspond with any of the original prohibited activities.

Eruv

When working out the prohibition about transporting goods from a public to private domain, or vice versa, the Rabbis noted that there could be a third type of domain. This third category which was neither private nor truly public was known as a *karmelit* ('neutral domain') and was invented by the Rabbis chiefly to avoid confusion. People were forbidden to carry in a karmelit unless it was surrounded by a visible, albeit notional, boundary colloquially referred to as an *eruv*. Ironically, this very attempt to avoid confusion has resulted in subsequent confusion and misunderstanding. This is well demonstrated by the division of opinion among Jews in Britain in the 1990s over the establishment of an eruv (literally 'a mixture' – of public and private property) in north-west London.

A public domain may be judged, said the Rabbis, to be an area which is entirely unrestricted, such as the wilderness. An area from which the world can be excluded can be regarded as no longer a public domain. So the city of Jerusalem, between its walls, and Manhattan, between its bridges, can each be regarded as a karmelit. The boundary of each is an eruv. This enables those needing to push (the equivalent of 'carry') prams or wheelchairs to move about on Shabbat whilst observing the regulations. Many members of modern Orthodoxy in Britain, including the former and the present Chief Rabbi, argue that having an eruv in north-west London helps young mothers and people with disabilities. It fulfils the original aim of the Rabbis of making the proper observance of Shabbat more possible. Most of the six-miles square area has natural boundaries of roads and railway lines, but for just over half a mile poles connected by thin wire are required to make clear just where the boundary lies.

There has been much rabbinic debate about what constitutes an eruv. In the Middle Ages, a natural boundary was required, such as that of a medieval city. Today, there are many Orthodox Jews who do not accept that the recently designated area meets the rabbinic requirements. These include the Ultra-Orthodox, and other members of the Orthodox community who feel that, unlike Jerusalem and Manhattan, north-west London does not have a clear boundary as a neutral domain (a karmelit). For one thing, it has major highways going through it making it thoroughly public. Since an eruv can only function in a neutral domain, they will not use this first British eruv. Nor will Sefardi Jews, who follow Maimonides' teaching that an eruv must have real boundaries, such as walls, and not purely notional ones.

All this illustrates something of the difficulty of understanding another faith. From the division of Jewish opinion and from some newspaper reporting, it could be argued that many Jews do not understand the purpose of the eruv. It is not surprising, therefore, that non-Jews are confused on this, as on other rulings which enable observant Jews to walk more than is normally permitted on Shabbat or to cook food on a holiday falling on a Friday for the Sabbath that follows it. From the outside, it is all too easy to conclude that the purpose of these rules is to evade or weaken observance. The crucial point for the Rabbis was, however, to make observance possible in all circumstances and to clarify it so that observance was not accidentally infringed. They made, as the Mishnah puts it, 'a fence around the Torah'.

Rest as a benefit

A major example of how Orthodox Jews attempt to continue this avoidance of the originally prohibited activities on Shabbat is not turning on an electric light. Activating an electric current is held to come under the category of kindling a fire and so is forbidden. Reports in the British Press on 1 September 1994 about a Jewish hotelier who lost his job for switching on the heating in a Jewish hotel on Shabbat further illustrate the difficulty of trying to understand the logic of the Orthodox position from the outside. Indeed, as *The Times* report for that day shows, the tendency is simply to leave the logic unexplored and, therefore, scorned. The opening line: 'A flick of a switch on the Sabbath cost the manager of a Jewish hotel his job' and the closing paragraph seem to invite derision:

> They [Orthodox Jews] do not smoke or drive a car [on Shabbat], for example, as this would constitute kindling a fire; they will read but not write; admire a

flower but not pick it. Traditional households that regard turning on a light as work operate their electrical supply on a time-switch.

It is true that starting a car engine is a long way from kindling a fire for building the tabernacle, but from the Orthodox point of view, the intention is the same. To suggest, as does this newspaper article, that there is something inconsistent about admiring a flower but not picking it, is odd. A park attendant would easily see the difference! It is in their determination to keep the Torah in its entirety that Orthodox Jews refrain from these activities. Those who sacked the hotelier argued that he had a licence to run 'a kosher hotel' where Orthodox guests could be sure that nothing which offended their rules would happen. If either the hotelier or the guests had, as he claimed, 'a more modern way of seeing his religion' then there were plenty of other hotels for them.

The time-switch raises another point about Orthodoxy and that is that maintaining the halakhah is combined with a constructive approach to the application of technological progress. 'The Sabbath is given to you, not you to the Sabbath' appears in a midrashic passage (Exodus Mekhilta 31:14; Yoma 85b). Christians tend to quote Jesus' comment: 'The Sabbath was made for man, not man for the Sabbath' (Mark 2:27) as marking a departure from rabbinic teaching in the first century CE, but indeed it is consonant with it. Other passages in the Gospels which are also often cited as demonstrating the alleged newness and superiority of the Christian religion (and indeed were written with that express purpose) also involve Sabbath-observance. A recurrent charge made against the Pharisees in these stories is that they criticized Jesus because he healed on Shabbat (e.g. Matthew 12:9–14; John 7:19–24). However, healing is not on the list of the 39 prohibited activities nor is it feared that it might infringe the work prohibition. On the contrary, the Rabbis (the successors of Pharisaic Judaism) actually encouraged healing on Shabbat to such an extent that they said that any or all of the 39 activities should be practised if a dangerous complaint required it. Danger to human life thus overrode all the prohibitions, and healing itself, even of complaints that presented no danger to life, was not forbidden. At some points, probably later than Jesus' lifetime, the use of medicines for trivial complaints was forbidden, not because of any prohibition against healing as such, but because it might lead to the actual grinding of medicinal ingredients on Shabbat.

Grinding *is* one of the 11 prohibitions in the first of the seven categories of melakhot. Jesus' healing activity and the arguments he adduces to defend it are very much along Pharisaic lines, so much so that some scholars, for example, Hyam Maccoby, suggest that the Gospel writers have, in some instances, confused the Pharisees with the Sadducees who are known to have applied the laws of Shabbat more harshly than the Pharisees.

From the Orthodox point of view, Shabbat is meant to be not a burden but a delight. To achieve this, anything which might constitute work is to be avoided. What is judged to be work is governed entirely by the list of prohibited activities. Thus an Orthodox Jew could, on Shabbat, carry something heavy in the house or garden, but not do the gardening, nor carry something as light as a handkerchief from home to synagogue, the last prohibition being specifically of carrying anything from a private to a public place or vice versa. There is, however, an additional category of work which relates to the amount of effort involved. Anything which by the effort needed to carry it out may be judged as not in keeping with Shabbat is prohibited.

As already seen in the Talmud, there is one eventuality when all Shabbat regulations must be set aside. Doctors, nurses, and other emergency services must do everything to save life. Other Jews are expected to take such actions as using lifts or driving vehicles if by so doing they can save human life. There is also leniency with rabbinic prohibitions in order to assist animal life.

Redefining 'rest'

Non-Orthodoxy lays no less stress on setting apart Shabbat as a day of refreshment. The substantial departure comes, however, in defining the nature of work. What was work at the time of Exodus 35 or in rabbinic times has clearly changed. Rubbing sticks together to kindle fire is work, but using a switch or a button to activate lighting, heating, cooking appliances, or lifts is no longer work. It does not detract from the relaxation which is the original purpose of the day. It may, in fact, enhance it.

Preserving the spirit of the original command for a day on which Jews rest from normal work lies behind the re-definition of work attempted by the Reform writer Dow Marmur in *Remember the Sabbath Day* (1983). Domestic chores which *feel* like work should, for example, be avoided. Travel, which has the associated tension of crowds and jams, and major cooking tasks are also considered unhelpful, but it is accepted that there will be a variety of decisions as members of Reform communities evaluate how best to promote their personal refreshment. Some activities, such as commercial business, are strongly discouraged, whilst others are judged according to their purpose. Thus, driving to attend the synagogue or to visit relatives is allowed whilst driving to go shopping is not.

Conservative Judaism concentrates attention on the positive practices of observance, such as lighting candles and attending services on Shabbat rather than on the various prohibitions. Trying to revitalize the halakhah in keeping with the demands of the times, it has found it hard to reach agreement on precisely what is permitted. In a split decision, the Law Committee of the Rabbinical Assembly has sanctioned the use of electricity and, more radically, has permitted travel on Shabbat for the specific purpose of attending the synagogue (which is, after all, an obligation for men and women) but only if attendance would otherwise be impossible. There is a clear difference at this point from Orthodoxy in which someone unable to walk to the synagogue is obliged to stay at home.

The Reconstructionist position stresses individual fulfilment, permitting activity 'which the individual is unable to engage in during the week, and which constitutes not a means to making a living but a way of enjoying life' (*The Guide to Jewish Ritual*). Rather than frustrate 'a legitimate and deeply felt ambition' even work connected with one's career may supersede Sabbath observance.

Observing Shabbat in home and synagogue

One of the positive mitzvot of Shabbat is to surround the day with beauty. In order to achieve this, intense preparation is needed as the day approaches. Settling disputes and clearing up bad feeling are part of this. Some very pious people immerse themselves in the mikveh (ritual bath) to help prepare themselves spiritually. Physical preparations include shopping and cleaning, which must be completed so that Shabbat is not interrupted. The meals need to be prepared and the table laid for the Friday evening meal. This is an important family occasion.

Friday evening

Shortly before sunset, two Shabbat candles are lit, usually by the mother of the household, accompanied by daughters and any young children. This act ushers in Shabbat and sometimes those present draw the light from the candles towards their face three (or more up to seven) times as if beckoning it into the home. The mother may shield her eyes as she says the berakhah (blessing):

> *Blessed art Thou, King of the Universe, who hast hallowed us by the commandments, and commanded us to kindle the Sabbath lights.*

Usually a blessing over the performance of a mitzvah is recited *before* the mitzvah is performed, but since this berakhah indicates that Sabbath rest has begun the kindling of flame needs to take place first. By shielding her eyes, she ensures that she does not see the result of the act until after the berakhah.

Meanwhile other members of the family welcome Shabbat in the synagogue. As the evening service begins, Shabbat is ushered in as a queen or a bride. One of the most popular hymns on this theme is *Lekhah Dodi* ('Come, my friend'). The friend is invited to 'Welcome Bride Sabbath.' After the service, and throughout Shabbat, the usual greeting is *Shabbat Shalom* ('a peaceful Sabbath') or the Yiddish *gut Shabbos* ('a good Sabbath'). This greeting is exchanged as those who have been to the synagogue return home. The story is told that on Sabbath eve two angels, one good and one bad, accompany a man home from synagogue. If he finds everything ready for the Sabbath and the right atmosphere, the good angel says: 'May the same happen next week', and the bad angel has to respond: 'Amen' ('so be it'). But if the household is not ready for Shabbat, the bad angel has his say: 'May the same happen next week', and the good angel, against his will, has to respond: 'Amen' (Shabbat 119b). As they gather round the table, the family sometimes sing *Shalom Alekhem* ('Peace be with you'), a greeting to the angels. Often the children are blessed with the priestly blessing from Numbers 6:24–26, the parents concluding with the prayer that God will make the boys like Ephraim and Manasseh (Genesis 48:20) and the girls like Sarah, Rebekah, Rachel, and Leah, taken as good exemplars of their faith. Then the man recites Proverbs 31:10–31 praising the woman of the house as model wife and mother, a 'woman of worth' (*eshet hayil*).

Before the meal, *kiddush* ('sanctifying' or 'hallowing') is recited, as it is at the synagogue at the close of the Sabbath evening service. This sets the time apart as holy. The first part of the kiddush is the reciting of Genesis 2:1–3 which recalls God's resting after creating the world. God is blessed first for wine, then for giving Shabbat to Israel, and finally for the bread. The wine symbolizes the sweetness and joy of the day and the bread is a reminder of the double portion of manna given to the Israelites on Shabbat in the wilderness after the exodus (Exodus 16:4–36). The Sabbath loaves are plaited to symbolize the double portion. The plaited loaves (*hallot*, singular *hallah*; in Yiddish, *halles*) usually have a white cloth over them, taken by some to symbolize the dew which covered the manna. Like the two candles, the two loaves are also a reminder of the two injunctions, to 'remember' and to 'observe' Shabbat. After the blessing, a piece of the bread is dipped in salt and given to everyone present. This often includes guests, especially those without a family of their own. (With increasing numbers of people living away from their families, some synagogues encourage their members to organize communal Sabbath activities, such as the Friday night meal or Saturday lunch. It is certainly very difficult for someone to gain much of a sense of celebrating Shabbat without company.) After the meal a Sabbath grace is recited. All this and the *zemirot* ('table songs') celebrate the Jew's dependence on God for his creation of the good things in life. The song below, quoted here from *Forms of Prayer*, captures the purpose of Shabbat well, with its refrain:

> *This day for Israel is light and is joy,*
> *a Sabbath of rest.*
> *You commanded our fathers who stood at Mount Sinai*
> *to keep Sabbath and seasons for all of our years,*
> *to share at our table the choicest of food,*
> *a Sabbath of rest. Refrain*
> *Treasure for the hearts of a wounded people,*
> *for souls that have suffered, a soul that is new,*
> *to soothe away sighs from a soul that is bound,*
> *a Sabbath of rest. Refrain*
> *You have made this the holy, most blessed of days;*
> *In six days you finished the work of the world,*
> *this day the saddest find safety and peace,*
> *a Sabbath of rest. Refrain*

The order of these Friday evening activities may vary, especially among non-Orthodox communities. There is an emphasis on the home celebrations. This may mean having the meal first or, for some people, saying the service at home, preferably at the same time as the synagogue service starts in order to show identification with the community. In Reform synagogues, this is usually at a set time throughout the year. Some begin at 6.00 pm or 6.30 pm and cater for those who prefer to have an early service and then return home for the kiddush and family meals. Others begin at 8.00 pm or 8.30 pm for those who prefer to attend the service after they have welcomed Shabbat at home and had their meals.

The start of Orthodox services is governed by sunset. The recurrent phrase in the first chapter of Genesis: 'And there was evening and there was morning' is taken in talmudic tradition to mean that night precedes day. For this reason, the day begins, for religious purposes, at nightfall and lasts until the next nightfall. On Shabbat and other festivals, the day begins at sunset as the twilight period is a legally doubtful one and there is an obligation to extend these festive days. Jewish calendars, consequently, give the time of Shabbat as beginning just before sunset and ending when it is fully dark. (In the absence of a calendar, this is when three average-size stars appear in close proximity in the night sky.) In Israel, sunset occurs at a reasonably consistent time throughout the year, between 5.00 pm and 7.00 pm. In Britain, however, sunset can range from 3:30 pm in the winter to 9.00 pm in the summer.

Saturday

The main service of the week is on the Saturday morning. In Orthodox synagogues, this starts with shaharit (morning prayer) and is followed by musaf (additional prayer), the whole service lasting from about 10.00 am till 12 noon. (See Chapters 10–11 for further details of the synagogue service.) In non-Orthodox synagogues, the service is usually shorter. Everywhere, it is very much a family occasion and the chief bond uniting Jews and keeping them part of a worshipping community. After the service, there is kiddush (a slightly different one from that on Friday evening), at the synagogue or at home, preceding a meal – again with the singing of zemirot and the grace after meals.

The afternoon is unstructured, designed for relaxation and visiting. The only games which are forbidden are those which infringe Shabbat regulations. For example, card games, chess, billiards, table-tennis, snooker and ball games at home are allowed, whilst playing for money, writing down the score, and public ball games are not. There is also an afternoon service in the synagogue. The unusual feature of this, unlike the weekday afternoon services, is that the Torah is read. The Kaddish, the Alenu, and the Sabbath Amidah are said at this, as at the other two Sabbath services. The following prayer, recited in the afternoon service, states the ideal of Shabbat:

> . . . *thou hast given unto thy people . . . a rest granted in generous love, a true and faithful rest, a rest in peace and tranquillity, in quietude and safety, a perfect rest wherein thou delightest. Let thy children perceive and know that this their rest is from thee, and by their rest may they hallow thy Name.*

At any time after nightfall comes the evening service followed by the ceremony marking the end of Shabbat. This is conducted in both home and synagogue and, like the welcoming ceremony, it uses wine and light. Showing the distinction between the holy day of Shabbat and weekdays, the ceremony is known as *Havdalah* ('separation' or 'division'). There are berakhot (blessings) over wine and then over sweet-smelling spices. The spices, contained in a box, are passed round. Some take this as a way of sweetening the deeds of the coming week, others as a way of helping the memory of Shabbat to linger. A rabbinic saying suggests that on Shabbat people are given an additional soul, bringing them nearer to God. Perhaps the spices are to refresh the departing soul or to revive the body as it feels weak when the extra soul departs. Shabbat being over, a plaited candle is lit and hands are spread out towards the light as a third blessing is said. This is a reminder that the first thing God created was light to be used to good purpose. With the going out of Shabbat, the 'first day' of creation begins. All the physical senses are used in Havdalah to heighten the sense of the spiritual. In the essential prayer of Havdalah, God is praised for separating secular from sacred; dark from light; pagan nations from Israel; the six days from Shabbat. The candle is extinguished with the wine as one last blessing is said concluding the ceremony. There often follow songs, notably one about Elijah, prophet and herald of the Messiah.

13

the rhythm of the year – festivals and fasts

In this chapter you will learn:

- about the importance of annual commemoration in Judaism
- about the calculation of months and years in the Jewish calendar
- about the minor festivals and the fast of Tishah B'Av.

A sense of time

There is in Judaism a strong sense of the passage of time. We have seen this in the pattern of daily prayer and particularly in the weekly separation of Shabbat (the Sabbath) from the rest of the week. This sense, especially of historical time, is particularly strong in the annual remembrances of Judaism. At specific times each year, historical events are not just commemorated but recreated and so, the aim is, re-lived. Time is *experienced*, in both seasonal and historical terms, so that an awareness of time and of its significance is cultivated. With the exception of the Day of Atonement, all the special days in the Jewish year are designed to call to mind God's activity in nature or history or both.

History

The opening verses of Leviticus 23 tell us about Shabbat. This chapter goes on to institute other 'appointed festivals', presenting, in effect, a summary of the Jewish religious calendar. These festivals are 'holy convocations', that is, gatherings of the people specifically to hear the Torah read. They are *appointed* times or seasons, moments in time when the eternal, spiritual world can be glimpsed. The rituals and prayers associated with each festival, from biblical times until now, are a means to a spiritual experience, ways of appropriating the significance of God's activity in the history of a people and making it your own. Clearly, observing the rituals and saying the prayers do not automatically convey spirituality. It is possible for Jews, as for the adherents of any other religion, to go through the motions. The way in which the Jewish year is punctuated by a number of festivals, however, each contributing particular qualities to the Jewish way of life, has extraordinary potential. Festivals, and especially the meals associated with them, are what non-Jews tend to know about Judaism. They should not be viewed, however, as simply an indulgent string of parties. Rather they give the year a religious rhythm.

The details of behaviour and practice given in the halakhah are designed to amplify the intention of the biblical source. Festivals stemming from post-biblical times similarly celebrate events important in the history of the Jewish people. Though there is variation of local custom and liturgy, all groups jointly recognize the festivals as marking various experiences of the Jewish people and as responding to the emotional needs related to these experiences, thereby offering comfort, inspiration, and a general sense of meaning in Jewish history.

Season

The stress is primarily on the historical event, bringing it to life so that the sense of divine activity in the past is, ideally, experienced afresh in the present. Yet there remains in the Jewish year a sense of the seasonal and agricultural. Just as the year includes the full range of natural possibilities through the sequence of the seasons and the agricultural cycle, so the festivals harness a rich variety of psychological and spiritual qualities. Many scholars stress the agricultural origin of the festivals, believing their historical significance to have been developed later. They point to the similarity between the biblical festivals and those of other countries in the ancient Near East. What soon became vital for the Jewish people was the affirmation of God's work in human history, even if these celebrations of historical events may first have been more general agricultural feasts. Certainly, the ancient seasons, counted according to the phases of the moon yet inevitably determined also by the effects of the sun on the crops, explain the two basic series of celebrations.

The first series falls in the spring and early summer. Preparation for the spring holiday of *Pesah* (Passover) begins on the tenth day of what is sometimes counted as the first month (Nisan) and the festival itself commences on the fifteenth day of the month, the day of the full moon and lasts a week (or eight days). Beginning with the second day of Passover, according to Pharisaic tradition, a period of 49 days is counted out, culminating in the festival of *Shavuot*, ('Weeks' or 'Pentecost') celebrated for one day or two. Balancing these spring holidays is a series of autumnal festivals a half-year later. The first of these is *Rosh Hashanah* ('the New Year') observed for two days, at the beginning of the seventh month (Tishrei). It is followed 10 days later by *Yom Kippur* ('the Day of Atonement'), a one-day fast. On the fifteenth of the month, *Sukkot* ('Tabernacles') is celebrated for a week (or eight days), culminating in the additional one day festival of *Simhat Torah* ('Rejoicing of the Law').

Major and minor

A division which needs to be understood in the Jewish calendar is that between its major and minor focal points. Each major festival is a 'holy day', *yom tov* (literally, a 'good day'). A yom tov is characterized by three things: rejoicing which includes resting from work and ceremonial meals; special prayers and synagogue rituals; ceremonies and customs related to the subject of the festivals. By

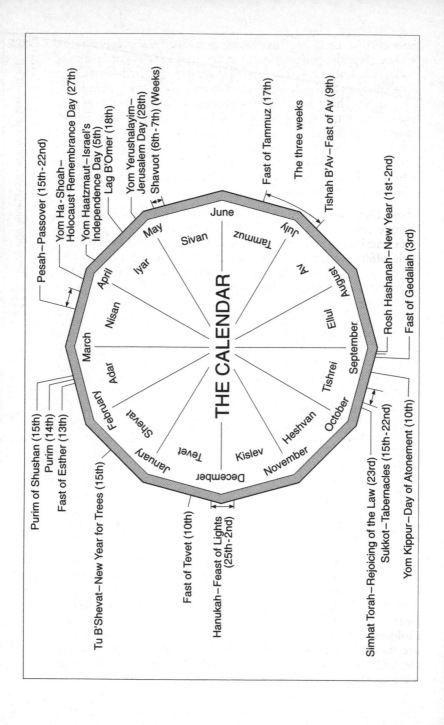

THE CALENDAR

Pesah–Passover (15th–22nd)
Yom Ha-Shoah–Holocaust Remembrance Day (27th)
Yom Haatzmaut–Israel's Independence Day (5th)
Lag B'Omer (18th)
Yom Yerushalayim–Jerusalem Day (28th)
Shavuot (6th–7th) (Weeks)
Fast of Tammuz (17th)
The three weeks
Tishah B'Av–Fast of Av (9th)
Rosh Hashanah–New Year (1st–2nd)
Fast of Gedaliah (3rd)
Yom Kippur–Day of Atonement (10th)
Sukkot–Tabernacles (15th–22nd)
Simhat Torah–Rejoicing of the Law (23rd)
Hanukah–Feast of Lights (25th–2nd)
Fast of Tevet (10th)
Tu B'Shevat–New Year for Trees (15th)
Fast of Esther (13th)
Purim (14th)
Purim of Shushan (15th)

March — Nisan
April — Iyar
May — Sivan
June — Tammuz
July — Av
August — Ellul
September — Tishrei
October — Heshvan
November — Kislev
December — Tevet
January — Shevat
February — Adar

these criteria, there are three major festivals: Pesah, Shavuot, and Sukkot. (Strictly speaking, only the first and last days or Pesah and Sukkot are 'holy days'. The intermediate days are 'half-festivals' on which services are held and when only essential work is permitted.) They depict three stages of the exodus, with the liturgy of each festival speaking of it as 'a memorial of the Exodus from Egypt'. Passover marks the freedom of the exodus itself, Weeks gives freedom its spiritual connotation by marking the giving of the Torah on Mount Sinai, and Tabernacles stresses that true security is found in God's presence by marking the journey through the wilderness to the promised land.

These three are called Pilgrim (or Foot) festivals because, in Temple times, Jews would make a pilgrimage to Jerusalem to offer sacrifices. Since the destruction of the Temple in 70 CE, such offerings are no longer made, but the festivals are still important and involve many celebrations in the home and the synagogue. In Israel, the Pilgrim festivals retain their agricultural connection, falling at the appropriate season of the year: Pesah at the time of the barley harvest; Shavuot at the time of the wheat harvest; and Sukkot at the ingathering of crops. In other countries too, the celebrations of the Pilgrim festivals ingeniously interweave the historical, agricultural, and personal. At Pesah, for example, there are thoughts of the freedom of people from political bondage, the liberation of the earth as it springs to new life, and the yearning of most people to escape the oppressive or even just the mundane in life. Taking a rather different character are the festivals of Rosh Hashanah and Yom Kippur. They are major, in respect of originating in a biblical injunction and having work restrictions, but they are solemn rather than joyous festivals. Together the three days of Rosh Hashanah and Yom Kippur are called the 'High Holy Days' or the 'Days of Awe'. The stress is on the awesome demands of God in each Jew's relationship with him and with other people. Yom Kippur, which is also a major fast, is the most important festival of the year.

All the other festivals and fasts of Judaism are minor, not in the sense of being unimportant, but in that they are not commanded in the Bible and consequently are not subject to the same restrictions as the biblical festivals and fasts. Some of these, viz. Israel's Independence Day, Jerusalem (Reunification) Day, and Holocaust Remembrance Day, are modern observances. Others are ancient, notably the festival of Purim which, though based on the biblical book of Esther, is held to be post-biblical and hence a minor festival.

The lunar calendar

Length of the month

The Gregorian calendar, with 12 months of slightly varying length, is based on the movement of the sun. The Jewish calendar is also solar, in the sense that the agricultural seasons of the year were, and are, determined by the position of the sun. When the ancient Israelites worked out their calendar, however, they based it mainly on the movements of the moon. The moon takes approximately 29.5 days to orbit the earth. As it gets to the end of its orbit, less and less of it is seen, until it disappears altogether and then it reappears. It is the *re*appearance of the moon, the new moon, that marks the new month for Jews. The Hebrew word for 'month' is *hodesh* which means 'that which is renewed'. The moon is what is renewed and with it the month. The Jewish calendar is then essentially lunar.

Length of the year

Clearly a month cannot last 29.5 days, but each pair of months will add up to 59 days, so the months are taken in pairs, the first having 30 days, and the second 29 days and so on. (There are sometimes slight variations in this.) This gives 354 days in an ordinary Jewish year, 11 days fewer than in the solar year. If this were left, the Jewish calendar would fall behind by 11 days each year until the lunar year was months behind and the festivals would eventually fall at the wrong time of the year. Deuteronomy 16:1 says that the Passover celebration of the exodus falls in the month of *Aviv* ('ripening'). This is understood to mean that it must always fall in the spring. To ensure this and the appropriate seasonal timing of Shavuot and Sukkot an intercalation is made, keeping the lunar year in step with the solar year. This is achieved by adding an extra month, a sort of leap month, seven times in a cycle of 19 years. It is the last month of the Jewish year, *Adar*, which is doubled. In the third, sixth, eighth, eleventh, fourteenth, seventeenth, and nineteenth year of every 19-year cycle, there is a 'second Adar', *Adar Sheni*. Jewish festivals and fasts occur at set dates in this calendar. For example, Pesah lasts from 15 to 22 of the month called *Nisan*. The months of the Jewish year are often numbered from Nisan because it occurs in the spring, at a time of new beginnings. Exodus 12:2 gives the occurrence of the exodus as determining this as the first month. (It should be noted, however, that the Jewish New Year festival actually comes in the Autumn.) The dates to which 15–22 Nisan correspond in the non-Jewish calendar will vary slightly from year to year. For instance, in 2007, Pesah falls on 3 April–10 April, whilst in 2000, it fell on 20 April–27 April. The names of the months of the Jewish year are Babylonian and go back to the Jewish captivity in the sixth century BCE.

Numbering the years

So far as the numbering of the years themselves is concerned, there was no uniform method of dating until the Middle Ages. The current practice was then adopted of reckoning from the creation of the world *Anno Mundi* (AM), which medieval Jewish scholars calculated from the biblical account to have occurred in the year 3760 BCE. It is debated in the Talmud whether the creation took place in the first month (Nisan) or the seventh month (Tishrei). For dating purposes the latter view is followed, so the new year, and hence the Jewish New Year festival, falls on the first day of Tishrei. To convert dates from CE to AM, 3760/1 needs to be added to the CE date. Thus 2000 CE becomes the year 5760 from 1 January–29 September; from 30 September (the date of the Jewish New Year in 2000) the Jewish year is then 5761. This method of dating is used in Jewish legal documents, letters, and newspapers, but it has no doctrinal significance. Its use, therefore, does not normally disturb those who prefer to interpret the biblical record differently to allow for a belief in the vast age of the earth implied by science.

The new moon

Even though the new moon is marked in most diaries, few non-Jews pay much attention to it. In ancient Israel, however, the appearance of the new moon was of great importance. People watched out for it in order to know when the next month started and when, therefore, to celebrate their festivals. The new moon would be expected on the twenty-ninth or thirtieth day of the month. On the thirtieth day, the Sanhedrin, the great legislative court in Jerusalem, would assemble and wait for two reliable witnesses to come and testify that they had personally seen the crescent moon in the sky. Satisfied with the report of the witnesses, the Sanhedrin would announce the thirtieth day as the new moon, *Rosh Hodesh* (literally 'the head of the month'). Should weather conditions prevent this testimony to the moon's reappearance, the court in Jerusalem would automatically declare the thirty-first day of the month Rosh Hodesh. The message was spread throughout Israel by lighting beacons and sending messengers.

A problem arose with the reliability of this procedure when Jews settled outside Israel. There would inevitably be a delay before these Diaspora communities, notably in Egypt and Babylon, had it confirmed whether the rabbinical court had announced the day after the twenty-ninth as Rosh Hodesh or had waited for the next day. Jews in these communities, therefore, celebrated the thirtieth as Rosh Hodesh and on those occasions when they were informed of its postponement to the thirty-first they observed this as a second day of Rosh Hodesh. In order to be quite sure that they were observing the festivals on the right date, these Jews automatically observed each festival for an extra day. Pesah became eight days, Shavuot two days, Rosh Hashanah two days and Sukkot eight days. The one exception was Yom Kippur which, because of the hardship of fasting for two days, lasted only one day. Those living in Israel still adhered to the time lengths stipulated in the Bible, except for Rosh Hashanah which was given an extra day as it fell on the first day of the month and so it was difficult to publicize its arrival in time even in Israel.

When the supreme court in Jerusalem no longer existed to announce the new moon, a permanent calendar was worked out. This system, still used today, was permanently established under Hillel II, Patriarch of Palestinian Jewry, about 360 CE. Even after the calendar was fixed, the talmudic sources state that the Jews of the Diaspora were advised to hold fast to the custom of their ancestors and keep the 'two days of the Diaspora' (Betzah 4b). Orthodox Jews outside Israel still follow this practice. They regard it as a means of expressing the special holiness of the land of Israel where they keep to the exact dates laid down in the Bible. Reform Jews, in whatever country, do not observe the extra days (though most observe Rosh Hashanah for two days in order to be in harmony with the practice in modern day Israel), since they believe that knowing the precise occurrence of each festival renders the talmudic advice unnecessary. Some Conservative Jews also argue for the abolition of the second day of the Diaspora because of the anomaly of treating as a holy day a day that is not observed as sacred in Israel.

The new moon today

Numerous biblical passages mention the new moon alongside Shabbat and other festivals (e.g. Numbers 28). In early times, it was clearly treated as a festive day when people did only essential work. Over the centuries, different ideas developed about just what work was allowed on the day. Today the new moon is little different from any other day. It is regarded as a minor festival by Orthodox Jews and its approach is solemnly announced in the synagogue on the previous Shabbat, rather like it was announced in the Sanhedrin. On the day itself, certain features in the service distinguish Rosh Hodesh from the ordinary weekday. Amongst the prayers is one that the new month will be 'unto us for good and for blessing, for joy and gladness, for salvation and consolation, for support and sustenance, for life and peace, for pardon of sin and forgiveness of iniquity.' The account of the ancient sacrifices offered on Rosh Hodesh (Numbers 28:1–15) is read from the Torah. (When the new moon falls on Shabbat, this reading follows the Torah portion for the week.) Also, part of the *Hallel* is recited. *Hallel* is the Hebrew for 'praise' and the word is used to mean Psalms 113–118. These are especially joyful psalms and are, therefore, sung during most festivals. (Only part of the Hallel is read on Rosh Hodesh when labour is permitted and on the last six days of Passover when it is considered unfitting to sing the full praises of God as the Egyptians drowned.)

The festivals of Hanukah and Purim

Though minor festivals (on which there are no work restrictions), Hanukah and Purim hold considerable importance for what they commemorate historically and for the attitudes they celebrate. Both highlight loyalty and courage in the face of persecution, the importance of religious freedom and survival, and the power of right to conquer might. Hanukah especially speaks to those nationalist and secular Jewish circles, in which other religious festivals are minimized, because it expresses a fight for Jewish identity and independence.

Maccabees and the Festival of Dedication

The spirit and purpose of Hanukah are summed up in its name. *Hanukah* is the Hebrew for 'dedication' and the festival commemorates the dedication of the Temple, or rather, the *re*dedication of the Temple after it had been desecrated by opponents of the Jewish faith in the second century BCE. In the fourth century, the powerful Alexander the Great tried to unite his subjects under Greek ways and beliefs. This process of Hellenization brought some benefits to the Jewish people of the time, but it also posed a threat. There was the temptation to abandon Jewish tradition and adopt Greek ways.

After Alexander's death in 323 BCE, his empire was divided among different rulers. The land of the Jews, by now called Judea, became part of the Seleucid (Syrian-Greek) Kingdom. In 175 BCE, Antiochus IV, the ruler of the Seleucid Kingdom, stepped up attempts to force the Greek religion on Jews who had remained faithful to belief in one God. He proclaimed himself a God, taking the title Antiochus Epiphanes ('god manifest'), and urged the Jewish High Priest, (Jason and then Menelaus) who in effect governed Judea, to spread Greek influence among the Jews.

In the following years, Antiochus became fierce in his opposition to the Jewish religion, issuing decrees, for instance, banning circumcision, the study of the Torah, and Sabbath observance. Pagan altars were erected throughout Judea and unclean animals sacrificed on them. Finally, in the month of Kislev (December) 167 BCE, he set an altar to the God Zeus in the Temple court and ordered that pigs be sacrificed. This sparked off a rebellion led by Mattathias, an elderly priest in Modin, a village outside Jerusalem. Mattathias and his five sons launched guerrilla attacks on the Greek units. After Mattathias' death in 166, the loyalist Jews were led by his third son, Judah, nicknamed 'Maccabeus'. The name 'Maccabee' suggests 'hammer' and possibly refers to Judah's heroism against the Greek forces. By December 164, Judah and his men had gained control of Jerusalem. There they restored and rededicated the Temple.

The story of the rededication of the Temple, and of the Maccabean Revolt which led up to it, is told in 1 and 2 Maccabees, the main story coming in 1 Maccabees 1–4. The climax came when, on 25 Kislev 164 BCE, Judah and his men entered the Temple and tore down the altar which had been desecrated exactly three years before. They built a new altar and relit the great menorah (the seven-branched candlestick). After the original purifying and rededication ceremonies, it was agreed that there should be an annual celebration of this event (1 Maccabees 4:59).

The Talmud and the Festival of Lights

Besides being the festival of Dedication, Hanukah is also known as the 'festival of Lights'. This relates to a story in the Talmud (Shabbat 21a) which tells of a miracle in the Temple when Judah and his men rededicated it. When they entered the Temple, they found just one jar of oil that had not been defiled and with this they lit the menorah. This amount of oil would normally last only one day but, the story goes, it miraculously lasted eight days, giving time for fresh, pure oil to be prepared.

The Talmud says that to celebrate this miracle a lamp should be lit on each of the eight days of Hanukah. These eight lights have become the main symbol of the festival. In fact, there are nine lamps or candles as one candle is used to light each of the eight special candles, which must not be used for any practical purpose. The lighting-candle is called the *shamash* ('servant'), and it is placed in the middle of the Hanukah menorah, sometimes called a *hanukiah*. On the first night of Hanukah the first candle (furthest right on the menorah) is lit. On the second night, another candle is added. The servant candle lights the new candle and then the one on its right and so on, until by the last night all the lights are burning. Placing the candles from right to left but lighting them from left to right gives equal importance to both sides of the hanukiah, indicating that God's presence is everywhere. The Talmud instructs that the lights burn outside where people can see them (Shabbat 22a) and so a hanukiah is often to be seen in the windows of Jewish homes at Hanukah.

The candle-lighting takes places when all the family is together. There are special songs, notably *Maoz Tsur* ('O fortress, rock', addressed to God). The song recalls successive deliverances: from Egypt, from the Babylonian exile, from Haman's threat of extermination (see below), and, lastly, from the terror of Antiochus Epiphanes. Its point is the one central to the Haftarah (reading from the Prophets) on Hanukah: 'Not by might, nor by power, but by my spirit, says the LORD of hosts.' (Zechariah 4:6). Presents are also given; foods fried in oil are often eaten, chiefly *latkes* ('potato pancakes'). A traditional children's game is played with a *dreidle* ('spinning-top'). Each of the top's four sides has on it a Hebrew letter. Together the letters stand for the Hebrew phrase: 'A great miracle took place there'. That Hanukah is a festival of light, has special songs, presents, foods, and games, and falls in December (sometimes the 25th Kislev actually coinciding with the 25th December) sometimes leads non-Jews to think of Hanukah as the Jewish Christmas. This is an unhelpful comparison both for Christians and for Jews. The central meaning of Christmas, that God became incarnate in the man Jesus, is vital to Christians and unacceptable to Jews. The central meaning of Hanukah resides in the resistance of Judaism to assimilating ideas and practices from other religions.

Esther and the Festival of 'Lots'

Purim is the other minor festival which remembers a difficult period in Jewish history and urges hope and trust in God. Like Hanukah, this festival is not commanded in the Torah but stems from the decision of the Rabbis to commemorate an historical event. Purim is based on the story vividly told in the book of Esther – a book accepted in the canon of the Bible only after much rabbinical dispute (Megillah 7a). The name of God nowhere appears in the book (a feature which has rendered artists free to illuminate the scroll). Modern scholarship is inclined to regard the book as a fictional short story, perhaps with an historical core, composed in Maccabean times to bolster Jewish patriotism. The first mention of Purim in Jewish literature occurs when 2 Maccabees 15:36 mentions the 'Day of Mordecai', celebrated on the 14 Adar. Some attach greater authenticity to its purported setting in Persian times. Its importance in the Jewish Year is not dependent on such speculations, however. Purim is the most light-hearted of the festivals and it teaches with a refreshing jollity the lesson, repeatedly needed in Jewish history, that oppressors will not have the last word against goodness and truth. In the early days of Liberal Judaism, the movement deleted Purim from the calendar. It was considered inappropriate to encourage Jewish nationalism and to applaud the characters of the book of Esther all of whose motives may be criticized.

The festival derives its name from the word used in the book of Esther for 'lots'. These lots were drawn by the villain of the story, Haman, to decide on what day to slaughter the Jews. This day, 14 Adar, became in the event the day of his own execution. The essence of the story of Esther is that she married the fifth century BCE king of Persia, Ahasuerus (thought to be Xerxes 1), concealing her Jewish identity. Esther's only relative, Mordecai, uncovered a plot to kill the Jews and told Esther. This plot came from Ahasuerus' Prime Minister, Haman, who hated the Jews. Mordecai, who worked for the king, refused because of his Jewish faith to bow down to Haman and Haman, therefore, persuaded the king that his Jewish subjects were not loyal. His plot seriously backfired when Ahasuerus was informed of it by his own wife, Esther. Impressed by his wife's risking her own safety by admitting her Jewishness, he executed not the Jews but Haman himself.

The carnival atmosphere of Purim is captured particularly by the children. They often dress up and enact humorous plays based on the story of Esther. They also boo, stamp, and wave *greggers* (rather like football rattles) every time Haman's name comes up in the reading in the synagogue. Reading the whole of Esther in public is one of the four mitzvot (obligations) of Purim. It is read not from a book but from a scroll. Because the Hebrew for 'scroll' is *megillah*, the book of Esther is often called simply 'the Megillah'. The Megillah is read both in the evening and the following morning. The most famous of the traditional foods associated with Purim are three-cornered pastries made of sweet dough, and filled with a mixture of poppyseeds and honey. Made by all Jewish communities, these cakes are known by a variety of names and are supposed to represent Haman's hat, Haman's ears, or Haman's pockets (in Yiddish *hamantashen*).

Esther 9:22 speaks of the contrast between sorrow and gladness, mourning and holiday. To try to capture this contrast, Jews observe a fast on the day before Purim. They are remembering the fast of Esther before she went to plead with her husband to spare his Jewish subjects (Esther 4:16). The other three mitzvot of Purim itself are: festivity and rejoicing (a festive meal is usually part of the day); gifts to the poor; and gifts to each other. Esther 9:18–19 gives these mitzvot. The passage also explains why Jews in Jerusalem celebrate Purim on the 15 Adar, one day later than Jews everywhere else. The antiquity of ancient Jerusalem's wall from the days of Joshua renders it, according to the Rabbis, 'a walled city', equivalent to the ancient Persian capital of Shushan (or Susa) which won its victory a day later than the Jews of the provinces. The festive day is called *Shushan Purim*. In a leap year, Shushan Purim and Purim are celebrated on the fifteenth and fourteenth of the thirteenth month, Adar Sheni.

Other festivals

There are three other festivals related particularly to the land of Israel but also remembered by Jews elsewhere.

The New Year for Trees

The first of these is ancient and goes back to when the agricultural New Year was considered to begin. In modern life, we speak of the calendar year (beginning in January), the financial year (beginning in April), and the academic year (beginning in September). Ancient Israel also had more than one New Year according to what aspect of its life was being measured. Farmers had an obligation to set aside each year a proportion of their crops for the priests and the poor. There needed to be a date from which these contributions or tithes were counted and this was fixed as 15 Shevat, in Hebrew *Tu B'Shevat*.

The Talmud suggests that the reason for this choice of date was that it marked the end of the rainy season in Israel (Rosh Hashanah 14a). The sap of the trees became active again, bringing new life, and so a new crop of fruit, to the trees. The festival is often called the New Year for Trees and in Israel is marked by tree-planting. Jews living in other parts of the world often contribute money to such tree-planting projects. They also express their ties with Israel by eating fruit particularly associated with Israel, such as pomegranates and olives. It is a tradition to try to eat fifteen kinds of fruit. Nowadays, Tu B'Shevat is a celebration of thanksgiving for the fruit of the ground.

Israel's Independence Day and Jerusalem Day

The modern festivals of *Yom Haatzmaut* (Israel's Independence Day) and *Yom Yerushalayim* (Jerusalem Day) fall on 5 and 28 Iyar respectively. 5 Iyar 5708 (14 May 1948) was when David Ben Gurion declared the creation of a Jewish state to be named 'Israel'. In 1949, the Chief Rabbinate of Israel declared it a public holiday and established special orders of service for evening and morning worship. Some Orthodox Jews do not recognize Yom Haatzmaut as a new festival but many Jews throughout the world do observe it. In Israel, sirens herald a two-minute silence in which those who died in the conflict surrounding the Declaration of Independence are remembered. If the date coincides with Shabbat, Yom Haatzmaut is celebrated on the preceding Thursday. 28 Iyar (7 June) was the third day of the Six Day War in 1967 when the Israeli defence forces captured the portion of Jerusalem which had been in the Arab sector since partition in 1948. In this section of the city was the Western Wall, the only part of the Temple left after 70 CE and the holiest place of Jews. The chief chaplain of the forces blew the ram's horn, whilst the Defence Minister placed within the Wall's crevices a slip of paper on which he had written the prayer: 'Peace be upon Israel'. Now an annual day of celebration, Yom Yerushalayim sees huge crowds gathering at the Western Wall. Many Jews around the world celebrate in the synagogue the reunification of the old and new sections of Jerusalem.

Fasts

An important part of celebrating for Jews is eating. When wanting to do the opposite of celebrating, Jews stop eating and fast. There are five public fast days in Judaism. (There are also fasts which are limited to specific groups or individuals. The day before Pesah is a fast for the first-born, remembering the sparing of the first-born Israelites in Egypt (Exodus 12). Another is that of a bride and groom before their wedding ceremony, expressing the beginning of a new stage in life.) Only one is commanded in the Torah and this is Yom Kippur (see Chapter 15) during which Jews express sorrow for wrongdoing. Jewish tradition has added four fast days, all commemorating sad events in Jewish history. Some judge these to have agricultural roots like the festivals.

Fasting for the loss of the Temple

The most important fast after Yom Kippur falls on *Tishah B'Av* ('9 Av'). On this date in 586 BCE, the Babylonians destroyed the first Temple and, in 70 CE, the Romans destroyed the second Temple. Other tragedies in Jewish history also occurred on Tishah B'Av, notably the fall of Bar Kokhba's fortress in 135 CE, the expulsion of the Jews from Britain in 1290 CE, and the expulsion of the Jews from Spain in 1492 CE. Some synagogues commemorate the Holocaust destruction on Tishah B'Av. Others prefer to set aside a different date for this, 27 Nisan, known as *Yom Ha-Shoah* (see Chapter 16). Like Yom Kippur, Tishah B'Av is a 25-hour fast. (All other fasts are from dawn to dusk.) It is marked by an intense atmosphere of sadness in the synagogue. The curtain is removed from the ark and the covers from the reading desk. Lights are low and the biblical book of Lamentations, lamenting the destruction of Jerusalem, is chanted mournfully. At the morning service, prayers are said quietly without the adornments of tallit and tefillin. Amidst the sadness, there is hope for the future and, in the seven weeks following Tishah B'Av, each Shabbat service includes messages of consolation and promise, beginning with Isaiah 40.

Non-Orthodox Jews do not think it right to emphasize the Temple and to pray for its restoration. They observe Tishah B'Av in recognition of the Jewish suffering involved in the two Temple destructions and other black events in Jewish history, but they do not observe the other fasts lamenting the loss of the Temple. Orthodox Jews, however, believe that the Temple was such a vital sign of God's presence with his people that it must remain a focus of Judaism. Psalm 137:5–6 expresses this:

> *If I forget you, O Jerusalem,*
> *let my right hand wither!*
> *Let my tongue cling to the roof of my mouth,*
> *if I do not remember you,*
> *if I do not set Jerusalem*
> *above my highest joy.*

They, therefore, observe the additional fasts of 10 Tevet, which marks the beginning of the Babylonian siege of Jerusalem, and 17 Tammuz which is the date when the Romans breached the walls of Jerusalem in 70 CE leading to the destruction of the Temple and the related fast of 3 Tishrei, known as the Fast of Gedaliah. After they had destroyed the Temple and deported many Jews in 586 BCE, the Babylonians appointed Gedaliah as governor over the people remaining in Judah. Rivals murdered him, shattering hopes of any continuing Jewish community. For Orthodox Jews, the three weeks following 17 Tammuz are the saddest time of the Jewish year, with mourning customs (for example, not listening to music) intensified as Tishah B'Av approaches. In many communities, there is no eating of meat and no drinking of wine from the 1–9 Av inclusive.

14
the pilgrim festivals

In this chapter you will learn:

- about the origins of the three major festivals of Passover, Weeks, and Tabernacles
- about the importance of reliving the experiences of gaining freedom, receiving the Torah, and depending on God
- about the rich symbolism and ceremonies of these festivals.

Passover – the festival of unleavened bread

Preparations for Passover entail great time and effort. The home is thoroughly spring-cleaned and the essence of this process is the removal of every trace of leaven. This is in response to Exodus 12:7–19 which (in verse 17) calls Passover 'the festival of unleavened bread', *Hag Ha-Matzot*. *Matzah* ('unleavened bread', plural *matzot*) is bread made from flour kept specially dry. It must be baked within 18 minutes of coming into contact with water, ensuring that it does not rise. Bread made of any of the five grains (wheat, rye, oats, spelt, or barley) which has been in contact with water for 18 minutes before baking is *hametz* ('leavened'). Matzah is the only grain product that Jews can eat at Passover. The strict view is that the whole process of making matzah must be constantly supervised from cutting, milling, sifting, transporting, kneading, and baking. All foods prepared with the guarantee that they have no hametz content are labelled 'Kasher for Pesah'.

Removing all hametz from Jewish premises involves varied procedures. Many families have special kitchen utensils, crockery, and cutlery for the festival – used only at Pesah and stored away for the rest of the year. Biblically and in rabbinic tradition, a Jew is commanded not to eat or to possess hametz, so an Orthodox Jew gets rid of it. For someone whose livelihood involves large supplies of hametz, an attempt is made to accommodate the law by selling the hametz to a non-Jew (who is not under the obligation to keep Pesah). He is likely to help by not closing on the purchase and, therefore, returning the hametz after the required period. Alternatively, an Orthodox Jew might lock the hametz away and give the purchaser the key. Reform practice prefers sealing such products in a box and storing it away from domestic use, for example in a garage, cellar, attic, or shed. They stress the point that hametz must not be eaten, whilst the Orthodox follow the injunction of Exodus 12:19 believing that since hametz is not non-kosher during the rest of the year a Jew could easily forget that it is Pesah and eat it. They also regard simply sealing it as still having possession of it. The Orthodox and non-Orthodox practices here illustrate well one of the differences of approach.

A common ritual is for pieces of hametz to be deliberately hidden. On the 14 Nisan a ceremonial search is made, often involving the whole family. Any remaining leaven is then put aside and burned (as a symbol of destroying all that hametz stands for) on the following morning, before Pesah begins in the evening (15 Nisan). The purpose of all this avoidance of leaven is to recreate for the Jew of whatever time and place the physical conditions of the exodus from Egypt. According to Exodus 12:34, unleavened bread was eaten by the Children of Israel just before they escaped from slavery in Egypt, there being no time to wait for the bread to rise. Following the command of Exodus 12:18 to eat unleavened bread, Jews specifically eat matzah during this period, at least on the first day (for Orthodox Jews outside Israel on the first two days) of the festival. It is a way of entering physically into the experience of their ancestors of being enslaved and then free.

The spiritual significance attached to leaven is also obvious. Because it makes bread rise, it has come to symbolize the tendency in human beings to become proud and self-reliant. Not eating hametz and eating matzah is a reminder of the Jew's dependence on God. With the physical spring-cleaning should go a cleaning out of what is unacceptable in their lives. The significance of these rituals usually features in the rabbi's sermon on the Shabbat before Pesah.

Freedom – then and now

The meaning of 'Passover'

Some maintain that the festival of unleavened bread and the festival of Passover were originally two distinct occasions. Unleavened bread was an agricultural festival (revolving round the need of farmers in the ancient Near East to get rid of old bread and leaven from the previous year's crop), whilst Passover was essentially pastoral. They link the name 'Pesah' with the Hebrew verb meaning 'to skip' which might have been used of new-born lambs. Certainly, in the early spring (in Hebrew *Aviv*, which before the Babylonian name was adopted for the month also denoted Nisan) the crop-farmers of ancient Israel would celebrate the barley harvest and the shepherds the lambing season. What is important for the Jewish faith, however, is that these celebrations were, at some point, combined with historical celebrations. The essential springtime occurrence commemorated at Pesah is the exodus from Egypt.

Exodus 12:3–6 tells how on the eventful night every Israelite family was commanded to offer and eat a lamb. The Torah later commanded the Israelites to sacrifice a lamb every year to recall this (Deuteronomy 16:2, 6–7). This was called the 'Paschal' (of the Passover) lamb. (Deuteronomy 16:3 refers to unleavened bread as 'the bread of affliction' remembering the Egyptian oppression.) Whilst God's control of nature is deliberately recalled in this springtime festival, it is the historical event of the first 'Passover' that Pesah celebrates most of all. The focus is on God's control of history, in particular his liberating the Israelites from slavery.

The book of Exodus narrates the story of a series of plagues sent by God on the Egyptians, each intended to persuade the Pharaoh to let the Israelites go. The final deadly plague was the killing of the Egyptian first-born. We read in Exodus 12 of how the Israelites were to mark the doorposts of their houses with blood from the lamb, so that God would know that they were not Egyptians. He would 'pass over' them and not kill their first-born. The story tells that this plague did eventually persuade the Pharaoh to release the Israelites, but that before they had got very far he changed his mind, perhaps regretting the loss of his slave-labour. Exodus 14 gives a dramatic account of how the Israelites got across the Red Sea. (This is the traditional rendering of the Hebrew expression *yam suph* in Exodus 13:18. *Yam suph* refers to the Red Sea in 1 Kings 9:26 and in Exodus 10:19. Some, however, think it connotes the 'sea of reeds' and consequently envisage the Israelites crossing expanses of reed beds somewhere along the line of the modern Suez Canal.) The pursuing Egyptians drowned. The name of the festival as 'Pesah' is then taken to mean 'pass over' and derives from God's passing over the homes of the Israelites.

Thus Pesah is the celebration of freedom. Without the events commemorated by this festival, there would be no Jewish people. In the kiddush on Shabbat and on other festivals, Jews remember the exodus from Egypt. The Ten Commandments open with the statement: 'I am the LORD your God, who brought you out of the land of Egypt, out of the house of slavery' (Exodus 20:2). But it is Pesah which more than anything celebrates the beginnings of the nation.

The *Seder*

The most colourful feature of the festival is the celebratory meal which takes place in the home on the first night. Orthodox Jews outside Israel have another such meal on the second night. To this are invited relatives and other guests, especially people who would otherwise be on their own. (Reform communities, and increasing numbers of Orthodox and Liberal, hold a communal celebration in the synagogue.) Sometimes this celebration is like a family 'get together' with accompanying rituals playing only a small part. Many Jews, however, are committed to recreating the exodus experience for everyone present. To help them do this the meal follows a set 'order', in Hebrew *seder*. The order is the seder *Haggadah* ('order of telling'). What is told is the Exodus story of slavery and freedom, as enjoined by Exodus 13:8: 'You shall tell your child on that day, "It is because of what the LORD did for me when I came out of Egypt." ' The celebration has thus come to be known as the *seder* and it proceeds according to a unique liturgical and educational text known as the *Haggadah*. The *Haggadot* (plural) usually have the Hebrew text accompanied by a translation in the language of those celebrating the seder. They are often beautifully illustrated. They may include stories of more recent Jewish experience, but their basis is the biblical account of the exodus with phrase-by-phrase midrashic commentary. At the heart of this is the account from Deuteronomy 26:5–8 which begins: 'A wandering Aramean was my ancestor . . .' Everyone present is given a copy of the Haggadah and may take it in turn to read from it. The aim is that they celebrate their existence as part of the Jewish people. As the Haggadah puts it: 'In every generation the individual should regard himself as if he personally had come out of Egypt.'

The atmosphere and the effort that goes into the preparation of the seder raise the obvious question: 'Why is this night different from all other nights?' In the course of the evening, this question is asked and answered in typical Jewish educational fashion – not only with words but also with things to see and taste. One such symbol is a cushion placed beside the person leading the seder. This symbolizes the comfort of being free to eat in a relaxed position, as in ancient times free people would recline to eat.

With the children lies the future of the Jewish people and it is appropriate that it is the youngest child present who asks why this night is special. The general question leads into four specific questions about the evening's rituals:

Why on this night do we eat unleavened bread?
Why on this night do we eat bitter herbs?
Why on this night do we dip our herbs?
Why on this night do we recline?

The leader of the celebration, usually the father, gives the answers to these questions as he points to the various symbols. On the seder table will be three matzot (pieces of unleavened bread). Tradition has read different connotations into this, but one matzah is broken to symbolize 'the bread of affliction' (since this is how a poor man eats his bread). Part of this is put away – often hidden for the children to find later. The fun of this may help them to stay awake on what is a very long night. This matzah is called the *Afikomen*, which is probably a Greek word meaning 'dessert', the last taste of the meal. It is fitting that this should be matzah, as unleavened bread is the central symbol of Pesah.

Further symbols are designed to recreate the experience. The most usual green herb is parsley or long lettuce, whose bitter-sweet taste recalls both slavery and freedom together. Horse-radish is often one of the bitter herbs, its particularly bitter taste providing a powerful reminder of the misery of slavery. The green herbs are dipped in salt water, a symbol of both the tears of the slaves before they were freed and the sea they crossed to freedom. Another symbol combining both slavery and freedom is the *haroset*. This mixture of fruit, nuts, spices, and wine is seen to resemble the mortar with which the slaves had to make bricks. When eaten, haroset gives the sweet taste of freedom. The bitter herbs are dipped in it.

These items of food are usually placed on a special seder dish. With them are two more symbolic items but they are not eaten. One is an egg, hard-boiled then roasted. This is a reminder of the sacrifices offered in the Temple. Another reminder of sacrifice is a lamb bone. This stands for the Paschal lamb, the lamb slaughtered at Pesah. (Step 10 of the 15 steps of the seder is to eat a sandwich made of two pieces of matzah filled with bitter herbs. This is a reminder of Rabbi Hillel, who is said to have eaten matzah and bitter herbs at the same time. Some include haroset in the sandwich.)

The symbolism extends into the four cups of red wine which everyone has to drink during the course of the meal. The red wine perhaps symbolizes the lamb's blood used to mark the Israelites' houses at the first Passover or perhaps simply the value of freedom. The Talmud says that the four cups stand for the four promises of Exodus 6:6–7. Here four different verbs are used as God promises Moses that he will rescue his people. He will 'bring out, deliver, redeem, take'. All the emphasis in the Haggadah is on God's activity. Moses is mentioned only once and that in passing. A fifth promise is given in Exodus 6:8 and this is symbolized by another cup. In talmudic times, people disagreed about whether a fifth cup of wine should be drunk. A compromise was reached by pouring out a fifth cup but not drinking it. When the Rabbis had a question that could not be resolved, they would leave it to be answered by the Prophet Elijah when he returned. Elijah is expected to herald the Messianic Age when all disputes will be resolved and true freedom and peace will reign. So this cup, standing on the table in Elijah's name, came to be Elijah's cup. There also arose the custom of opening the door to encourage Elijah's arrival.

The wine is also used to make a further point during the seder. When each of the ten plagues is mentioned, each person spills a drop of wine to express sorrow at the suffering of the Egyptians. The celebration is of the Israelites' deliverance, not other people's suffering. Remembering that there are countries where Jews still experience oppression, the seder ends with the words:

> The redemption is not yet complete . . .
> Peace, shalom . . .
> Next year in Jerusalem,
> Next year may all be free.

The whole event blends seriousness with jollity, as seen particularly in the lively songs which round off the evening. These include the very popular *Had Gadya* ('One Little Goat') which allegorizes Jewish history in terms both of recurrent persecution and God's final purposes.

Counting the days

The *omer*

On the second day of Pesah, Jews begin counting the days to the next festival, Shavuot. Whilst Pesah gave them their physical freedom, it was at Shavuot that they gained their spiritual freedom by being given God's Law, the Torah. This counting from Pesah to Shavuot is called 'counting the Omer', though it is actually counting *from* the Omer. An *omer* was a measurement of barley. The Torah commands that 'from the day after the sabbath' (taken by the Pharisees to mean the second day of Pesah) when a sheaf of barley is brought to the Temple in Jerusalem 50 days be counted and then the first fruits of the wheat harvest are offered (Leviticus 23:15–16). The wheat harvest thus begins seven weeks after the barley harvest and thus takes the name 'Shavuot' (Weeks). Whilst counting the weeks gives the festival one name, counting the days gives another, 'Pentecost', the Greek word for '50'. Nowadays Shavuot falls on a fixed date, 6 Sivan and, outside Israel, also 7 Sivan, but the days of the Omer period are still counted to capture the sense of looking forward to receiving the Torah.

Since this period is one of anticipation, it may seem odd that the first 32 days of it are regarded as a sad period by Orthodox Jews. This includes some features linked with mourning the dead, such as not cutting the hair or celebrating weddings. The origins of this mourning are obscure, but one explanation is that many of the disciples of Rabbi Akiva, in the second century CE, died from a plague during the Omer period. On the thirty-third day, apparently, the epidemic ended. Also on this date there was a victory in the Bar Kokhba Revolt. The fast, which had marked the sadness of the plague and the Bar Kokhba Revolt, was lifted. This date, *Lag B'Omer* ('the thirty-third of the Omer') has, therefore, become a minor festival. Mourning turns then to celebration and there is often a surge of hair-cuts and weddings on this day. For mystics, the date is significant as the anniversary of the death of the great mystic, Shimon bar Yohai, a disciple of Akiva and alleged author of the medieval mystical work, the Zohar. The celebration is, therefore, one of his soul's being united with its mystic source on high. The sombreness of the Omer or *sefirah* ('counting') season is also interrupted in modern times by Israel's Independence Day festival (5 Iyar), and Jerusalem Day (28 Iyar). Non-Orthodox Jews generally do not believe in following the mourning restrictions of the period.

Combining the wheat harvest with the giving of the Torah

The Bible does not say when Moses was given the Torah on Sinai. On the basis of Exodus 19, however, it has been calculated to have been the third month, that is, Sivan. Since the sixth day of Sivan is Shavuot, the two events, the beginning of the wheat festival and the revelation on Sinai, became one festival. The historical explanation seems to have been added to the natural ones derived from the land and its life. Even now, when its chief significance for Jews is theological, Shavuot (like Pesah) still includes echoes of a harvest festival. There are no special rituals (like eating unleavened bread at Pesah) but customs which developed over the centuries. One of them is to decorate the synagogue with flowers and plants, representing the flowering of Mount Sinai when the Torah was given.

Another custom is to eat dairy dishes, especially cheesecake. Various explanations have been offered for this. One is that, until the laws about meat were given, Jews could be confident only of milk dishes. Another is that eating milk products is a reminder that God brought them out of Egypt into 'a land flowing with milk and honey' (Deuteronomy 26:9). Deuteronomy 26 stresses gratitude for the land and its produce. The Israelites are to remember their humble and harsh beginnings (verse 5) and offer God the first fruits (that is, the best) of the harvest (verses 1–3, 10). 'The festival of First Fruits' is, in fact, another name for Shavuot. The thought remains that, though there is no longer a Temple in which to offer first fruits, the harvest should not be taken for granted.

Freedom to obey – Shavuot

The Rabbis refer to Shavuot as 'the concluding festival' to Pesah. This expresses the thought that the deliverance from slavery remembered at Pesah was not an end in itself. God says to Moses when assuring him that he is sending him to deliver his people: '. . . when you have brought the people out of Egypt, you shall worship God on this mountain' (Exodus 3:12). What the people are being given is not freedom to do nothing, but freedom to serve God. According to Maimonides, liberty without law is a doubtful blessing. This link between freedom from slavery and freedom for service is expressed at many points during Shavuot. First, many people stay up throughout the night, studying the Torah. (Many Reform synagogues now follow this tradition and organize study groups culminating in breakfast and a dawn morning service.) They may study one particular topic or read from an anthology of written and oral law specially compiled for 'the night of Shavuot'. On the second night, the book of Psalms is often read.

Secondly, the readings in the synagogue focus particularly on God's revelation. Central to the service on the first day of Shavuot is the solemn reading of the Ten Commandments from Exodus 20:1–17. On the second day, the Torah passage is Deuteronomy 15:19–16:16 which commands all three Pilgrim festivals. The passages from the Prophets and the Writings also express the need for obedience to God's commands, notably the book of Ruth. This Moabite woman is taken as the paradigm of a whole-hearted convert to Judaism as she joins the covenant people by accepting God and the Torah (Ruth 1:16). Confirmation ceremonies often take place in Reform and Conservative synagogues at Shavuot as an appropriate time for those who have been studying in a post-bar/bat mitzvah class to demonstrate a commitment to Judaism. This helps reinforce the significance of this festival which, perhaps because it lacks ritual and a home-base, does not have the popularity of the other two Pilgrim festivals.

Where true security lies – Sukkot

The last of the Pilgrim festivals is a deliberate reminder of the Jewish people's dependence on God. 'Sukkot' means 'huts', 'booths', or 'tabernacles' and the festival takes its name from the period when the ancient Israelites had no permanent homes but only temporary shelters. This was during their long journey through the desert after the exodus from Egypt to the land of Canaan. Like Pesah, this festival attempts to recreate the conditions of the past in order for the events to become present experience. In Leviticus 23:42, Jews are commanded to 'live in booths for seven days' and so the festival of Sukkot is observed as a re-enactment of this original dependence on God. The psalmist speaks of God hiding him 'in his *sukkah* in the day of trouble, . . . under the cover of his tent' (Psalm 27:5). Thus the sukkah becomes a symbol of reliance on God for protection and strength when all other security is gone. So the central feature of this festival is the building of a sukkah.

A sukkah must have certain characteristics. It must have at least three walls – the fourth side may be left open – made of material that can withstand the wind. Often the wall of the house or garage forms one wall and the others are of a temporary nature. It must have a particular kind of roof with features deliberately designed to encourage Jews to reflect on God as creator in contrast to the solidity of a permanent house in which people are more naturally inclined to put their trust. The roof must be made of plants which cannot be used for food. These plants must be in their natural state (boards of wood cannot be used) and detached from the ground (the branches of a growing tree cannot be used). It must be possible to see the sky through it and it must not be so dense that a heavy rain cannot come through. It must not have an additional covering, for example, an overhanging balcony.

Synagogues often have a room with a sliding roof which can be drawn back. In place of the roof is positioned a covering, made according to the requirements for the roof of a sukkah. This room then becomes a sukkah. The Rabbis speak of adorning the mitzvot. So the sukkah, whether in a private garden or synagogue, is made as attractive as possible especially with hanging fruit.

Since Sukkot, like the other two Pilgrim festivals, is also a harvest festival (Leviticus 23:39 refers to the gathering in of 'the produce of the land' at this time), the sukkot could well represent the shelters of the farmers bringing in the harvest, who lived on the job. Certainly God's provision of the harvest is still recalled at Sukkot. It is the final harvest of the year and takes place from 15–22 Tishrei, in the autumn. Like Pesah, the first and the last days of the festival are holy days, on which all work except the preparation of food is prohibited. (Conservative and Reform operate the same guidelines as to what should and should not be done at the festivals as those suggested for Shabbat.) There is some variation in practice as to how much time needs to be spent in the sukkah to fulfil the precepts of the Torah. In Israel, many Jews sleep in the sukkah for the seven days. However, in countries like Britain and America where the climate in late September or early October can be quite cold, most Jews simply eat in it. Even this mitzvah does not apply to someone who is ill or if it is raining. The Talmud is critical of someone who tries to prove his piety by staying in the sukkah at times not required by the Torah. Nonetheless, some effort has to be made. This is why the festival is celebrated not in the spring, when the exodus occurred, but in the autumn, when sitting in a sukkah is more likely to entail some discomfort through cold. Hospitality is an essential aspect of the sukkah and people often visit friends to share refreshments.

The four plants

The second most distinctive ritual of Sukkot is holding in the hand four plants. The mitzvah for this, as for the sukkah, comes in Leviticus 23. In verse 40, we read:

*On the first day you shall take the fruit of majestic
trees, branches of palm trees, boughs of leafy trees,
and willows of the brook; and you shall rejoice before
the LORD your God for seven days.*

Since this festival concludes the harvest in Israel, these plants are
symbols of God's provision. The meaning of the Hebrew
rendered 'fruit of majestic trees' is uncertain but it is taken to
connote the *etrog*, a citrus fruit which looks rather like a lemon
but tastes and smells quite different. The 'branches of palm trees'
are called the *lulav* and the 'boughs of leafy trees' are represented
by myrtle. These, together with willows, constitute the 'four
species', the *arba minim*. Why these four particular plants were
originally chosen is not altogether clear, but they are understood
by the Rabbis to be the biblical requirement.

Many Jews think that there is symbolism attached to the arba
minim, though, as often with such matters, they are not agreed on
what it is. One midrash links each species with a different part of
the body, taking the etrog as the heart, the lulav as the backbone,
the myrtle as the eye, and the willow as the mouth. Another
interprets the four plants as indicating different types of character,
taking taste as standing for the Torah and scent as standing for good
works. On this interpretation, the etrog, having both taste and
scent, represents someone who knows the Torah and practises it;
the fruit of the lulav, having taste but no scent, represents someone
learned in the Torah but who does not do good deeds; the myrtle,
having scent but no taste, represents someone who does good deeds
but does not know the Torah; and the willow, having neither scent
nor taste, represents someone who is both ignorant and selfish.
This, the most popular of the many interpretations, suggests that no
one must be left out of the Jewish community. Each person, with his
or her strengths and weaknesses, combines with others to constitute
God's people. In terms of humanity at large, this reflects a generous
yet realistic view of human nature. The arba minim symbolize that
it takes all sorts to make a world. On each day of the festival, the
four plants feature during morning prayers in the synagogue (except
on Shabbat in Orthodox communities owing to the restriction on
carrying in a public domain). The etrog is held in the left hand,
whilst in the other are three myrtle twigs and two willows tied to the
lulav. A blessing is recited for the command to take the lulav (as the
largest, representing the whole group). Many communities not only
hold but also wave the lulav as they recite the Hallel (festive psalms).
This waving is done in all directions, probably symbolizing that
God is everywhere.

The obligation to rejoice

Sukkot is called 'the season of our rejoicing' in response to the command in Leviticus 23:40. The emphasis on rejoicing is seen in Judaism at many points, for instance, in rites of passage and on Shabbat. It is particularly strong at Sukkot and on the days which conclude the festive season begun, three weeks before, with the New Year. In ancient times there was, during Sukkot, a festive procession to and from the spring which supplied the water for the Temple. Water was poured on the altar as a great offering of thanks for the rainy season about to begin. In celebration of water vital for any future harvest, there would be dancing to flutes, harps, and cymbals. The exuberance of the water-offering is reflected in the Mishnah's comment: 'He who has not witnessed the joy of the water-drawing has never in his life experienced real joy' (Sukkah 5:1). There is still today a meal in the evening celebrating the water-drawing. On the seventh day of Sukkot, there is a procession with the Torah scrolls and the lulav and etrog round the bimah in the synagogue seven times. Prayers are recited with the refrain *Hoshanah* ('Save us'). This day now has the name *Hoshanah Rabbah* ('the Great Hosannah'). After the final circuit, the willows are beaten against the floor or chairs until the leaves fall off, suggesting the shedding of sins. The penitential mood of the High Holy Days thus resurfaces, as seen in a number of features such as the wearing of the white kittel (shroud). The plea is thus for God's saving.

Simhat Torah

The same sense pervades the eighth day of the festival commanded in Leviticus 23:39 and Numbers 29:35 as a day of complete rest. This is, in effect, a separate festival and so, like all festivals, it begins with the kiddush and ends with the concluding Havdalah. It is called *Shemini Atzeret* ('the eighth day of assembly'). A central feature of the musaf (additional service) on Shemini Atzeret is the prayer for rain. Orthodox Jews outside Israel observe Shemini Atzeret for two days. The second of these two days came, sometime after the eleventh century CE, to be known as *Simhat Torah* ('the Rejoicing of the Law'). In Israel, Shemini Atzeret and Simhat Torah are celebrated on the same day. Reform Jews, also keeping Shemini Atzeret for only one day, celebrate Simhat Torah on the same day. This is the only occasion when Reform celebrates a festival on a different day from that kept in Orthodox synagogues in the Diaspora.

Simhat Torah can only be described as an explosion of joy. Whilst the festival of Shavuot commemorates the giving of the Torah and the whole festival of Sukkot is characterized by rejoicing, it is this day which above all expresses the joy of the Jewish religion. The synagogue becomes a place of great exuberance. All the Torah scrolls are taken out of the ark and carried round the bimah seven times (taken to represent the march round Jericho described in Joshua 6), with everyone singing, dancing (sometimes out into the streets), and clapping as they process. Many people are called up to read from the Torah. The greatest honour goes to the one who reads the final portion of Deuteronomy and to the one who then reads the first portion of Genesis. They are called 'bridegrooms' and they represent the community joined to the Torah as a bridegroom to a bride. There is sometimes a tallit (prayer shawl) over the heads of the readers like the hupah at a wedding.

The description of the scene which is best known to non-Jews comes from the seventeenth-century diarist, Samuel Pepys. Following his visit to a Sefardi synagogue in London 1663, he writes:

> *But Lord, to see the disorder, laughing, sporting, and no attention, but confusion in all their service, more like brutes than people knowing the true God, would make a man forswear ever seeing them more; and indeed, I never did see so much, or could have imagined there had been any religion in the whole world so absurdly performed as this.*

There may well have been services at Simhat Torah where riotous behaviour has been granted too much licence, but Pepys' description assumes a western, aesthetic point of view. We have a different viewpoint in Chaim Potok's account of Simhat Torah, in his novel, *In the Beginning*. A vivid paragraph concludes:

> *The noise inside the synagogue poured out into the night, an undulating, swelling and receding and thinning and growing sound. The joy of dancing with the Torah, holding it close to you, the words of God to Moses at Sinai. I wondered if gentiles ever danced with their Bible.*

Simhat Torah is a post-talmudic festival. It is based on a story about King Solomon celebrating when he finished reading the Torah. So the final portion of the Torah, Deuteronomy 33:1–34:12

is read and, so that the cycle is not broken, the first portion of the Torah, Genesis 1:1–2:3, follows. The festival is an expression not of logic but of jubilation at God's having given the Jewish people his Torah by which to live. Whether the festivities are fitting depends, as a rabbi once said in his Simhat Torah sermon, not just on whether we 'rejoice with the Torah' but on whether we 'conduct ourselves so that the Torah rejoices with us'.

15

the New Year and the Day of Atonement

In this chapter you will learn:

- how the New Year and the Day of Atonement came to be the most important days in the Jewish calendar
- about the music and words used to express a sense of repentance and a new start
- about the origins and purpose of fasting on the Day of Atonement.

The importance of The High Holy Days

Jews regard the first day of the month of Tishrei as beginning a new calendar year. Leviticus 23:24 says that 'a day of complete rest, a holy convocation commemorated with trumpet blasts' is to be observed on 'the seventh month, on the first day of the month' (compare Numbers 29:1). Counting Nisan (the time of the exodus) as the first month, this brings us to 1 Tishrei. It is only in post-biblical Jewish literature that this day is designated *Rosh Hashanah* ('the New Year', literally 'the Head of the Year'). In the Mishnah we find this day marking the beginning of a penitential season (Rosh Hashanah 16b). It is celebrated as the birthday of the world and, in particular, of the human race. Attention is, therefore, focused on God as creator, to whom people are answerable for how they live. Final judgement for the year will be passed on the tenth and last day of this season of penitence, giving people time to reflect and repent. So the recurrent phrase in the liturgy of this season is: *'Remember us unto life, for You, O King, delight in life; inscribe us in the Book of Life, for Your sake, O God of life'* and the greeting exchanged among Jews at this season is: 'May you be inscribed and sealed for a good year.'

Everything about this period is designed to help the individual members of the Jewish community to appreciate their significance in a sort of cosmic drama and to encourage the strenuous effort required if they are to recognize all that is wrong in their relationships with God and with other people, and to make amends. It is, then, a time when serious new year resolutions are built into the liturgy and customs of the calendar. The ten days of penitence culminate in *Yom Kippur* (the 'Day of Atonement'), the holiest day of the Jewish year. Rosh Hashanah, observed in Israel as well as in the Diaspora for two days, and Yom Kippur constitute the 'High Holy Days'. Stressing the need for reverence of God, they are also referred to as *Yamim Noraim* (the 'Days of Awe').

Getting to the heart of the 'matter'

It could well be argued that to understand the High Holy Days is to understand Judaism. Repentance and atonement stand at the height of Jewish spiritual life. Many would say, though perhaps using different terminology, that they lie at the heart of human life in general. Certainly, the need to face up to mistakes, to let go of resentments, to feel that others have let go of resentments towards you, and to feel the genuine chance of a fresh start are vital parts of much experience. From the Jewish point of view, the designer of the whole enterprise is the one to whom to turn for such renewal.

There are, however, two difficulties in trying to understand these days from the outside. First, it may be asked: 'Whose High Holy Days are we looking at?' For there is great variety of concept and observance. Some would lay the greater stress on obligation whilst others would lay it on emotion, as illustrated by the story about a Hasid who was the only one in the synagogue able to blow the ram's horn. When he stood up to blow, he was so moved that he burst into tears. A Lithuanian rabbi said to the Hasid: 'We are commanded to blow, so blow.' What of the many Jews not affiliated to any synagogue and yet who make a special effort to be present at this period especially on Yom Kippur? And what does the liturgy of this period, with its affirmation that God organizes and judges his world, mean to Jews after the Holocaust? Secondly, it may be asked whether it is actually possible to plumb someone else's faith. This series, *Teach Yourself World Faiths*, rests on the assumption that it is possible at least to get some inkling of it. The best way of getting close to the experience of the High Holy Days is through their liturgy.

Creating the atmosphere

The sound of the *Shofar*

Both words and the music of the services create the mood. The highlight of Rosh Hashanah and the characteristic sound of the whole period is the *shofar* ('ram's horn'). For an entire month before Rosh Hashanah, the shofar is sounded every morning except Shabbat. The purpose of this is to convey a sense of what is coming and a sense of something changing in the month of Ellul, leading up to the New Year. Some associate the shofar with the story of the binding of Isaac in which a ram is caught in a thicket by its horns (Genesis 22:13). The story of Abraham's readiness to sacrifice is read on the second day of the festival. But no such association is needed for the sound to have its plaintive, pleading, and challenging effect. Maimonides stresses the capacity of the sound to rouse the spiritually inert.

Many imaginative explanations have been offered, encouraged perhaps by the three different kinds of note sounded. Since the third century, these notes have been combined to form a well-defined series. The first, *tekiah*, is a long, drawn-out, uninterrupted blast, representing a call for attention and a march in a new direction. The final tekiah is particularly long. The second, *shevarim*, consists of three broken sounds, and the third, *teruah*, has nine staccato sounds. Both shevarim and teruah are taken to represent the weeping of the penitent. Repentance is the overall aim and the overall sound matches the aim. The following prayer from the Rosh Hashanah Musaf (additional service) captures the sense of awe:

> *The great shofar is sounded; a gentle whisper is heard; the angels, quaking with fear, declare: 'The day of judgement is here to bring the hosts of heaven to justice!' Indeed, even they are not guiltless in thy sight. All mankind passes before thee like a flock of sheep. As a shepherd seeks out his flock, making his sheep pass under his rod, so dost thou make all the living souls pass before thee; thou dost count and number thy creatures, fixing their lifetime and inscribing their destiny.*

Interspersed with the blowing of the shofar at the Rosh Hashanah service are scriptural verses celebrating God's kingship and judgement with the sound of the shofar. These include Exodus 19:16, where God reveals himself and initiates the covenant at Sinai, Isaiah 27:13, where God will gather people from other lands to worship him in Jerusalem, and Psalm 81:4–5, where the shofar proclaims the new moon. The Saadiah Gaon offers as one of ten reasons for the blowing of the shofar the use of trumpets at a king's coronation. So, at the beginning of the year God is crowned as King. Certainly, the theme of kingship is vital to Rosh Hashanah. As creator, God is not to be thought of as simply having set the world going but also as the one who constantly calls human beings to obey his rule.

Prayers of penitence

Throughout Ellul, *selihot* ('penitential prayers') are said early in the morning. The aim is to summon up the concentration and spiritual energy demanded by the High Holy Days. The selihot cultivate self-examination and anticipation. The Reform Mahzor (prayer book for festivals) incorporates short readings and meditations for the whole period. A prayer of confession from a selihot service includes the words:

For not listening to Your voice within us
For denying the needs of our soul
For making this world a god
Forgive us, pardon us and grant us atonement . . .
For hoarding grudges and insults
For refusing to let go
For abandoning hope
Forgive us, pardon us and grant us atonement.

There is a certain ambiguity about the mood of Rosh Hashanah, stemming from the emphasis on God's kingship, which includes both judgement and compassion. We can see this in the following meditation where the opening mood of awe and unworthiness changes to a sense of divine love and joy:

Poor in worthy deeds, I am horribly frightened in thy presence, who art enthroned and receiving praise from Israel . . . May our defaults be pardoned by thy love, since love draws a veil over all wrongdoing. Turn thou all afflictions into joy and gladness, life and peace, for us and for all Israel.

Yet this combination of the misery of estrangement and the joy of returning is crucial to the whole period. It is strikingly expressed in the way in which some communities sing, on Yom Kippur, a long communal confession of awful sins. A further tale sheds light on this. Hearing about a certain rabbi following this practice, the Baal Shem Tov:

sent after the rabbi and asked him, 'Why do you sing the confessions joyfully?' Said the rabbi to him, 'Lo, a servant who is cleaning the courtyard of the king, if he loves the king, is very happy cleaning the refuse from the courtyard, and sings joyful melodies, for he is giving pleasure to the king.'

So on Rosh Hashanah too there is a great sense of festivity combined with an emphasis on the awe-inspiring day of judgement to come. It is not always easy to keep the balance, but it is important for the significance of the whole period where the key thoughts are human sin and divine grace in equal measure.

God the King

The liturgy of Rosh Hashanah itself focuses less on human beings as sinners and more on God as king. Sin is scarcely mentioned, in fact. There is in the Musaf, a series of benedictions known as 'kingships'. In the Reform Mahzor, these open as follows:

> Let us think of the forces which rule our lives, the currents of instinct and longing which rise from the depths of our being, the tides of ambition and desire which sweep away our will, the little waves of habit and routine in which our vision drowns – yet the Lord is greater than these, and His still small voice louder than their roaring. On the New Year we acknowledge Him as king; may He reign over us and within us.

The image of an old man on the throne can create difficulties, but the language was designed to restore a sense of God in the world, the sense of the spiritual which is a prerequisite for atonement. One might expect the train of thought to be in the opposite direction and the liturgy to start with cleaning out the sins and then to focus on the spiritual. Maimonides, for one, however, saw the danger of this. It could end in total self-preoccupation, as if God were somehow incidental to the process.

Returning

The concept which provides the vital link is repentance. The Hebrew for this, *teshuvah*, means literally 'returning'. This returning to God can be in a very simple sense or it can involve profound inner development. An important expression of this in the liturgy comes in Psalm 51. Verse 10 reads:

> Create in me a clean heart, O God
> and put a new and right spirit within me.

Between Rosh Hashanah and Yom Kippur fall the penitential days of the Fast of Gedaliah and *Shabbat Shuvah*, (the 'Sabbath of Returning'). On Shabbat Shuvah, the reading from the Prophets is Hosea 14 which appeals for Israel's return to God and promises attendant forgiveness and prosperity.

There is in Judaism a tremendously profound sense of sin and yet it is always emphasized that sin is transient, for we have the choice and the capacity to turn back to God and achieve spiritual purity. The thought in Judaism is not of some innate tendency always to do wrong (unlike the concept of 'original sin' in Christianity), but of a constant struggle between good and bad inclinations. As Maimonides emphasizes: 'Free will is bestowed on every human being. If one desires to turn toward the good way and be righteous, he has the power to do so.'

True repentance

In his *Laws of Penitence*, Maimonides is optimistic about change, but the change must be in attitudes, qualities and actions. Teshuvah is thus the focal-point of this ten-day period, in the sense not simply of feeling sorry for certain wrongs done but also of a spiritual transformation, a recentring of life in God and his ethical demands. God's gracious forgiveness is contingent upon sincere personal contrition and deep resolve on the part of the penitent. Only then can God keep the promise of Isaiah 1:18: '. . . though your sins are like scarlet, they shall be like snow; though they are red like crimson, they shall become like wool.' Not forgiveness, however, but reparation is the ultimate purpose and in this process choice and responsibility loom large. In the so-called 'Literature of Introspection', which comes from the Lithuanian talmudic academies of the late nineteenth and early twentieth centuries, we find a realism about this. There, Israel Salanter says that it is easier to study the entire Talmud than to correct a single aspect of one's character. Salanter founded the movement known as *Musar* ('discipline'), which strove to bring the religious world and its ethics into one's own life and culture. The choice is put starkly in one of the Torah portions for Rosh Hashanah, Deuteronomy 30:

> *See, I have set before you today life and prosperity, death and adversity. If you obey the commandments of the LORD your God that I am commanding you today, by loving the LORD your God, walking in his ways, and observing his commandments, decrees, and ordinances, then you shall live . . . I call heaven and earth to witness against you today that I have set before you life and death, blessings and curses. Choose life . . .* (verses 15–16,19)

Tashlikh

A simple ceremony, carried out after the afternoon service on the first day of Rosh Hashanah (or, if this falls on Shabbat, on the second day), gives a very good sense of what can sometimes seem rather complicated ideas. It is known as *Tashlikh*, ('casting away'). Jews gather, often as a community, by a stream or sea to recite Micah 7:19 where God casts all sins 'into the depths of the sea'. Some find it helpful to make a physical demonstration of casting away all that is bad about their lives by emptying out crumbs or dust from their pockets. Long established in Orthodox communities, tashlikh has become increasingly common in Reform in recent times.

Kapparot

Another symbolic preparation for the Day of Atonement is observed now only by the very Orthodox. This is known as *kapparot* ('atonements'), from the same root as *Kippur*. It is based on the ancient Temple ritual of this day, as described in Leviticus 16, whereby a goat was driven out of Jerusalem into the wilderness. The goat was thought to carry the sins of the people. After the destruction of the Temple, the custom developed of slaughtering a chicken instead and giving it to the poor for the festive meal held before Yom Kippur. Most people now give not a chicken but money instead. The ancient idea is remembered as people recognize that they have done wrong and need to make amends. Kapparot is never performed in Reform communities. Instead, charity is strongly encouraged in the form of inviting the lonely and needy to break the fast of Yom Kippur in someone else's home or communally at the synagogue.

Fasting

The purpose of Yom Kippur

One mark of a festival is a special meal. This is particularly true of Judaism. Rosh Hashanah is no exception. After the festival is welcomed with kiddush, it is customary to eat food containing honey, such as cake and biscuits, or apples dipped in honey. The hope is thus expressed that the new year will be a sweet one. Yom Kippur, however, is not only a festival but also a fast day and so cannot include any food or drink. It may seem odd to fast on a festival, but the point of the fast is not to punish yourself by making yourself miserable. The aim is to take your mind off physical needs to assist concentration on the spiritual. This is linked to three other reasons for fasting on Yom Kippur. It can be a penance for wrongs done, demonstrating a sincerity about one's protestations of remorse. It can encourage self-discipline and self-control, much needed if the New Year resolutions are to be kept. It can promote compassion by giving a knowledge of what it means to go hungry if only for one day, and an awareness of the need to alleviate suffering. In all regards, fasting is not seen as an end in itself but as a way of fulfilling the purpose of Yom Kippur. The passage read from the Prophets on the day (Isaiah 57:14–58:14) makes plain that there is nothing automatically good about fasting:

> *Look, you fast only to quarrel and to fight and to strike with a wicked fist.*
> *Such fasting as you do today will not make your voice heard on high.*
> *Is such the fast that I choose, a day to humble oneself?*
> *Is it to bow down the head like a bulrush, and to lie in sackcloth and ashes?*
> *Will you call this a fast, a day acceptable to the LORD?*
> *Is not this the fast that I choose: to loose the bonds of injustice, to undo the thongs of the yoke, to let the oppressed go free, and to break every yoke?*
> *Is it not to share your bread with the hungry, and to bring the homeless poor into your house:*
> *when you see the naked, to cover them, and not to hide yourself from your own kin? . . .*
> *Then you shall call, and the LORD will answer:*
> *you shall cry for help, and he will say, Here I am.*
> (58:6–7,9)

The origin of Yom Kippur

It is Leviticus which gives the authority and the name for Yom Kippur. In the Talmud, it is simply called 'The Day' (Yoma 14b), indicating the rabbinic understanding of the day as the most important in the Jewish Year. Leviticus 23:27–8 reads:

> *Now, the tenth day of this seventh month is the day of atonement; it shall be a holy convocation for you: you shall deny yourselves . . . and you shall do no work during that entire day; for it is a day of atonement, to make atonement on your behalf before the LORD your God.*

This verse clearly commands that no work be done, as on Rosh Hashanah and the first day(s) of other major festivals. (On Rosh Hashanah, Orthodoxy follows the same prohibitions as for Shabbat except that food can be cooked if it is to be consumed on the same day. Reform makes the same re-evaluation of prohibited activities as with Shabbat, regarding travel and the use of electricity, for example, as no longer constituting 'work'.) The command in Leviticus 23:27 for self-denial or, as it is sometimes rendered, 'affliction', is interpreted by the Rabbis to forbid sexual intercourse, anointing (washing), the wearing of leather shoes (a sign of comfort), and, chiefly, eating and drinking. This is, then, the most important fast in Judaism, observed, except by the very young or where there is any threat to health, for 25 hours.

Atonement

Again it is through the texts that we can get closest to the significance of Yom Kippur. For every book on theology in a Christian study there will be in a Jewish study a bookcase on Law, that is, the Talmud. It is from the tradition and its expression in prayer that Jewish theology can be derived. This applies to the theology of atonement. Sin in Judaism is seen as separating and alienating people from God. As we have noted, the main purpose of this period of penitence, culminating in Yom Kippur, is not only forgiveness, significant though this is, but restoration. Teshuvah suggests a returning to the pristine purity of what we are. Through this, the thought is, the world may become as God intended and be re-sanctified. (The mysticism of Martin Buber and Abraham Isaac Kook in varying ways expands on this notion.) We see here then the two dimensions of the day. Unlike Tishah B'Av and other fasts, Yom Kippur is not a sad day. Because of the restoration aspect, there is joy in the day, as seen in the story of the man singing as he cleaned out the king's courtyard.

Kol Nidrei

What he was singing, namely a confession of all sorts of sins, still forms the central feature of the Yom Kippur liturgy. Before the confession can begin, however, the worshippers need to feel released from the vows or promises which they have not been able to keep during the past year. To make a vow in Judaism is a solemn undertaking. Not being able to keep it can thus leave a sense of wrongdoing which needs to be erased. So on the eve of Yom Kippur the synagogues are full for a long service. The service begins with *Kol Nidrei* ('All vows'), a prayer calling upon God to cancel all vows which have not been fulfilled. This prayer cannot be used to cancel commitments which Jews have simply failed to fulfil, such as repaying someone a debt. It relates only to vows between themselves and God, such a voluntary fast (see Chapter 13) or other religious obligation, which they were unable to keep for good reason. Historically, the clearest example of such a vow comes from the Spanish Inquisition, when Jews were required to swear allegiance to the Christian Church to avoid persecution. The Kol Nidrei prayer enabled such Jews still to worship God without feeling that they had denied him. The ancient tune used for this prayer is a haunting reminder of the difficulties which Jews have often faced in being faithful. The thirteenth-century rabbi, Judah the Pious said:

> *Chant your supplications to God in a melody that makes the heart weep, and your praises of Him in one that will make it sing. Thus you will be filled with love and joy for Him that seeth the heart.*

Prayers of confession

After the cancelling of religious vows, the focus moves to sin. This is a different matter requiring not cancellation but forgiveness and absolution. Attention is firmly fixed on the responsibility of each member of the Jewish people to keep certain ethical demands. The prayers of confession list, in greater and lesser detail, the sins to be forgiven. Like most Jewish prayer, the plural 'we' is used throughout, remembering that each person shares the sorrow and, often, the consequences of other people's sins, but there is a pause after each section for each to confess particular sins privately. The longer form of the confession in the Reform prayer book lists 44 sins. It begins:

> *For the sin we have committed before You by foolish speech.*
> *And for the sin we have committed before You by misusing our minds.*
> *For the sin we have committed before You by the demands of business.*
> *And for the sin we have committed before You by using violence.*
> *For the sin we have committed before You by bribery.*
> *And for the sin we have committed before You by compulsion.*

The Orthodox confession similarly catalogues damaging acts: hasty condemnation, envy, tale-bearing, to name but three. Again, there is nothing automatic about confession bringing anyone back to being at one with God. Judaism is very clear that God does not forgive anyone any sin against someone if he or she has not tried to put things right. As the Mishnah says:

> *For transgressions between man and God, the Day of Atonement atones; but for the transgression between a man and his fellow man, the Day of Atonement does not atone unless he has first reconciled his fellow man.* (Yoma 8:9)

In the theology of Atonement which emerges from this, divine grace requires human engagement. A contemporary rabbinic authority, J. B. Soloveichik, has evoked the essence of Yom Kippur in a poetic description of Moses standing on Mount Sinai after the disaster of the golden calf (Exodus 32). Alone and desolate, Moses shivers in the unbroken silence of a dark desert night. Only as he trembles is a distant faint sound heard. Once Moses seeks him in prayer and supplication, God appears. The conclusion is drawn from this account that something is expected of the human being, however slender, before 'at-one-ment' can occur.

Other expressions of repentance

The Haftarah during the afternoon service on Yom Kippur universalizes God's longing for repentance. It is the Book of Jonah, where the prophet is commanded to preach to the people of Nineveh. Both Jonah and the Ninevites have to change – their conduct as well as their attitudes. The Mishnah points out that it was when 'God saw what they did, how they turned from their evil ways' (Jonah 3:10), and not when God saw their sackcloth and fasting that he revoked his punishment (Taanit 2:1).

Many Jews spend the whole of Yom Kippur in the synagogue, though some may emerge for a breath of air or absent themselves during the afternoon. The focus is on atonement throughout. White, a symbol of both festivity and purity, predominates. It is seen in the dress of the rabbi and the cantor and in the curtains of the ark. Some men wear a white kittel over their clothes. (Some will have been to the mikveh on the eve of Yom Kippur as a sign of spiritual cleansing. See Chapter 9.) In non-Orthodox synagogues, the liturgy is equally long. Although mentions of sacrifices, the physical resurrection of the dead, and a personal Messiah are omitted as theologically obsolete, a vast range of material, both ancient and modern, is substituted.

Neilah

The final service, at the end of the afternoon, is called *Neilah* ('closing'). Its title refers to the closing of the Temple gates, when prayers were offered in ancient times. The thought of the Neilah service which has grown from this is of the closing of the heavenly gates of God's judgement. The gates, open for repentance, are symbolized by the doors of the ark being open throughout the service. Ezekiel 18 centres attention on the individual's responsibility to keep God's command and challenges him with the whole point of the High Holy Days:

> *Have I any pleasure in the death of the wicked, says the Lord GOD, and not rather that they should turn from their ways and live?*

(Ezekiel 18:23)

A single long blast of the shofar announces the end of the fast. At home or communally, Havdalah is performed and fast broken. Some people then proceed to begin to build a sukkah for the next festival. By this immediate preparation to keep the mitzvah of Sukkot, they are expressing the essence of the Jewish faith: God has given them mitzvot by which to live as he intends.

the Holocaust

Questioning

Most people suffering great pain or loss find themselves asking the question: 'Why?' It is not that they always articulate this. Nor do they necessarily expect anyone to answer their question. Indeed, any answer given would run the serious risk of banality, insensitivity, even cruelty. Rather, the question arises as a protest against something which threatens life's meaning, something which, they believe, just should not be. It has often been said that the death of one child raises the question just as acutely as the death, as in the Holocaust, of a million children. No one can doubt that for those who love that child this is true. For many, however, the Holocaust throws up particularly violently a challenge to meaning. If we believe in the unique value of every human life, then the greater the loss of life the more desperate for an answer we may feel.

Questions old and new

There are those, great Jewish thinkers among them, who contend that the Holocaust raises new questions and not just the old questions on a bigger canvas. They argue for the uniqueness of the attempted genocide not only in its scale but also in its cruelty. In particular, they ask the question 'Why?' about the Nazi determination to humiliate and dehumanize Jews, and other groups singled out as inferior, before they killed them. There is debate about whether or not the Holocaust should be described as unique. Knowing in recent years the vicious cruelty and massive 'ethnic cleansing' in the former Yugoslavia and in Rwanda, and the apparent impotence (some would add indifference) of world powers to prevent it, we perhaps use the word 'unique' reluctantly. If there is a case to be made for its uniqueness, it would seem to rest on the aim of its perpetrators, namely, the total elimination of a race. Certainly it is not helpful to plead superior suffering of the Jews above anyone else's or to satanize Hitler as against other wicked rulers. There is little debate, however, about the fact that the knowledge of the Holocaust does raise immense and, many would say, unanswerable questions. This chapter is concerned with identifying these questions and assessing their importance for the Jewish faith.

The purpose of frank questioning

Rabbi Albert Friedlander maintains that it is vital that the questions be asked. Even if, as he believes, there are not sufficient answers to be found for our time, ignoring the questions, not facing up to the evil of Auschwitz, will go on poisoning the atmosphere. Friedlander considers some of the responses made by Jewish theologians, religious leaders, novelists, and psychologists – Orthodox and Progressive. These he calls *Riders towards the Dawn*, the title of his book on the subject published in 1993. These are those who, he says, as Jews, have entered the darkness, many of them having suffered the camps themselves or having lost family there. They are the messengers to whom present-day Jews must listen if they are 'to move out of the shadow of the Holocaust'. But he thinks that this movement *from ultimate suffering to tempered hope* (the book's subtitle) is incumbent not only on Jews. Indeed, he considers at many points the role of Christians. This is significant for many reasons: first, the part played by the anti-Judaic teaching of Christianity in the rise and culmination of anti-Semitism; secondly, the contributions in action and theological thought from Christian opponents of Hitler; and thirdly, the need for self-criticism and fresh approaches from present-day Christians if healing is to come.

Friedlander is not alone in wanting to draw non-Jews into the discussion. The British Orthodox rabbi Norman Solomon has written of the duty of theologians and philosophers and of 'ordinary' Jews and Christians to talk about the Holocaust. Honest co-operation on this is, he maintains, essential for the building of a happier future. Certainly, Jews and Christians should be clear about the purpose of such talk. Further causes for hostility abound if Christians display an ignorance of the culpability of the Church in condoning anti-Semitism and, in some cases, fostering it or if Jews simply lay their resentment at the feet of Christian audiences in schools or public meetings. It is surely the responsibility of the leaders and writers of both faith communities not only to communicate the facts but also to find ways forward rather than simply to instil guilt in each other.

Remembering

There has been considerable disagreement in recent years over the rightness of teaching the Holocaust in schools and colleges. It is clearly very difficult to strike a balance between making sure people know the facts of the Holocaust, especially in the face of revisionists denying them, and leaving them weighed down with horror and despair. 'Remembering for the Future' was the title given to international conferences on the Holocaust held in Oxford and London in 1990 and 2000. It aptly sums up the purpose of researching and teaching the Holocaust. Forgetting is clearly not possible for its survivors. Nor is it permissible for its perpetrators; neither should it be countenanced for those living since. How best to remember, however, is something which divides Jewish opinion and this division reminds us that there is no single Jewish answer. It is significant that, for 20 years afterwards, very little was said about the Holocaust in theological terms, though there were attempts at artistic and literary expression. Jonathan Sacks describes it as 'a mystery wrapped in silence'. Even those who, since the Eichmann trial in 1961, have written substantively about it are reluctant to call themselves Jewish theologians. Holocaust theology is not a discipline in its own right and no one has written a systematic theology which looks analytically at the event and the diverse responses, offering a coherent and critical account of theological sources. Non-Jews are rightly wary of claiming to understand. But Jews also feel the utter incomprehension of it all. Again, Jonathan Sacks sums it up when he asks both how one could dare to speak and yet how one could dare not to speak on so unfathomable an experience.

Holocaust memorials

Yet, the very notion of remembrance is problematic. What is the object of those who built the great museum of the Holocaust in the USA and of those who visit it? The same question can be asked of Yad Vashem, the Holocaust museum in Jerusalem which is the 'World Centre for Teaching the Holocaust'. There, educationists, psychotherapists, and others with the necessary skills for such sensitive matters, hold seminars and courses. There, too, world leaders and ordinary tourists are taken when visiting Israel. Few such visitors could fail to be shocked and moved by what they see at Yad Vashem, but remembering, especially for Jews themselves, goes beyond this. There are Israelis who oppose taking children to Yad Vashem or engaging in its programmes. They ask what children are expected to do with these 'memories' of the Holocaust. Some Jews, of course, in Israel and elsewhere, are generally against what they see as focusing on the past. They fear that it simply recreates resentment and presents the Jew as someone who has been, and, therefore, could well be again, victimized. But hidden resentments are surely more dangerous, as evidenced by the explosion of hatred in Yugoslavia in the 1990s which, far from being sudden and inexplicable, stemmed from the failed 'reconciliation' between ethnic groups of 50 years ago.

There are clearly risks in continued talk about the iniquities of the Holocaust, especially if they are divorced from other manifestations of racism. The frequency with which the subject of the Holocaust comes up in meetings and journals aimed at Christians or Christians and Jews with interfaith interests can backfire. 'Not again' can be the response of those who, having no Jewish experience, find it hard to grasp why it cannot be said to be over and done with. Simon Wiesenthal, for instance, is sometimes criticized as vengeful in his pursuit of Nazi criminals. He and those who support the work of his foundation would maintain otherwise. They see the inadequacy of shelving these crimes against humanity (erroneously referred to as war crimes) for God's later dealings. Rather, justice must be done in the here and now. They also doubt any easy talk of forgiveness, not least because it is doubtful whether 'forgiveness' can be offered by others on behalf of the millions killed. The Centre in Los Angeles, named after Wiesenthal, houses the Museum of Tolerance, and tolerance and compassion are precisely what the Wiesenthal foundation pursues. Justice in the Jewish tradition, and perhaps in other religious traditions, is not the opposite of mercy. Such

the Israeli President speaking at Yad Vashem on Yom Ha-Shoah, 1990

ancient wrongs cannot simply be forgotten, but require something more concrete and positive.

Yom Ha-Shoah

A clue to why Jews need specifically to 'remember', as if they are
likely to forget, perhaps lies in the setting aside of a special day
of commemoration, *Yom Ha-Shoah* ('Day of the Shoah'). The
Hebrew word, *Shoah*, means 'whirlwind' and the term is more
commonly used by Jews than the term 'Holocaust'. Originally
called 'The day of Holocaust and heroism', this day was
established by the Israeli Parliament in 1951. It is observed
annually, on 27 Nisan (the anniversary of the Warsaw ghetto
uprising) by most Jews, except the Ultra-Orthodox. Since it was
declared by a secular body, the Knesset, many Jews (including
the present British Chief Rabbi Sacks and his predecessor,
Jakobovits) are hesitant about having a special memorial day
with special memorial prayers. They would prefer to assimilate
remembrance of the Holocaust into the existing fast of Tishah
B'Av which commemorates earlier 'destructions', notably of the
first and second Temples in Jerusalem.

Challenges to Jewish faith

This raises an important question. Should the Holocaust be
viewed as one event in Jewish history, albeit extraordinarily great
in its destruction, or should it be singled out as unique? This is
one of the questions to which theologians address themselves and
they arrive at different answers. Perhaps this illustrates the fact
that even in what is sometimes described as a post-theological age
in Judaism (and in Christianity) essentially the same questions are
being asked by the 'ordinary' member of the community as by
their theologians. Considering the impact of the Holocaust on
the Jewish world is a difficult task, not least because there is not
one Jewish world but many Jewish worlds. The USA, Israel, and
east European Jewry constitute just three of the major ones. The
sheer physical impact was to wipe out centres of Jewish population
and with them their culture, and to concentrate the decimated
Jewish population in the USA and Israel. The psychological and
spiritual impact is much harder to measure. It could be argued,
however, that it made certain assaults on faith which are common
to Jews of many different communities and of many different
religious perspectives, including those who, to all intents and
purposes, have thrown off formal religion.

The questions raised, though they may not be expressed in recognizably theological form, do, in fact, cluster around that ancient question 'Why?' They revolve round certain beliefs, still held, half-held, or reluctantly abandoned, that God is good, that God is powerful, and that he has a special purpose for the Jewish people in the history of the world. One may take the view that the Holocaust is, on its particular combination of facts, unique or one may argue that essentially no radically new theological challenge is posed. Either way, it is undeniable that this immense evil, whether pondered over theologically, or struggled through psychologically, or simply reaching one through a form of popular culture (such as the novel, *Schindler's Ark* and the Hollywood-style film *Schindler's List*) eats away at the vitals of a belief in a benevolent creator working out his purpose in human history and giving the Jewish people a special role in the scheme of things. The Holocaust, together with the founding of the State of Israel, events powerfully connected in the Jewish imagination, has had an enormous impact on Jewish self-understanding.

In this book, written essentially for non-Jews who are trying to teach themselves about the Jewish faith, the focus for this brief consideration of the Holocaust's impact on Jewish life needs to be the theological tradition. There we see writers trying to wrestle with the very questions which we identified at the start of the chapter. In their varied responses, the theologians represent the main ways in which people have come to terms, theoretically at least, with aspects of the Holocaust. Assimilation, denial of traditional belief to concentrate on a sort of existential Judaism, regarding it as punishment or a way of sanctifying God, are all possibilities expressed by the theologian, the creative artist, and the ordinary believer alike. Some of their main threads repay attention, for these theologians at least try to avoid a general cynicism about God and human beings, not addressing the questions at all, which is surely dangerous as a sort of festering wound. Questions about innocent suffering, divine and human purpose and responsibility arise for all theists but for Jews particularly the questions sharpen. They concern the nature and existence of God, the place of the Holocaust in the history of world Jewry, and the relevance of Jewish belief and practice 'after Auschwitz'. There is the sense that this experience calls into question the three co-efficients of traditional Judaism: God, the Torah, and the people of Israel.

Questioning and remembering combined

'Remember' is a key word in Jewish observance. Whether it is on the many festivals or fasts based on historical events or whether it is on the major festival and fast of Rosh Hashanah and Yom Kippur, remembering does not comprise simply recalling the past. Rather it entails appreciating the significance of the day. There may be dangers in a box-office hit like *Schindler's List* or even a tour of the first permanent Holocaust Exhibition in Britain (opened at the Imperial War Museum in London in June 2000), but unless we are to retreat into ignorance and apathy, then the realities of the Holocaust need to be presented. For this really to be remembering, however, means going beyond the facts into some sort of exploration into their meaning or, if need be, meaninglessness. The rest of this chapter aims to give some idea of how some writers have attempted to do just that. It is not intended to be a summary of the full range but rather a sample, especially of two writers. These are taken as representing contrasting approaches as they seek to inspire Jewish living after the Holocaust. They are not only presenting Holocaust theologies, but also feeling after post-Holocaust theologies (many of them are still developing), demanding that Jews go beyond the Holocaust so that they do not allow themselves to be permanently imprisoned in it.

A radical answer

The 'death' of God

The first and major writer is Richard Rubenstein. (There is a sense in which all the writers after him are coming to terms with the challenge he presents.) His thought has, in fact, developed over 20 or 30 years as seen in the 1992 edition of *After Auschwitz* subtitled *History, Theology and Contemporary Judaism*. The first edition of this book in 1966 was subtitled *Radical theology and contemporary Judaism*. So radical was it that it caused absolute uproar in his native America, shaking, as it did, the entire foundations of traditional Jewish belief. In reply to the difficulty of reconciling the Holocaust with the notion of a God acting in history, particularly the history of the Jewish people, Rubenstein simply maintains that they are irreconcilable. The biblical image of a saving God has to go. God is rather 'Holy Nothingness'. Hence the title 'death of God' theologian for Rubenstein. In effect, he systematizes the intuition: 'I can no longer believe.' Unlike those who are determined to hang on to a belief in God's covenant by somehow seeing Auschwitz as divine providence and Hitler as an agent of God's punishment (a sort of modern Nebuchadnezzar), he finds it impossible to celebrate Passover with all its assumption of divine concern and intervention.

The life of the people

Rubenstein's argument is that Judaism will survive and people will not follow through the logic of the Holocaust. This is indeed largely what has happened in the Jewish world. For some however, he has coherently articulated what they feel. The focus is no longer God, but rather, the community of Israel. Drawing heavily on existentialist writers, he believes that Jews have to create meaning and not assume that existence derives meaning from the divine. He argues for a return to primal origins, for the importance of nature, especially in the land of Israel, and the sanctity of bodily life. In recent years, he has struck a more optimistic note than in 1966, emphasizing a notion of God as ultimate reality rather than as radically transcendent or even non-existent.

Rubenstein's offering people a way of maintaining Jewish identity, one based on religion in the form of rituals and practices but not on theistic faith, has perhaps a certain honesty about it. But there is also surely a dishonesty, or at least an evasion, about recommending going to synagogue to offer prayers as a sort of group therapy, if one finds the content of the prayers meaningless and moreover one does not believe in a God to whom to pray. He stresses the need to pass on authentic Jewish rites of passage, but is he right in thinking that this is separable from the beliefs therein expressed? Completely secular or social expression of identity would surely make more sense? And yet, there are people who do find value in the ritual whilst having lost (or maybe never having had) the belief (see Chapters 1 and 17). What he suggests does seem to be true for some, that is, that religion functions psychologically.

Difficulties with Rubenstein's response

There are, however, other difficulties about Rubenstein's solution to the questions. The chief are his evaluation of history and his limited knowledge of the biblical faith. He takes the Shoah as *the* decisive event of Jewish history. This he takes as conclusive evidence for the non-existence of God. Logically, he should take the founding of the State of Israel, on which he lays so much stress, as equally decisive evidence for God's existence. In the 1992 edition of *After Auschwitz*, Rubenstein does, in fact, draw on the historical events from the Six Day War of 1967 up to the present and there is a new notion of covenant coming through, but still the idea of God entering history is denied. One might reiterate: 'If events destructive of Israel demonstrate the absence of divine providence, what do constructive events demonstrate?' Nor is he right in assuming that his question about God's activity in history is new. The biblical material is more varied then he recognizes. There is at many points (e.g. Jeremiah 12:1) the cry about why the good suffer and the wicked prosper.

A traditional response

The most significant writer opposing Rubenstein is Eliezer Berkovits and the most cited work is his *Faith after the Holocaust* (1973). So determined is he to counter Rubenstein's radicalism that his theological argument is at times contrived. Some judge that he evades the question raised by Rubenstein by producing a description of the world which, whilst retaining old certainties, in no way relates to the facts. Others point out that Berkovits himself does not claim to answer the agonizing questions directly but that he gives hope by claiming that future acts of redemption will give answers. He is, after all, concerned with *faith* after the Holocaust and not with statements admitting logical demonstration or verification. The scholar, Steven Katz, says, in *Post-Holocaust Dialogues* (New York University Press, 1985), that it is 'to Berkovits's credit that he has formulated several important theological theses that, even if "faith" statements, are suggestive in a Jewish theological context after Auschwitz.' He speaks of his courage in dealing with the 'meaning' and reality of the Shoah and, for all the gaps in his argument, is pointing us 'in the direction of important truths that need further reflection and development'. His conservatism has enabled him to give, writes Katz, 'one of the most theologically and Jewishly convincing "responses" of all those who have taken part in the discussion.'

God 'hiding his face'

Berkovits starts with the very strain in the biblical tradition which Rubenstein ignores, namely, the protest that God seems to be absent from the experience of the faithful. At the heart of Berkovits's thinking is a verse which, he maintains, celebrates the presence of the God who can and does hide in the world in order to enable human responsibility and freedom: 'Truly, you are a God who hides himself, O God of Israel, the Saviour' (Isaiah 45:15). The need for God to give space in order for people to develop as moral beings is central to his argument. This 'justification' of evil, the so-called free-will defence, is an ancient and a common one in both Jewish and Christian thought, but Berkovits makes very particular use of it in relation to the calamities of Jewish experience. God 'must absent himself from history', he writes, and not intervene even when his freedom is grossly misused. But God only appears to be absent. He is nonetheless present as the saving God of Isaiah 45:15. Berkovits refers to certain Psalms of lament which speak of God's 'hiding his face' and this without any human cause such as sin. In Psalm 44:24, for example, the community, after lamenting their suffering and the unfairness of it all cry:

> Why do you hide your face?
> Why do you forget our affliction and oppression?

Berkovits here rejects one of the traditional notions still put forward by some theologians and still held by some, namely, that the Holocaust was a punishment. 'Because of our sins' is the explanation offered for God's hiding his face in some biblical passages, notably Deuteronomy 31:17–18. The prophets of the Hebrew Bible also interpret the destruction of the Temple as punishment for the people's violating the Sinai covenant. Flowing from this there is the lingering idea in some people's minds that, in the Holocaust, the ever-just God must be punishing someone for something. Most of these people would be hard-pressed to identify what the 'something' was. Was it unfaithfulness to Judaism in assimilation, secularism, or even Zionism? One would have to be very strenuously opposed to these three things even to contemplate such an equation. Further contradictions arise. How would one explain, for instance, the fact that many of those who perished were the most pious? In *With God in Hell* (1979), Berkovits gives moving testimony to the religious faithfulness of many in the camps. (The book's dedication indicates the personal cost to Berkovits, as it is to his mother, a brother, and two sisters who all perished.) And, more fundamentally, what sins could possibly have merited such appalling 'punishment'?

The Holocaust and old questions about faithfulness

Like most Orthodox thinkers, Berkovits does not believe that the Holocaust was unique, except in the 'objective magnitude of its inhumanity'. He insists that it be seen in the context of history as a whole and the distinctive history of the Jewish people in particular. He here draws on another biblical notion, that of Israel as a suffering servant. In the book of Isaiah, notably in 52:13–53:12, the servant suffers not for his wrongs but for other people's and his suffering is somehow part of God's purpose for the world. Contrary to some other thinkers, Berkovits believes that Israel must not become 'a nation like other nations', powerful and justified in her very survival.

Other elements from biblical and rabbinic responses to suffering in the Jewish tradition explored by Berkovits are *Kiddush Ha-Shem* ('sanctification of the name') and the *akedah* ('binding') of Isaac. Kiddush Ha-Shem relates to those who surrender their lives rather than betray their Judaism, the martyrs or *kedoshim* ('holy ones'). But the pious, the convert to Christianity, and the atheist all perished alike in the Holocaust. They were not martyrs, electing to die for their Jewish faith, but victims who died involuntarily because of their Jewish blood. Berkovits and most Jews, though not all, reject Kiddush Ha-Shem as having any bearing on the Holocaust. He does apply, however, the ancient story of the binding of Isaac (Genesis 22), where Abraham is presented as undergoing a test of faithfulness.

Difficulties with Berkovits's response

Whilst there are aspects of Berkovits's response that will ring true to many Jews, the criticisms of it ring true to perhaps many more, and not just those on the Progressive wing of Judaism. Against him, it can be argued, the Nazis took freedom away from the Jews. Thus the freedom of those who chose the good was destroyed by those who chose the bad. There is further the worrying corollary that if such things as selfless love, forgiveness, fortitude and faith are unavailable unless they are a reaction to such inhumanity then the Nazi regime was actually assisting Jews in their moral development. It could even follow that yet greater corruption in the future could promote yet greater Jewish virtue. Even if it is accepted that the all-powerful and all-good God could not create people free to do right without creating people free to do wrong, the question arises: 'Is it worth it?' Given the extent of the evil of the Holocaust (and, of course, other times when the results of freedom run riot) might it not be preferable to do without human beings capable of courage and faith?

As do other theologians (such as Fackenheim), Berkovits appeals to the book of Job as offering biblical precedent for someone suffering immense injustice and yet going on believing in God's providence. The parallel is a poor one, however, for Job, unlike the majority of Jews under Hitler, lived to tell the tale, and with all his health and happiness restored. In the six million by contrast, all potential for moral growth was destroyed. It is on this ground that some thinkers say that no 'answer' to the Holocaust carries conviction without reference to some sort of after-life. Berkovits himself concedes:

> . . . all this does not exonerate God for all the suffering of the innocent in history . . . There must be a dimension beyond history in which all suffering finds its redemption through God. This is essential to the faith of a Jew.

Dan Cohn-Sherbok thinks that a neglect of Jewish belief in life after death is what is lacking in all the major Holocaust theologies. It could be argued, however, that unless this is very carefully worked out, such belief is simply a crutch, a way of letting God off the hook. There has not yet emerged a thoroughgoing approach to this which avoids the proverbial 'pie in the sky when you die'.

The way in which Berkovits tries to fit the vision of Israel into his vision of the powerlessness of the Jewish people as the suffering servant carries little conviction. Presenting the State of Israel as the proof of the vindication of the forces of good over evil, light over darkness, contradicts some of his central points. Berkovits's contention that, when Jews suffer historical calamity God is curbing his power so as not to overwhelm human freedom, does not seem to square with his belief that God is at work in the State of Israel. How can God be seen to be at work in the estab-lishment of a human State in 1948, it may also be asked, and centuries ago in the escape from Pharaoh, whose treatment of the children of Israel was far less troublesome than Hitler's? If Israel is the witness to the final judgement of history by a moral God, why could not this witness have come a little earlier? One further wonders what Berkovits would say should the State of Israel be destroyed. Would it be that God was again hiding his face? Logic would surely demand this. He maintains that the exodus was a miracle, a 'one-off' but, by sidelining this event, one which after all is crucial to the Jewish experience, Berkovits ends up with a vision of God and the world which is anything but traditionally Jewish. One of the recurrent dangers for the State of Israel is that some claim theological justification for its existence whilst ignoring all aspects of the theology. As we shall see in the next chapter, certain brands of Zionism (Jewish and Christian alike) decidedly 'use' God with precious little reference to his will as distinct from theirs.

Survival and beyond

Other theological contributions

While Berkovits could be said to exemplify both the best and the worst of suggested lines of thinking for coping with Jewish life after the Holocaust, brief mention should also be made of a number of other contributors. Emil Fackenheim thinks that the attention should not be on any traditional theology or theodicy (reconciling God's power and love with the reality of evil), but on working out how Jews can respond. They should not spend time trying to bail out God's reputation, but concentrate on their obligations. In addition to the 613 obligations of the Torah, there is now a 614th mitzvah. There comes from Auschwitz, he says, a commanding voice to survive and thus not to give Hitler a posthumous victory. Jews are 'forbidden to despair of the God of Israel, lest Judaism perish'. He too believes that 'the saving God of the past saves still' and he centres his hope on the continued existence of the people of Israel and in Israel. In his later writing, Fackenheim suggests that God is somehow present in the world and people must discern his will in order to 'mend the world'. His thought centres on the idea that the world ruptured at creation, that the spiritual and physical worlds parted company. When Jews fulfil their obligations, they restore the world and bring it back to what God intended.

Representing a new generation of American rabbis, Eugene Borowitz also tries to present a breadth of covenant for those yearning for a faith which can have some meaning after the battering of the Holocaust. His writing reflects his understanding of the complex relationship of Israel to her Palestinian neighbours in trying to work out what it is to 'renew the covenant'. Irving Greenberg urges continued belief in the God of Israel but on new terms, with a covenant, which is voluntary. Ignaz Maybaum tries to build on Fackenheim's insight of God's revelatory voice from Auschwitz by arguing that the State of Israel not only guarantees Jewish survival but also defines the purpose of Jewish existence. Incorporated into this deep faith in progress, however, is the ghastly concept that the Holocaust was essential to bring eastern European Jewry into the modern world.

Psychology and literature

From the point of view of trying to understand the struggles of Jews coming to terms with the Holocaust in thought and experience, writers other than theologians have much to offer. Only in the last decade have many Holocaust survivors begun to talk about their experiences in response to their third generation grandchildren. That they are able to, often owes much to the work of psychotherapists. Of great significance is 'logotherapy', which has been called the third great Viennese school of psycho-analysis, as developed by Viktor Frankl. He tells movingly of how he himself discovered meaning precisely in Auschwitz and Dachau where the oppressor sought to deprive the life of the Jew of all meaning and value.

If it is impossible to give, in a few lines, any adequate sense of theologies and psychologies dealing with the subject of the Holocaust, it is even more outrageous to try to capture the thought of a novelist. Yet, it could be argued, when faith is not entirely a matter of reasoned response, it is the novelist who can perhaps help most. Chief amongst those who have tried is Elie Wiesel. In a series of novels, published first in French and then in English, Wiesel speaks for the millions of murdered Jews and for the silent survivors. He also depicts the Jewish tragedy as a paradigm of the universal human experience. Using biblical and Hasidic (his own background in Hungary) tales, his novels have four main interwoven themes: witness, silence, laughter, and dialogue. But the theology which comes through his stories imposes no systematic structure. It is rather full of great tension and has thus enabled people to talk more honestly about their experience of the Holocaust and its impact on faith.

In an essay on belief, Wiesel refers to his childhood certainty that the world was intelligible in terms of God's providential intervention in human affairs. He would recite the 13 principles of Maimonides, including the last one which affirms belief in the coming of the Messiah 'even though he tarry'. But, he says, an abyss separates him from the child he once was. The last festival he celebrated at home before he experienced Auschwitz was Passover. But, he asks, how does one read the story of Passover after Auschwitz? How does one celebrate the festival of Purim in which God intervenes to deflect a wicked plan? Judaism is shot through with the notion of holy history, where clear explanations are offered for exile in terms of punishment, where God hears prayers to deliver travellers.

In an age where traditional theology is under attack for many reasons besides the Holocaust, it is not surprising that some judge asking the questions to be more fitting than suggesting answers. There certainly is no satisfactory system of explanations. But the writers touched on in this chapter have sought those aspects of their tradition, which they believed could support them and their fellow-Jews in a sceptical pluralistic age. Chaim Bermant seems to resent the faith of these 'riders towards the dawn'. In *The Jewish Chronicle* of 31 December 1993 he writes: 'It must be good to be God, for the Orthodox give Him the benefit of their certainties, and the Liberals the benefit of their doubts'.

It must be said, however, that both those with the certainties and those with the doubts still struggle to find a response which is at the same time honest and sustaining.

17

Israel

In this chapter you will learn:

- why Israel carries such significance for Jews
- about the varieties of viewpoint represented in Israel
- about the major difficulties of achieving peace.

A focal point for Jews

Since the establishment of the State of Israel in 1948, the question: 'What does it mean to be Jewish?' has sharpened its focus. The answers given have important practical implications for those seeking to emigrate to that country. About one-third of the world's 15 million or so Jews live in Israel, but also for Diaspora Jews, Jewishness defined in relation to a land – its laws and its policies – raises questions of identity which are at the same time both theologically ancient and politically modern. Every Jew has a view on the matter. Some maintain that, now the State is a reality, Diaspora Jewry should relinquish the right to comment on Israeli affairs, for example, Jonathan Magonet, Principal of the Leo Baeck College, in *An Explorer's Guide to Judaism* (Hodder and Stoughton, 1998). After all, such Jews are no longer 'in exile'; they are abroad by choice. There is a sense, of course, in which everyone has the right to comment on Israeli affairs, provided he or she has the complex facts to hand. The contention that it is well-nigh impossible for anyone living in the western world – even a Jew – to understand and interpret these facts should, however, be taken seriously.

Crucial to the perspective must be the recognition that for many Jews the Holocaust and the State of Israel are always intertwined. They are bound up because of simple chronology, since the State was founded just three years after the Holocaust. If the Holocaust spoke of God's absence, the foundation of Israel spoke of God's presence. For many, it offered some restoration of faith and still does. This immediate background is essential to acquiring any sense of the triumph of Zionism in the Jewish imagination. For other Jews, the significance is not so much theological as Jewish in the sense that the State of Israel restores Judaism to what might be considered its original state – that of being not merely a religion but a people with a language and a culture. Israel as it now exists is clearly not a theocracy but a democracy. As such, the entire *demos*, people, is involved in giving an answer to the question: 'What does it mean to be Jewish?' The reply may be bewilderingly diverse but the sense of peoplehood is surely vital and a focal point of this sense of peoplehood is the land of Israel.

No attempt to consider the essentials of Judaism, which is the purpose of this volume, can ignore Israel. For everyone who espouses this faith, the land of Israel has significance. This has been so since the recorded beginnings of what eventually became known as Judaism (see Chapter 1). This ancient significance, however, is not to be equated with what has become known as Zionism. The word 'Zionism' covers a wide variety of responses which are well documented in historical and political accounts. The primary focus here, however, is a religious one in an attempt to get some inkling of what Israel means in Jewish belief.

The development of Zionism

The term 'Zionism'

The term *Eretz Yisrael* ('Land of Israel') itself originates in religious belief. As the name given to the patriarch, Jacob, 'Israel' expresses a belief in God's promise to Abraham of a land for his people (see Chapter 2). That this physical arena was to enable the covenant people to live out God's requirements is reflected in the term *Eretz Hakedoshah* ('The Holy Land'). After King David made it his capital, Jerusalem took on special significance, eventually as the place where all sacrificial worship was centralized. One of the hills on which the city was set was Mount Zion and the name came to connote the whole city and moreover the whole land. When many of its people were exiled in Babylon, this city and its land were the centre of painful longing (Psalm 137:1). The ingathering of the exiles and the restoration of the land were hopes constantly expressed (as in Isaiah 51:3; 52:1–2; 57:7–10 where the term 'Zion' is used throughout). The term 'Zionism' could thus be used of these beliefs and hopes. What it has come to denote, however, is something altogether more political and an identification of State with Land, of Zionism with Judaism, is the source of much conflict and confusion. The whole weight of the biblical promise, with the collective hope of ingathering, lies behind the Jewish association with Israel, the land. 'The Holy Land' is one to which you make *aliyah* ('ascent'), the term used generally now of 'immigration' to Israel. But any line of continuity with what is now understood as Zionism in terms of Israel, the State, is not a straight one.

Different origins of Zionism

Its roots lie in the emancipation offered in the modern period (see Chapter 5). To this 'gift', the Jew could react in a range of ways. He could reject the new freedoms and continue to live a distinctively religious existence separated from non-Jewish society. He could do the exact opposite: assimilate totally by abandoning not only Jewish practice but also Jewish belief. This thoroughly secular approach amounts to: since the Messiah has not come, we no longer believe that he is coming (or as a song has it: 'The Messiah doesn't even call.'). The response of the majority, however, was both to take the emancipation and to keep the religious belief. Certain adaptations were needed as we saw in the origins of modern Orthodoxy, Reform, and Conservatism. But Judaism remained a religion, in what Neusner has called 'the Protestant model'. By this, he means that the religion is one which is essentially a private matter: it affects the individual and the family. But in the public sphere, nothing distinctive emerges. The believer may be transformed by 'private messages' but does not translate these into a particular political role.

Not everyone, of course, would accept Neusner's portrayal of either Judaism or Protestantism in North America. There are certainly Jews and Protestants in Britain who will say that they devote much time and energy to translating their beliefs into political action. But the truth of Neusner's description, whether it be a grain or a mountain, emerges when we consider a fourth reaction which some Jews had to emancipation. There were those who found anti-Semitism to be remaining in their so-called modern, emancipated lands, those who gave up being distinctively Jewish but who were nonetheless rejected on the single ground of race. For some with this experience, the logic was to become not primarily Englishmen or Frenchmen, 'of Mosaic persuasion' but to become nationalistically Jewish, that is, to create a state in which a Jewish language could be spoken and a Jewish culture lived. The beginnings of modern Zionism were then political, secular, and nationalistic. If a nation has the right to become a state, then (so the originators of Zionism maintained) the Jewish people must have a state – one based not on the coming of the Messiah but on modern nationalism.

Political Zionism

The main thrust towards Zionism came from this last group, those who wanted self-emancipation rather than anything dependent on the whims of particular governments. In east European countries there were Jews who had not yet attained political rights. There were also those who had experienced a taste of freedom only to find it taken away again. In Russia, a combination of poverty, pogroms, and laws limiting Jews to the Pale of Settlement led, between 1882 and 1903, to the first aliyah (immigration to Israel). Many more Russian Jews emigrated to western Europe and the USA, but this small and eccentric minority of about 24,000 who went to Palestine were the real pioneers of Zionism. They were highly secular in the way in which they drew on the prophetic ideals of the Bible, yet they were steeped in Jewish culture and were, therefore, not happy with the straight Socialism of some Russian Jews. The latter, in fact, constituted some of the fiercest opposition to early Zionism, forming the Socialist Bund in Poland, pressing for a revolution in their own country. The former preferred to blend their socialist ideals with Zionism. These 'Lovers of Zion', as they were known, created the nation. By their decisions and efforts were established, for instance, labour unions, large-scale industries, health organizations, the free press, and the army. Some of these were fleeing the Russian pogroms which had convinced them that building security for Jews from within was simply not possible and that a separate identity was needed.

Many of these early settlers were essentially practical Zionists. The first ever Zionist tract to elicit any response was Leon Pinsker's pamphlet *Autoemancipation* (1882). It was his sense that Jews would remain as alien minorities in each country unless they had their own territory as an independent nation which informed their thinking. So desperate were they after one pogrom that they would have settled for any country to which they could flee. But Pinsker, like Theodor Herzl later, moved from thinking that the location need not necessarily be Palestine to believing that only this land could inspire the emotional drive needed for Jewish self-emancipation. When the British Government declared itself willing to allocate a territory for Jewish resettlement in Uganda as a Jewish homeland, it was the most secularized Jews who insisted against Herzl, at the sixth Zionist Congress in 1903, that not only was Uganda unsatisfactory but that it had to be Israel-Palestine.

The second aliyah between 1904 and 1914 and the third, from Poland and Rumania as well as Russia, between 1919 and 1923 revealed tensions which make modern clashes between the secular and religious in Israel look tame. Still profoundly Jewish historically and socially, these early settlers clashed with the religious farmers already in the land. There was friction between the secular Zionists and the religious Zionists who viewed each other as an embarrassment or even a hostile force. The efforts of

Abraham Isaac Kook (1868–1935), who was part of the second aliyah and became the first Chief Rabbi of Palestine, were directed at healing the rifts, but even today in Israel there are posters decrying Kook as a heretic and bookshops which will not stock his writings. Kook wrote powerfully about the universalist aspect of Judaism, but there were and are those who have lost (or perhaps have never had) this idealism. This Zionist thrust from eastern Europe involved both Chaim Weizmann and David Ben Gurion both of whom were to play such a major role in translating the dream into reality.

By the turn of the nineteenth century, west European ideas began to feed into Zionist thinking. Countries where anti-Semitism still surfaced, even though ostensibly outlawed, included France, where in 1895 a Jewish army officer was found guilty of spying for the Germans, publicly disgraced, and sentenced to life-imprisonment. By 1906, Captain Dreyfus was totally vindicated after a struggle which rocked French political life. Covering his trial had been the Viennese journalist, Theodor Herzl (1860–1904). By his own account, his shock at this manifestation of anti-Semitism added strength to his conviction that the only answer was a Jewish State. This Herzl claimed to have founded in effect by his establishing the Zionist Organization in Basle in 1897. At its first congress, Herzl announced that the world would see this within a half-century and he was proved right. As defined by Herzl in his essay *The Jewish State*: 'the aim of Zionism is to create for the Jewish people a home in Palestine, secured by public law.' The name 'Palestine' comes from a rendering of the Hebrew for 'Philistia', the coastal strip of the land of Canaan (Israel). The term for this Philistine coastal strip only occasionally in biblical times refers to the whole land (Exodus 15:14). As a name for the area, 'Palestine' owes its prominence first to the Romans who renamed it 'Syria Palestina' and then to nineteenth century British usage which acquired political force as seen in the Balfour Declaration of 1917 which declared: 'His Majesty's Government view with favour the establishment in Palestine of a national home for the Jewish people.'

Cultural Zionism

Another of Zionism's founding-fathers was Asher Ginzberg (1856–1927). Adopting the pen-name *Ahad Ha-am* ('One of the people'), Ginzberg centred his attention not so much on the physical survival of Jews as on the survival of their culture.

Drawing on his profound insights from an intensely religious family and education, he argued for a country as a centre of cultural creativity. Usually called 'cultural Zionism', Ahad Ha-am's programme was far more cautious and gradual than Herzl's. Despite his later religious agnosticism, his chief aim remained the establishment of Zion as the spiritual inspiration of Jews post-emancipation. In this he may be said to have explicitly claimed that Zionism would succeed Judaism (at least in any traditional sense). What was central was the life of the Jewish people and in this even religion was only instrumental. This contrasts sharply with a statement made one thousand years earlier by the Saadiah Gaon: 'The Jewish people is a people only for the sake of its Torah'. An important biblical passage for the whole matter of defining Zionism is Isaiah 2:1-4. At its centre are the words: 'For out of Zion shall go forth instruction [Torah], and the word of the LORD from Jerusalem.' The statehood Herzl and Ahad Ha-am were urging was a new conception not catered for in rabbinic Judaism and the religion which emerged from it. For, apart from the brief period 132–5 CE, Jews had not had statehood for 2,000 years.

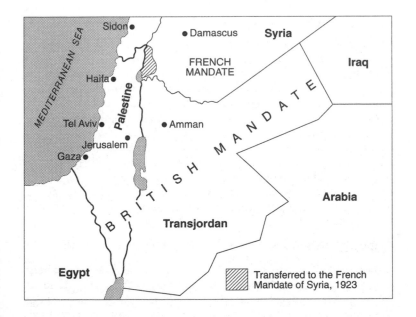

Transferred to the French Mandate of Syria, 1923

Opposition to Zionism came at first not only from the Socialist Bund and from some Ultra-Orthodox groups, but also from mainstream Orthodoxy and Reform in the USA and in Britain. Abraham Isaac Kook again played a major part in persuading many Orthodox Jews to support Zionism. Reform Jews who were enjoying the fruits of emancipation in western Europe or the USA were initially anxious about being told that their national home was really in Palestine. As we saw in the Pittsburgh Platform quoted in Chapter 5, they did not expect such a return to Palestine. Early Liberal Jewish opposition was voiced by one of Liberalism's founders, Claude Montefiore. Events, however, transformed many attitudes. Pogroms in eastern Europe were followed by attempted annihilation and it was the Holocaust which convinced Progressive Jewry. But for this, Reform Jews, especially in the USA where Zionism was at first seen as a retreat to a particularist view of Israel's role, would have retained their early opposition. For a Reform Jew to become a Zionist was a theological revolution, but this occurred and with it a transformation of the Jewish self-perception.

Religious responses to Zionism

Anti-Zionism

'Religious' responses to Zionism within the State of Israel cover a wide range. At one end of the spectrum are those who reject Zionism altogether. Members of the *Haredi* ('fearful', in the sense of religiously devoted) movement, for example, descended from the ghettos in Europe, believe that the land was given to the people of Israel by God and that it was taken from them because of their unfaithfulness to the covenant. When Jews again obey the Torah, they believe, God and only God will usher in the Messianic Age which will involve the restoration of the land to his people. They strongly oppose the notion that by settling in the territories Jews are in any way precipitating the redemptive age. Rather, they say, this shows an impatience with God's timing and competence to ingather the exiles.

The judgement of their early Zionist critics that, given time, the Haredim would emerge from their mediaeval ghettos and blend into modernity with everyone else was clearly unfounded. The Haredim used to be found only in traditional neighbourhoods such as Mea Shearim in Jerusalem. Today, however, their flourishing communities are to be found throughout Israel. Their

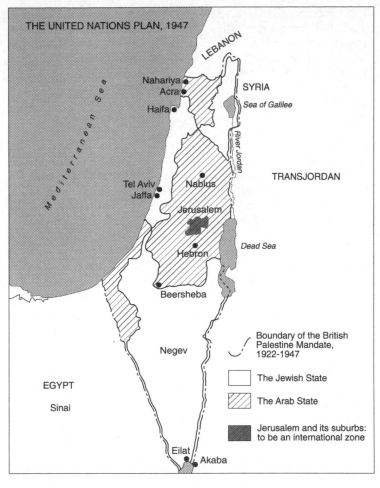

THE UNITED NATIONS PLAN, 1947

in November 1947, the United Nations General Assembly voted to partition Palestine

the Jews accepted the proposed boundaries for a Jewish State

the Arabs rejected the proposal for an Arab State and attacked Jewish settlements

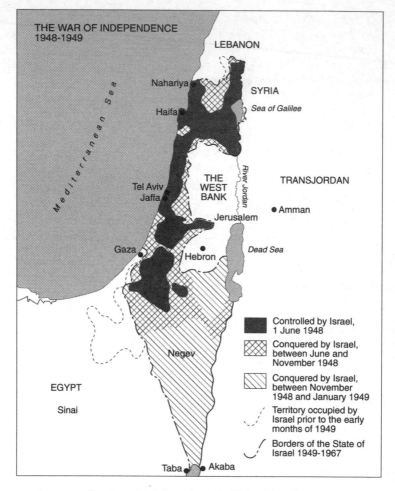

THE WAR OF INDEPENDENCE
1948-1949

LEBANON

Nahariya

SYRIA

Haifa

Sea of Galilee

THE
WEST
BANK

River Jordan

TRANSJORDAN

Tel Aviv
Jaffa

Jerusalem

● Amman

Gaza

Hebron

Dead Sea

Negev

EGYPT

Sinai

Taba ● ● Akaba

Mediterranean Sea

	Controlled by Israel, 1 June 1948
	Conquered by Israel, between June and November 1948
	Conquered by Israel, between November 1948 and January 1949
	Territory occupied by Israel prior to the early months of 1949
	Borders of the State of Israel 1949-1967

events surrounding the establishments of the State of Israel

growth in numbers and power of organization led them to win, in the 1996 elections, a record number of seats. Political allegiances – how far they are determined by religious conviction and how far by attitudes to peace with the Arabs – are very complex in Israel. Denying the legitimacy of the State, the Haredim, one might think, would not vote at all. Their main interest in the Knesset, however, is to capture public money to sustain religious schools and yeshivot. This they find to be consistent with their belief, held even more strongly than by Zionists, that the Jewish people has exclusive God-given rights in its biblical homeland. So, in 1996 by voting for the parties of United Torah Judaism and Shas, the Haredim, combined with the National Religious Party (a distinctly Zionist group), won 23 seats in the Knesset, not far short of the 32 seats of the winning party, Likud. Nonetheless, the 'religious', whether Zionist or anti-Zionist, retain great power by being able to bring down the government which, whatever its colour, always has to perform a delicate balancing act of coalition in order to retain power, given Israel's system of proportional representation. Whilst supported by some Haredim voters, Shas does not reject the legitimacy of Israel itself. Unlike the other Ultra-Orthodox groups in Israel, many of its leaders and most of its supporters have done military service. It deplores Israel's lack of religious observance and in this it stands alongside the anti-Zionist Haredim.

Even more adamantly anti-Zionist is the group *Neturei Karta* ('Guardians of the City') who say:

> *The Zionist State denies the Jewish people its essence and uniqueness, transforming it into a nation like all other nations, whose existence is not dependent upon the observance or abnegation of the Torah. The State before us was created as a substitute for the sanctity and Godliness of the People of Israel in order to transform its unique, deeply rooted essence into a territorial, gentile political one. The Zionist State represents total heresy uprooting the soul of our faith from its root and violating the covenant which God made with us in Horev.*

The accusation is that Zionism has changed the original concept of the promised land into one of nationalism, with land and language enabling people to be Jews without God.

Contrasting interpretations of religion

At the other end of the religious spectrum are those referred to as extremists or fundamentalists by their opponents. The *Gush Emunim* ('block of the faithful'), for instance, financed some of the first Israeli settlements on the West Bank (Judaea and Samaria) and the Gaza Strip after Israel had captured the territories during the 1967 War. They maintain that they have come back to certain areas to promote Jewish life and that this will hasten the arrival of the Messiah. Somewhere in between the Neturei Karta and the Gush Emunim are those who generally support the government but who do not see it in religious terms. The establishment of the State of Israel is not, in their view, a sign of the Messianic redemption. These groups, which include the Lubavitcher, support settlements and have opposed giving back parts of the West Bank. Indeed, they are particularly vociferous about this, but in what may be called ancient Zionist terms rather than political ones. Besides being concerned about security, their tenacity for the land rests on the religious belief that the land itself is holy, that is, given to Jews by God and, therefore, not theirs to hand over. It is their fierce opposition to handing back land which affords these groups their political clout in Israel, especially with right-wing politicians.

Also in between, but with very different attitudes to the land as God-given, come what may be called mainstream religious Zionists. One of their leaders, Rabbi Maimon (1875–1962) asserted: 'The Hebrew State must be established and conducted in accordance with the principle of the Hebrew Religion, that is, the Torah of Israel. Our conviction is clear: as far as we, the nation, are concerned, religion and state require each other.' The closeness of this perspective to the dominant biblical concept (that being given the land by God requires continued obedience to God) is undeniable. The conviction is that there is something divine, something transcendent in the way in which thousands of exiles have been 'ingathered' but that this entails living in accordance with Israel's moral mandate. This amounts to a reminder that Jews cannot have it both ways. Either the Jewish State is significant religiously in how its people live, or if they choose to live like any other people then their State becomes like that of any other people with no more claim on God's gift or purpose. In a sense, they believe that God's promises are his business. The Jew's business is to live in accordance with his requirements. This constitutes a warning against misusing the Bible as an Israeli charter for unending possession of 'the Greater Israel' with its widest biblical boundaries or indeed of any part of the land. It is no surprise that people of this persuasion have been among the fiercest critics of Israeli policy especially on human rights issues. This is not confined to them, of course. A member of one of the Knesset's entirely political parties is on record as saying:

Israel is duty-bound to preserve the basic Jewish moral lesson: what was hateful to us when we constituted a minority, what is bad for the Jews when they are scattered, will be hateful to us and harmful to us, even today, following our attainment of freedom and independence.

From different religious understandings of what it is to be a Jew, people draw different political applications of how to behave in a Jewish State. The understanding of the religious Zionist is reflected in the Declaration of Independence's reference to 'the prophets of Israel' as teaching what 'freedom, justice, and peace' mean. Yet it is striking that from a land which gave monotheism to the world comes a document in which the word 'God' never appears. The nearest to 'God' is 'faith in the Rock of Israel', a term which, it was judged, would not exclude the atheist, Ben Gurion himself included. The verbal gymnastics are clearly evident, however, when phrases such as 'the Ingathering of the Exiles' are combined with 'the development of the country for the benefit of all its inhabitants'. An Arab who is an Israeli citizen might be excused for wondering how the one could lead to the other, even if, as is pointed out by many Jewish settlers, they have developed the land to mutual benefit – particularly in the provision of water – in a way never attempted by the Arab population.

The whole question of settlements (especially those for immigrants) is still a vexed one. It is hard for Palestinians to take seriously the Israeli government's commitment to a peace process whilst continuing expansion. Why, they ask, have scores of settlements been built on disputed territory? Successive Israeli governments have been ambiguous in their attitudes, sometimes with pressure from the USA to halt settlements, yet between 1982–1992 there was a ten-fold increase. The Labour Government elected in 1999 drastically reduced budgets for settlements, but the Likud government of 2001 reversed this decision.

Identity in a Jewish State

As Israel approached 50 in 1998, much time was devoted in the world's media to an assessment of its birth and anniversary. A former member of the Knesset and a leader of the Israeli Peace Block, Gush Shalom, wrote:

When you are 50 years old, you should know already who you are. The state of Israel does not. What is it? A 'Jews' state', as the founder of the Zionist movement called the future state? A 'state of the Jewish people', as defined in one of Israel's laws? A state that belongs to its citizens? Or a 'Jewish and democratic state', as the official doctrine, endorsed by the Supreme Court, announces? And how can a state, whose every fifth citizen is a non-Jew, be Jewish and democratic at the same time? Who is a Jew? What does a 'Jewish state' mean?

Uri Avnery, 'Israel at 50: A Pronounced Case of Split Personality' in *The International Herald Tribune,* 7 April 1998

The Declaration of Independence

Though much has happened in and around Israel in the State's first 50 years which might account for the difficulty in giving a coherent answer to: 'What does a "Jewish State" mean?', it could be argued that confusion was inherent from the very beginning. As he declared an Independent Jewish State in May 1948, Israel's first Prime Minister, David Ben Gurion, was trying in some measure to address Jews belonging to each of the different persuasions outlined earlier. Ben Gurion announced:

Accordingly, we members of the People's Council, representatives of the Jewish community of Eretz Israel and of the Zionist Movement, are here assembled on the day of the virtue of our natural and historic right and on the strength of our resolution of the United Nations General Assembly, hereby declare the establishment of a Jewish State in Eretz Israel, to be known as the State of Israel. . . . The State of Israel will be open for Jewish immigration and for the Ingathering of the Exiles; it will foster the development of the country for the benefit of all its inhabitants; it will be based on freedom, justice, and peace as envisaged by the prophets of Israel; it will ensure complete equality of social and political rights to all its inhabitants, irrespective of religion, race, or sex; it will guarantee freedom of religion, conscience, language, education and culture; it will safeguard the Holy Places of all religions; and it will be faithful to the Charter of the United Nations.

This declaration is essentially a compromise document in which the wording represents attempts to give principles for Jewish identity which will accommodate all the widely differing viewpoints. It has in mind not only those Jews already living in the area but also those who might come and also those scattered across the world. Thus Israel is described as a Jewish State, that is a State belonging to the Jewish people wherever they are. Ben Gurion needed a single history according to which Jews could be united. He found such a history in the biblical presentation of a people who had been given a land, exiled, and returned. As he created the State, he harnessed the Jewish yearning for Zion which had originated in religious belief and yet his phrasing had to satisfy the many who by this time had broken radically with any belief in the redemption of the Messianic Age. The one unifying idea was that of peoplehood. Purpose or mission to the world did not enter into it. They were simply one people who had come from one place, travelled together, and were going back to that same one place. By calling the Jewish State 'the State of Israel', a clear statement was made that all Jewish history had been leading to this. Only some were still asking: what does it mean to be 'a kingdom of priests and a holy nation'? (see Chapter 2). Many were content simply to use theology as a backdrop to their claim to nationhood. But all were still asking: what does it mean to be Jewish? The answer for all the different groups, whether they centred on certain faith ideals or on being a member of the Jewish community, was rooted in the land of Israel as home-base.

Difficulties in defining 'Jewishness'

Continuing conflict on the issue of identity surfaces as a battle over the word 'Jew' takes place every single year in the Knesset and there have been a number of famous cases of people challenging the definition. Jewishness was originally defined in 1950 and 1954 in ways which reflected Hitler's definition (and other anti-Semitic persecution), that is, anyone with any Jewish blood. The case of Captain Shalit led ultimately to the 1970 amendment to the Law of Return, whereby 'Jew' means anyone who is born to a Jewish mother or who has been converted and who is not a member of another religion. In continuing debate, religious Jews want to add 'according to the halakhah' after the word 'converted'. The Chief Rabbis, one representing the Sefardi and the other the Ashkenazi community, want Jewishness to be defined in terms of one Jewish parent. They feel that many Jews from the former USSR have taken advantage of qualifying as immigrants by having a distant relative who is Jewish. Excluded from the rights of an *oleh* ('immigrant', plural *olim*) is 'a person who has been a Jew and has voluntarily changed his religion'.

By far the most celebrated and also the most revealing case in determining the present Law of Return, especially with regard to identity and religion, is that of 'Brother Daniel'. Born Oswald Rufeisen of Jewish parents in Poland in 1922 and reared as a Jew, he had converted to Christianity in 1941, entering the Carmelite Order in 1945. Wanting to join the Carmelite chapter in Israel, he insisted on his right to immigrate as a Jew. After some years, the case finally came to court in 1962. The arguments of the various judges make fascinating reading (as found in *Selected Judgments of the Supreme Court of Israel*, Special Volume, ed. A. F. Landau, Jerusalem Ministry of Justice, 1971), but two will be quoted as illustrative. (Others can be found in *Textual Sources for the Study of Judaism*, ed. Philip S. Alexander, Chicago University Press, 1990.) Judge Cohn argued:

> Never has there been such a revolutionary event in the history of the Jewish people, scattered and dispersed amongst the nations, as the establishment of the State of Israel. In the Diaspora we were a minority, tolerated or persecuted, but in our own State we are an independent nation like all other nations . . . This revolution is not merely of a political character; it renders imperative a revision of the values which we have imbibed in our long exile . . . There comes now to the State of Israel a man who regards Israel as his motherland and craves to find fulfilment within its borders, but his religion is Christian. Shall we therefore close the gates? . . . Should the State of Israel, 'based on freedom, justice and peace as envisaged by the prophets of Israel', act towards its inhabitants and those who return as did the evil rulers of some Catholic kingdoms in the past?

Judge Landau argued:

> First, the author of the dictum: 'Though he has sinned, he remains a Jew' which appears in Sanhedrin 44a, certainly never intended thereby to refer to a Jew who has changed his faith. It is doubtful whether Talmudic scholars, in speaking of an apostate, meant to include the extreme case of a Jew who has not only

committed idolatry but has renounced his faith and embraced another religion as well. Secondly, the wise interpretation given to this dictum by Rashi and by other authorities in the Middle Ages was due apparently to the desire to treat forced converts leniently and not to close the door upon them should they repent and return to the fold . . . The petitioner has excluded himself from the common fate of the Jewish people and has linked his destiny to other forces whose precepts he honours both in thought and in observance. That is the reality and that is still the feeling of the overwhelming majority of the Jews of today, both inside and outside the State, a feeling that springs from positive national sentiment and not from any desire to settle scores with the Catholic Church for its treatment of the Jews in days gone by . . .

In terms of cumulative credentials of Jewishness, Brother Daniel's case is impeccable. He is, therefore, accordingly a Jew and yet his case is rejected on the ground that he is not a Jew as popularly understood. It may be argued that what this case debates is the identity not so much of an individual but of the Jewish State. The judgement is made that who is accepted is not entirely a matter for the halakhah and yet every Jew has to accept halakhic norms as part of the structure of the society. The assumed objective stance of a judge disappears in this hearing, as he assumes the role of teaching the people the values of Jewish civilisation. Each judge, in fact, presents arguments which he will reject in order to offer a piece of teaching. The identity of the whole Jewish State and its legal system is herein being defined. Brother Daniel's case reveals the basic conflict of values which exists within the State itself. Both sides in the argument use traditional religious sources and modern Zionist literature, yet the final decision rests on a third source, that of popular conception of what a Jew is. One judge (Berison) spends three-quarters of his judgment showing how halakhically Brother Daniel is a Jew and then a quarter saying that he is not able to rely on this and will have to decide the other way. Similarly, Judge Silberg finally rejects the petitioner's case because: 'there is one thing that is shared by all Jews who live in Israel (save a mere handful) and that is that we do not cut ourselves off from our historic past nor deny our ancestral heritage . . . Our new culture in this land at the highest is merely a new version of the culture of the past.'

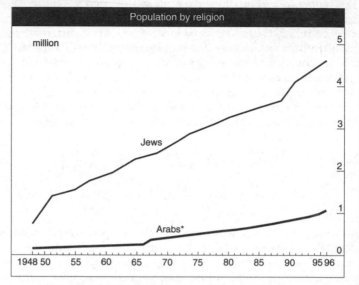

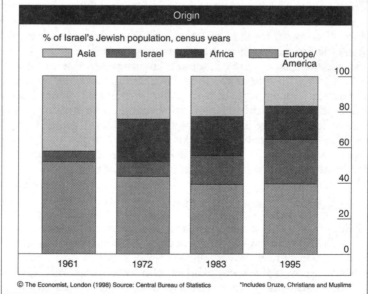

Ingathering the exiles

© The Economist, London (1998) Source: Central Bureau of Statistics   *Includes Druze, Christians and Muslims

The conflict between Israeli and Jewish law exemplified here stems from the way in which the State maintained the status quo, from the time of the Ottoman Turks, that personal status is a matter of religious jurisdiction whilst citizenship is different. The Law of Return is a secular law not within the jurisdiction of the rabbinic courts and its definition of Jewishness differs from the one used in these courts as they decide such issues as marriage and divorce. There are those who argue that Jewish religious law plays too little part in Israel, wanting the whole system of civil and criminal law which is provided by the halakhah to be operative.

The same issue of status and the 'freedom of religion' which is guaranteed raises the other most serious difficulty both in the Declaration and in subsequent statements of what it is to belong to the Jewish State. Of the 6.5 million Israeli citizens, 1.2 million are non-Jews, mainly Muslim Arabs. (Not all the Muslims are Muslim in observance any more than all the Jews are Jewish in observance.) Muslim, Christian, Druze, and Bahai enjoy equality before the law, a pluralism not always supported in other Middle Eastern countries. Seven different calendars of religious festivals (including Eastern and Western Christian and Samaritan) are recognized. Though there are disputes about the 'Holy Places' referred to in the Declaration, the difficulty with 'freedom of religion' is not so much with Muslims and Christians who both have autonomous religious courts in Israel but with non-Orthodox Jews. Jews who do not meet the Orthodox requirements are restricted in the areas of marriage and divorce (see Chapter 9). Civil marriage is effectively blocked, a situation which is deeply resented by Jews not in agreement with Orthodoxy.

Peace with justice and security

Turbulent years in the Middle East

| 1956 | Israeli forces occupy Sinai Peninsular. *Sinai Campaign*. British and French attack in Egypt. UN cease-fire. Israeli forces withdraw to armistice line. |
| 1967 | Egyptian blockade of Gulf of Eilat. *Six Day War*. Israel defeats Egypt, Jordan, and Syria and takes Golan Heights and West Bank of Jordan River. Partition in Jerusalem lifted. |

1969–70	Conflict over *Suez Canal*.
1973	Egyptians launch surprise attack on Day of Atonement. *Yom Kippur War*.
1979	Peace treaty signed between Israel and Egypt, following *Camp David Agreement* of 1978.
1982	Israel attempt to eliminate PLO by invading the Lebanon. *Lebanese War*.
1987	Palestine uprising begins. *Intifada*.
1990–1	Israel bombarded by Iraq in *Gulf War*.
1991	Madrid peace talks inaugurated. *Madrid Framework*.
1993	*Oslo Peace Accord*. PLO and Israel sign *Declaration of Principles on Interim Self-Government*. Vatican recognition of Israel, *Fundamental Agreement between the Holy See and the State of Israel*.
1994	Limited Palestinian self-rule as Israelis withdraw from Jericho and Gaza Strip. First meeting of (PNA) Palestinian National Authority. Israel and Jordan sign peace treaty.
1995	Cairo summit of leaders of PLO, Jordan, Israel, Egypt, and Syria to sign peace treaty (difficulty of Golan Heights taken by Israel in 1967). *Oslo II Accord*. Assassination of Israeli Prime Minister Rabin.
1996	Palestinian National Council election. PNA controls some towns and cities on West Bank and Gaza Strip. Right-wing government, Likud, elected.
1998	*Wye River Memorandum* restarts peace process – further West Bank areas, including villages, controlled by PNA. PLO revokes clauses in covenant calling for destruction of Israel.
1999	Moderate government, Labour, elected under Prime Minister, Ehud Barak.
2000	Papal visit to Israel-Palestine. Israeli withdrawal from the Lebanon. Death of Syrian President, Hafiz al-Assad and succession of his son, Bashar, leaving conflict over possession of Golan Heights unresolved. Palestinian-Israeli talks at Camp David break down over the status of Jerusalem. Second Intifada begins.
2001	Barak and Likud elected under Prime Minister, Ariel Sharon.
2002	Recurrent suicide bombings and retaliation. Elections called for early 2003.

Over four decades of conflict between Israel and her Arab neighbours have left a background of insecurity, mistrust, and aggression on both sides. To the onlooker it would seem as if their shared suffering could promote mutual understanding. Yet, personal experience is compounded by history, recollection, and the fearful prospects of modern warfare. On territorial disputes with such a long and complex history as this, it is not always easy to get at the facts, let alone to understand them. Conflicting statements about who originally lived where, who seized land from whom, and who created refugees, and so on are part of both the Palestinian and the Israeli propaganda machines. It is significant that the PLO and Israeli negotiators in the Oslo discussions of 1992–3 agreed that they could only make progress towards a peaceful future if they first agreed to set aside debates about the past. Those cynical about the whole peace process might argue that this was because one side or the other could not afford the truth to be told. But those involved gave a different reason. It was not that they were unaware of great injustices and deep resentments on the part of their people. Indeed, it was precisely such an awareness which led to their initial and repeated resolve. Whatever the past culpability of both Israel and the Arab nations, the need was to achieve justice and peace.

Peace for all and justice for all remain the quest. A recurrent theme in the various congratulatory messages in the world's press on and around Israel's fiftieth anniversary in 1998 was that Jews must no longer deny the Palestinians the very treasure which they themselves were celebrating, namely, the freedom to be a nation. Remembering the way in which the Arabs were largely responsible for the 'Catastrophe', as they refer to the war of 1948, by having rejected the 1947 United Nations' resolution partitioning Palestine into a Jewish and Arab State, the *Daily Telegraph* (29 April 1998) read:

> *In the ensuing war, they lost even more territory than had been apportioned to the Jews by the UN. With little sense of irony, Arabs now clamour for Israel to honour UN resolutions calling for its withdrawal from territories occupied in 1967.*

> *Yet Israel should be wary of falling prey to the same hubris which infected the Arabs. Decades of conflict with Zionism has forged a Palestinian nation which demands what the Jews have – the return from exile*

and the creation of their own state. ... The Jewish question has been resolved: the Palestinian question has not. Let us hope it will not take another 50 years.

the *Guardian* (30 April 1998) read:

Israel's independence was the Palestinians' catastrophe. This is not a case of spoiling the party by daring to mention the war(s). Conflict with the Palestinians and the wider Arab world remains the central, defining problem of Israeli life. Unresolved, it will remain not so much a blot on the country's achievements as a funda- mental, distorting flaw.

And Jonathan Sacks, the Chief Rabbi of the United Hebrew Congregations of the Commonwealth, wrote in *The Times Weekend* (18 April 1998):

If we search, as the prophets did, for the presence of God in human history, surely it is here. And it will be to God that on Israel's Jubilee we will give thanks. But the search for peace remains. Jews did not return home to make others homeless. Nor did they escape millennia of suffering to inflict suffering on others. Isaiah's words 25 centuries ago still define Israel's challenge and its hope: 'I will make peace your governor and righteousness your ruler. No longer will violence be heard in your land.'

Justice

We noted earlier the danger of Jews accepting the biblical promises of land whilst rejecting the accompanying demands for morality. That 'peace without justice is another form of oppression' is the chief claim of Canon Naim Ateek. In his book of Palestinian liberation theology, *Justice, and Only Justice* (Orbis, 1990), he writes as Pastor of the Arabic-speaking congregation of St George's Anglican Cathedral in Jerusalem. He is surely correct in his view that there can be theological justification for a political State and that the State of Israel cannot survive on injustice. If God's prophets are to be appealed to in a people's return to a land, then there must be genuine attempts to meet the covenant requirements: 'to do justice, and to love kindness, and to walk humbly with your God' (Micah 6:8). Ateek's point is, of course, the one made by the moderate religious Zionists. However, in a country where many have dropped at least the last part of the three-fold requirement, the emphasis must be on justice. Israel sometimes protests that a higher standard of morality is demanded of it than of any other State. Israel is, in fact, a State like any other of which neither a higher nor a lower morality should be demanded. The accusation is sometimes made that Jews above all people should avoid humiliating and oppressing those over whom they now have control. Taking this further, Zionism has been charged with being racist and the State of operating a system of apartheid. Those engaged in the actual struggle to find a way forward avoid this sort of emotive link with the Holocaust. One of the most impressive Palestinian representatives is Hanan Ashrawi, Professor of English at the University of the West Bank. She firmly rejects the analogy between Israel and Nazism but, as she said in the powerful television documentary series *The Longest Hatred*: 'I will not allow other people's suffering to give them the right to make me suffer.' As she went on, you cannot say who has suffered most since you cannot measure pain. Traumatized and scarred memories are no justification for further suffering. Rather, the causes of the pain and suffering of both peoples need to be avoided altogether.

Other requirements for peace

If justice is the starting-point, then what about peace? When Yitzhak Rabin and Yasser Arafat signed the document of mutual recognition between Israel and the PLO, Jewish responses ranged from jubilation at 'entering a new era' to 'condemning it as a black day for the State of Israel'. Verdicts from Arabs were similarly divided, with Chairman Arafat being described as both a hero and a traitor. One person's peace-maker is another's betrayer. One may feel that the *Intifada* (Palestinian uprising) was altogether justified given the refugee camps and the military confrontations experienced by Palestinians over the years but, as with any embattled hostility, the question is not whether it is justifiable but how to bring it equitably and permanently to an end. In his speech in Washington, Yitzhak Rabin spoke of how one makes peace with enemies, not with friends. His assassination in November 1995 by a right-wing Jewish extremist at a peace rally in Tel Aviv demonstrates not only the rift between Jews over what constitutes Jewish loyalty but also the cost of the compromises involved in such peace-making.

on the stones at this point on the Lebanese-Israeli border are the words in Arabic, Hebrew, and English: . . . *they shall beat their swords into plowshares, and their spears into pruning hooks; nation shall not lift up sword against nation, neither shall they learn war any more* (Isaiah 2:4)

just off the picture is the Lebanese flag

at the centre of the Israeli flag is the *Magen David* ('Shield of David') which has become a symbol for the Jewish people

Today, there are different perspectives on the Palestinian National Authority among both Israelis and Palestinians. Israelis of all persuasions are concerned about security implications and Israel retains control of strategically sensitive areas, albeit 'redeploying' outside Palestinian autonomous zones. Religious nationalists object strongly to the relinquishing of parts of the biblical heartland of Judaea and Samaria. More moderate Israelis believe that the transfer of power is essential to any long-term settlement and do not consider Israeli security to be threatened by the peace process. For Palestinians, initial euphoria tends to wear somewhat thin. Their areas are fragmentary and economic difficulties continue. The final settlement envisaged in the original accords has not been reached; the question of access to Jerusalem remains difficult. Israeli security restrictions weigh heavily and the Israeli army is still encountered on the routes that separate the different autonomous zones. Apart from access to Jerusalem, permits are required amidst considerable bureaucracy.

Long-time Israeli peace campaigner, Amos Oz adopted the slogan: 'Make peace not love.' He has consistently argued that the Palestinians deserve not love but peace and that this rests on a fair and decent division of the land. Many of his novels, for example, *In the Land of Israel* and *Black Box*, follow this line. Though Oz himself fought in the wars of 1967 and 1973, the latter he judges as marking the collapse of Israel's self-image as a dazzling success-story. In the 1980s, the invasion of the Lebanon and the massacres of the Sabra and Chatila camps which took place within Israeli military jurisdiction divided Jewish opinion both inside and outside Israel. Amos Oz once described Israel as 'neither a nation nor a country' but 'a fiery collection of arguments' and 'a tense and divided federation of dreams'.

Developments in the 1990s made this truer than ever. As a result, Israel became less embattled and this in two ways, showing the vital link between security and identity. First, its sense of survival and declining incidences of attack – both militarily from Arab terrorists and verbally from the rest of the world – help give it a feeling of security. Also important is international acceptance of Israel's civil rights record which is necessary for membership of the United Nations. In an article about Israel's recognition that security matters must no longer be judged by the military but now by the Supreme Court in Israel, *The Jewish Chronicle* of 5 May 2000 maintains: 'Israeli society is changing dramatically – becoming more open – not least because its sense of siege has been lifting. And along with key social values of the pioneering years, the consensus on security issues is also now open to challenge.' (Eric Silver, 'Another taboo goes: judges v generals'). Second, the changing ethnic and social geography of Israel renders it less likely to think of itself in terms of shared Jewishness over against the non-Jewishness of the Palestinians.

The range of Jewish identities described earlier has become even more diffuse in recent years. There is a tendency towards hyphenated identities along American lines. The massive immigration of Russian Jews (more than 700,000 since 1989, now amounting to more than 15 per cent of the population) was initially seen as a welcome reinforcement for Zionism. But these Jews have changed the face of Israel, notably by choosing to create the country's first successful ethnic party. Under Soviet communism they were hardly united in their Jewishness and yet they have contested elections as a Russian-Israeli party named *Ba'aliyah*. Their leader is Natan Sharansky who, as a consequence of trying to emigrate to Israel in the 1970s, spent nine years in a Soviet jail.

Other ethnic constituencies have also asserted themselves in political parties. Consequently, the European-Ashkenazi dominance of cultural life has come 'under siege', as one eminent academic has described it. Israeli Arabs are not the only ones who seek not so much social integration as equal status with those Jews who until now have determined how the State of Israel expresses itself 'Jewishly'. Country of origin is now accentuated, with people divided not only into hawk or dove, right or left, religious or secular, but also into Moroccan or Russian. There have always been distinctions, even divisions and inequalities, between western and oriental Jews in Israel. But Ashkenazim and Sefardim, respectively, now subdivide even more and voting patterns can be surprising, even for such an inherently surprising political system as Israel's. Zionist or non-Zionist is not always the defining character.

The term 'post-Zionist' is being increasingly used of Israel post-1998. The State has achieved its half-century. In a survey of Israel at 50, a writer for *The Economist* concludes that 'modern Israeli politics is not only about peace and war. It is also about what sort of society an Israel at peace intends to be' (Peter David in 'After Zionism', 25 April 1998). The State may yet, as its first Prime Minister claimed: 'prove itself not by material wealth, not by military might or technical achievement, but by its moral character and human values'. It all rather depends on what sort of peace Israel is aiming for. The motivation for withdrawal from the Lebanon in 2000 was, after all, to stop further loss of Israeli soldiers. It is no longer simply a question of where Israel's borders lie, but of what flows in and out of the country, literally and metaphorically. As has been remarked, the gap between Syria and Israel is only a matter of eight square miles, but this includes the shores of the Sea of Galilee which gives 40 per cent of Israel's water supply. The question now concerns the sort of society cultivated within Israel's borders. The biblical perspective, as expressed by Jonathan Sacks quoted earlier in the chapter, would go beyond this and ask what Israel hopes to give the world. This is essentially a religious question, the question of the purpose of the survival of Israel and the religion of Judaism. Whether or not religion can be in any sense a unifying rather than a divisive factor in Israel becomes all the more pertinent now that Zionism is no longer the strong binding force that it was when survival was everything. Israel has survived but survived for what? To satisfy both fidelity to the purposes of Judaism and political realism, the answer must somehow entail justice and security for all the inhabitants.

afterword

Since the aim of the series is avowedly practical rather than purely academic, it may be in order to hope that mention of some of the pitfalls may improve relations between Jews and people of other faiths. Most of these relate to Christian-Jewish encounter, since it is often those with Christian affiliation who have a particular interest in this religion and who perhaps make the most assumptions.

The first one is the assumption that Judaism and Christianity are fundamentally the same. This is a particular danger for those Christians who, quite rightly, have got the message that the roots of their own faith lie here. Though this is an improvement on the viewpoint reflected in such exclamations as: 'They even have our Psalms!', it can lead to a failure to see the very real and important differences. What has been described as a 'juxtaposed monologue' rather than a dialogue can be the consequence.

This sometimes surfaces in the surprise with which the news is received that a Jew may be unable to take part in occasions where Christian terminology or symbolism pertains. 'I cannot see why not, when we all believe in the same God' is more likely to be directed at Jews rather than at any other religious group. A sense of the power of the key Christian symbol of the Cross to evoke accusations of deicide, the Crusades, and later attempts to convert needs to be grasped. Not wanting to sing hymns and say prayers which focus on Jesus as the Christ, the Son of God, and the Suffering Servant should, by now, not be difficult to understand. The fact that Christians can see Jewish symbolism and recite Jewish liturgy without being similarly offended further adds to their bewilderment at Jewish non-participation. It can too easily seem as if Jews are being over-sensitive or plain awkward.

It was remarkable that, on the day in 1995 when the liberation of Auschwitz was being commemorated, an otherwise apt and sensitive religious service on the radio included a missionary hymn which included the lines: 'And where the gospel day sheds not its glorious ray, let there be light.' It might, of course, be argued that it was mainly Christians who would be tuned in to such a service but even to them, at a time when Christian culpability in the Holocaust was being much explored, this line might have had a hollow ring. Then a television newsman reported that at Auschwitz 'the Christian names' of the victims were being read out. That 90 per cent of these people would not have Christian names, while most of the perpetrators would, and that the silent yet knowing powers of the world included Christian leaders, made the phrase deeply unfortunate. In both these cases, no offence would be remotely intended and the choice of words would be much regretted once it was pointed out to those responsible.

A second pitfall is closely related to the first. It is the tendency of Christians to assume that Christianity is 'Judaism plus Jesus' or conversely that Judaism is 'Christianity minus Jesus'. In one sense, the first description is quite accurate. For people of a Jewish background who come to believe in Jesus as the unique revelation of God, their new religion is indeed Christianity. But the things which such a belief about Jesus does to their Judaism are far more radical than adding a sort of optional extra. Atonement, for example, is the key to Judaism and yet in Christianity the understanding of Atonement is something quite different. More importantly, Judaism can certainly not be summarized as Christianity without Jesus. It is good that much recent biblical scholarship has stressed the Jewishness of Jesus, but the religion which then developed from his teaching has quite a different focus (namely Jesus himself) from Judaism's focus in the Torah.

The third tendency sometimes follows on from this. It is to regard Judaism in a negative light, as being not just centred on the Law but oppressively legalistic. The cause of this is often that Christians derive their picture of Pharisaic Judaism not from rabbinic literature but from the New Testament. One would hardly expect to obtain an accurate picture of Christianity from someone who was deliberately wanting to convert you from it, nor would Salman Rushdie be the obvious choice for someone wanting a sympathetic treatment of Islam.

What Christians call the Old Testament constitutes the source of two further difficulties. First, in an effort to stress the newness and superiority of Christian teaching, what are perceived as good and positive qualities, such as love and forgiveness, are assumed to be absent from the Jewish scriptures. Hearing a Church reading about some bloody battle or unexplained law only serves to reinforce this impression.

Secondly, the very 'oldness' of it may give credence to the conviction that this religion has been superseded. (The fact that the religion of the New Testament is almost as old is often overlooked.) It is only recently that some important Church statements have withdrawn the claim of supersessionism. Until then, many Christians spoke of what Jews used to do rather than what they still do. Not only was there a new covenant for those who chose to enter it, but the old covenant had somehow died out. Alternatively, it should have done and these benighted Jews should be enlightened.

Some Christians see it as a necessary corollary of their faith that they should witness to others. Many of them see Jews as the obvious target since, they assume, there is a common starting-point, and there is good New Testament precedent for such activity. This is a logical position; indeed for many (though not for Jews) the only possible belief is that there cannot be a plurality of ways to God. This outright missionary endeavour is, I feel, less worrying than the variant on it, that is, the apparent quest for understanding of the Jewish faith, whilst, at some level, retaining a lingering feeling of antipathy towards it. This is not, of course, to say that no judgement should ever be passed on a belief or practice. Jews pass judgement on aspects of Christianity and of other religions. It is, rather, that assumptions are made that Judaism is the Old Testament religion with no developments since then. On the contrary, the roots of faith as found in the Hebrew Bible have been growing until now, as all the previous chapters of this volume have tried to indicate, particularly in the interpretative and evolutionary task of the rabbinic writings which are what a Jew, or at least his or her teacher, turns to for guidance about Jewish thought and practice. The Torah is not just the 'Old Testament' and, even if it were, one could do a lot worse.

A related danger is that Christians learn about one sort of Judaism, be it Ultra-Orthodox or Liberal, and assume that any departure in Jewish practice from what they have learned indicates a less than honourable representative of this religion. It is strange that this assumption is sometimes made by those whose own religion admits to so many possibilities of both belief and practice without necessarily impugning someone's sincerity.

Finally, a word about anti-Judaism, anti-Semitism, and anti-Zionism which obviously threaten understanding and harmonious relationships. The most recent of these, anti-Zionism is not generally found in Christian circles. (If anything, it may be argued, some Christian Zionism is in itself dangerous, since it tends to relate uncritically the State of Israel's land-claims to the theological promises of the Bible.) Considered criticism of a specific action of, say, an Israeli politician or soldier is not anti-Zionism. A regime which cannot brook such criticism is, indeed, one to be feared. Anti-Zionism as a denial of the right of Israel to exist at all is a position some people take, but assuming that it is in itself anti-Semitism is dangerous. Moreover, the term 'anti-Semitism' should be used, only with great care and accuracy, for the evil which it is and not just of anything that sounds vaguely critical of an individual Jew.

In Christian terms, it is anti-Judaism which is a very real possibility, if only because of its long and insidious presence in Christian liturgy, preaching, and legislation. The medieval blood libel, for instance, resurfaces – as evidenced by pamphlets in the 1990s, put out by groups claiming Christian affiliation. That the Lateran Councils provided Hitler with some of his legislation against Jews is well known, but it has taken parts of the Christian Church until very recently to formulate statements which eliminate the sort of anti-Judaism which can feed anti-Semitism.

The visit to Israel by Pope John Paul II in 2000 was of considerable significance in this regard. It did something to improve perceptions of Christianity in that country. The reluctance of the Vatican to recognize the State of Israel until 1993, combined with the Church's record on relations with Jews, will not easily be forgotten. Nonetheless, Israelis responded to the Pope's gestures of personal commitment on this visit and to his expressions of solidarity with Jewish suffering. He had a very delicate line to tread, since he was also visiting Palestinians and recognizing their suffering. That the Israeli Press generally reported favourably on the Pope may indicate that Jews and Christians, in and on Israel at least, can sometimes listen to each other and modify their views.

Further reading

This short list represents different types of book according to the reader's purpose. Details of more specialist literature are found within the body of this volume.

Cohn-Sherbok, Dan, *Holocaust Theology: A Reader*, University of Exeter Press, 2002
An extensive survey of responses designed to stimulate discussion and debate.

De Lange, Nicholas, *Atlas of the Jewish World*, Facts on File, 1999
An illustrated survey of Jewish history and culture.

Jacobs, Louis, *The Jewish Religion: A Companion*, Oxford University Press, 1995
A very clear and to the point introduction.

Glinert, Lewis, *The Joys of Hebrew*, Oxford University Press, 1994
A lively dictionary of Hebrew words with varied extracts illustrating how the words are used. Helpful with pronunciation.

Goldberg, David J and Rayner, John D, *The Jewish People: their History and their Religion*, Penguin, 1995
A succinct survey of Jewish history and literature and a thematic analysis of teachings and practices.

Mendes-Flohr, Paul and Reinharz, Jehuda (eds.), *The Jew in the Modern World: A Documentary History*, Oxford University Press, 1995
An outstanding anthology of primary sources in English covering religious and cultural developments.

Neuberger, Julia, *On Being Jewish*, Mandarin, 1996
A personal exploration of Jewish life and attitudes.

Neusner Jacob, *Judaism in Modern Times: an Introduction and a Reader*, Blackwell, 1995
A well-referenced presentation of concepts and expressions in modern Judaism.

Sacks, Jonathan, *The Dignity of Difference*, Continuum, 2002
Clear and readable arguments from an Orthodox Jewish perspective on the potential role of religion today.

Smith, Charles D, *Palestine and the Arab-Israeli Conflict*, Bedford Books, 4th edition, 2000
A useful and balanced approach.

Trepp, Leo, *Judaism: Development and Life*. Wadsworth, 2000
A wide-ranging consideration of Jewish belief and practice in its historical setting.

Wigoder G (ed), *The New Encyclopedia of Judaism*, New York University Press, New edition 2002
Wide-ranging and accessible entries, useful for reference.

Websites

www.jewish-studies.virtualave.net/
An Academic Jewish Studies Internet Directory. A gateway to 367 resources for the study of Judaism, including access to library catalogues and databases.

www.totallyjewish.com
For all information about the Jewish community in Britain.

Organizations and addresses

Board of Deputies of British Jews
6 Bloomsbury Square
London
WC1A 2LP

Council of Christians and Jews
5th Floor Camelford House
87-89 Albert Embankment
London
SE1 7TP

London Jewish Cultural Centre
The Old House
Kidderpore Avenue
London
NW3 7SZ

Manchester Jewish Museum
190 Cheetham Hill Road
Manchester
M8 8LW

Reform Synagogues of Great Britain (RSGB)
The Sternberg Centre
80 East End Road
London
N3 2SY

Sternberg Centre: as for RSGB

Union of Liberal and Progressive Synagogues (ULPS)
The Montague Centre
21 Maple Street
London
W1T 4BE

Yakar Educational Foundation
2 Egerton Gardens
London
NW4 4BA

glossary

Adar A month in early spring.

Adar sheni The extra month in a Jewish leap year.

Adonai Lord.

aggadah Narrative portions of Talmud and Midrash.

agunah Woman unable to remarry according to Jewish law because her husband has disappeared.

akedah Story of the binding (sacrifice) of Isaac.

alenu Concluding prayer of synagogue service.

aliyah Being called to read the Torah; immigration to Israel.

am People.

Amidah Important prayer (also known as **Shemoneh esreh** and **Tefillah**).

amoraim Rabbinic interpreters of the third and fourth centuries.

arba kanfot Small prayer shawl (also known as **tallit katan** or **tzitzit**).

arba minim Four species used at Festival of Tabernacles.

aron kodesh Part of synagogue containing Torah scrolls.

Ashkenazim Jews of eastern and western Europe.

Av A summer month of Jewish calendar.

avodah Temple service.

bar mitzvah Boy who has reached religious adulthood.

bat hayil Ceremony for girl of 12 years.

bat mitzvah Girl who has reached religious adulthood.

ben Son.

berakhah (plural **berakhot**) Blessing.

bet din (plural **batei din**) Rabbinical court.

bet ha-knesset Synagogue.

bet ha-tefillah Synagogue.

bet midrash Study hall.

bimah Platform from where Torah read.

brit milah Covenant of circumcision.

capel Yiddish word for skull-cap (also known as **yarmulkah**).

cohen Descendant of priestly family.

dayan (plural **dayanim**) Member of rabbinic court.

devekut Devotion.

Ellul Month in early autumn.

emunah Faith.

Eretz Yisrael Land of Israel.

eruv Boundary.

etrog Citron.

galut Exile.

gaon (plural **geonim**) Head of Babylonian academy.

gemara Rabbinic discussion of the Mishnah.

get (plural **gittin**) Divorce contract.

haftarah Synagogue reading from the Prophets.

Haggadah (plural **Haggadot**) Book read during the Passover meal.

Hag Ha-Matzot Festival of unleavened bread.

halakhah (plural **halakhot**) Jewish Law.

hallah (plural **hallot**) Special loaf used on Sabbaths and festivals.

Hallel Psalms 113–118.

hamesh megillot Five scrolls.

hametz Anything leavened, especially bread.

Hanukah Eight day festival.

hanukiah Hanukah menorah, nine-branched candlestick.

haroset Mixture of apples, wine, cinnamon, nuts eaten during the Passover meal.

hasid (plural **hasidim**) Member of a spiritual revival originating in the eighteenth century.

Haskalah Jewish Enlightenment movement.

Havdalah Ceremony at end of Sabbath and other festivals.

hazan (plural **hazanim**) Cantor.

heder (plural **hadarim**) Religion school.

heikhal Sefardi name for where the Torah scrolls are kept in the synagogue.

hekhser Kosher label.

hevra kaddishah Burial society.

hoshanah rabbah Prayer for salvation on the seventh day of festival of Tabernacles.

hukim Laws for which no reason is given.

humash First five books of the Bible in printed form.

hupah Wedding canopy.

kabbalah Jewish mystical tradition.

Kaddish Prayer said by mourner.

karmelit Neutral area, neither private nor completely public.

kasher (often **kosher**) Permitted food.

kashrut Food laws.

kavanah Intention in prayer.

kedoshim Martyrs.

kehillah Congregation, community.

ketubah (plural **ketubot**) Marriage contract.

ketuvim Writings, third section of Hebrew Bible.

kiddush Blessing recited over wine.

kiddush ha-shem Jewish martyrdom.

kiddushin Marriage.

kippah Skull-cap in modern Israeli usage.

Kislev Third month of Jewish calendar.

kittel Plain white garment worn by men on Day of Atonement.

kol nidrei Prayer on eve of Day of Atonement.

lag b'omer 33rd day of Counting the Omer (between Passover and Weeks).

lulav Palm branch.

maariv Evening service.

mahzor Festival prayer book.

magen david Six-pointed star.

mamzer Child of an illegitimate relationship.

mappah Comments on the Shulhan Arukh code.

Mashiah Messiah.

masorah Tradition.

masorti Traditional Jewish movement which accepts the findings of modern biblical scholarship.

matzah (plural **matzot**) Unleavened bread.

mazel tov Congratulations.

Megillah Scroll, biblical book of Esther.

mekhilta Rabbinic commentary on the book of Exodus.

melakhah Work forbidden on the Sabbath.

menorah Seven-branched candlestick or nine-branched version used at Hanukah.

mezuzah Parchment scroll fixed to doorpost.

midrash (plural **midrashim**) Rabbinic interpretation of Scripture.

midrash rabbah Midrash on books of the Pentateuch.

mikveh (plural **mikvaot**) Immersion pool.

minhag Custom.

minhah Afternoon service.

minyan Number required for saying certain prayers.

mishkan Sanctuary, Tabernacle.

Mishnah The Oral Law.

Mishneh Torah Law Code of Maimonides.

mishpatim Laws for which reason is clear.

mitnagdim Opponents of Hasidic movement.

mitzvah (plural **mitzvot**) Obligation, commandment.

mohel One who performs circumcision.

musaf The additional service.

musar Nineteenth-century ethical movement.

neilah Concluding service on Day of Atonement.

ner tamid Light kept burning in synagogue.

neviim Prophetic books of Hebrew Bible.

niddah Woman who is menstruating.

Nisan First month of Jewish calendar.

olam ha-ba The after-life.

oleh (plural **olim**) Immigrant.

omer Measurement of barley.

oneg shabbat Sabbath joy.

parashah (plural **parashiyot**) Weekly portion of Torah.

parev (or **parve**) Food neither milk nor meat.

Pesah Passover.

Pidyon Ha-Ben Ceremony for first-born son.

piyyut (plural **piyyutim**) Liturgical poem.

Purim Festival of Esther.

Rabbi (Hasidic **Rebbe**) Spiritual leader of Jewish community.

rimmonim Silver ornaments on Torah scroll.

Rosh Hashanah Jewish New Year.

rosh hodesh New Moon.

sandek Person holding the baby at circumcision.

seder Passover meal.

Sefardim Jews of Spanish origin.

Sefer Torah Torah scroll.

selihot Prayers for forgiveness.

Shabbat Sabbath.

shabbat shalom A Sabbath greeting.

shaharit Morning service.

shalom Hello; goodbye; peace.

shamash Candle for lighting Hanukah lights.

Shavuot Festival of Weeks or Pentecost.

sheheheyanu Celebratory blessing said on many happy occasions.

shehitah Jewish method of slaughtering animals.

sheloshim 30 day period after funeral.

Shema Jewish prayer declaring oneness of God.

shemini atzeret Concluding festival of Tabernacles.

Shevat A winter month of Jewish calendar.

shiur Religion class.

shiva Seven day period after funeral.

shoah Holocaust.

shofar Ram's horn.

shohet Ritual slaughterer of animals.

shul Yiddish word for synagogue.

Shulhan Arukh Law Code by Joseph Caro.

siddur Prayer book.

sidra (plural **sidrot**) Torah portion read in synagogue.

Simhat Torah Rejoicing of the Law.

smikhah Rabbinic ordination.

sofer Scribe.

sukkah Hut, tabernacle.

sukkot Festival of Tabernacles.

tallit Prayer shawl.

tallit katan (or **tzitzit**) Small tallit.

Talmud Mishnah and Gemara combined.

Talmud Torah Study of Torah.

tammuz A summer month.

tanna (plural **tannaim**) Rabbinic interpreter of first/second century CE.

targum Aramaic translation of the Bible.

tashlikh Prayer said at New Year.

tefillah Prayer.

tefillin Leather boxes and straps worn by Jewish men at morning prayer.

Tenakh Hebrew Bible.

teshuvah Repentance.

Tevet A winter month of Jewish calendar.

tevilah Ritual immersion.

Tishah B'Av 9th of Av.

Tishrei An autumn month of Jewish calendar (often counted as first month, but sometimes as seventh).

Torah First section of Hebrew Bible, Pentateuch; Jewish Law.

tosafot Mediaeval commentaries on Talmud.

tosefta Collection of rabbinic teachings from mishnaic times.

trefah Forbidden food.

Tu B'Shevat 15th Shevat, New Year for trees.

tzitzit Tassels at each corner of tallit.

yad Pointer for Torah scroll.

yahrzeit Anniversary of a death.

yamim noraim Days of Awe.

yarmulkah Skull-cap.

Yehudi Jew.

yeshivah (plural **yeshivot**) Religious study centre.

index